electronic day trading to win

WILEY ONLINE TRADING FOR A LIVING

Electronic Day Trading to Win / Bob Baird and Craig McBurney

Day Trade Online / Christopher A. Farrell

Trade Options Online / George A. Fontanills

How I Trade For a Living / Gary Smith

electronic day trading to win

BOB BAIRD
CRAIG McBURNEY

John Wiley & Sons, Inc.

New York • Chichester • Weinheim • Brisbane • Singapore • Toronto

This book is printed on acid-free paper. ∞

Published by John Wiley & Sons, Inc.

Published simultaneously in Canada.

This publication is designed to provide accurate and authoritative information
in regard to the subject matter covered. It is sold with the understanding that
the publisher is not engaged in rendering professional services. If professional
advice or other expert assistance is required, the services of a competent
professional person should be sought.

Library of Congress Cataloging-in-Publication Data:

Baird, Bob, 1956–
    Electronic day trading to win / Bob Baird, Craig McBurney.
      p. cm.
    Includes index.
    ISBN 0-471-35072-9 (cl. : alk. paper)
    1. Electronic trading of securities.   2. Stocks—Data processing.
  I. McBurney, Craig, 1963– . II. Title.
  HG4515.95.B35   1999
  332.64'0285—dc21   99-30534

Printed in the United States of America

10 9 8 7 6 5 4 3 2 1

*If you didn't make more money
during the bear market decline of 1998
than at any other time,
then you weren't day trading!*

*"There's a lot of very, very sore egos around here," said one
Merrill broker, who asked not to be identified, "We have been
insulted one too many times. They basically called us dinosaurs."*
—Merrill Lynch broker (average annual salary $300,000) upon
learning that Merrill was offering online trading, in article
"Brokers Jittery Over Their Pay," *Wall Street Journal,* 6/2/99.
(See cartoon on back cover!)

contents

preface xi

acknowledgments xvii

introduction 1

chapter 1
enter the day trader: the markets, and where the day
trader fits in   **12**

Day Trading Benefits   15

The Basics   22

Market Participants   24

Other Participants   34

Economic and Political Factors: Overview   35

chapter 2
what makes it all possible: the small order execution
system (soes)   **39**

A Short History of SOES   39

SOES Today   53

SOES Tomorrow   56

chapter 3
entering the market: electronic communications networks
and how they operate   **58**

Using ECNs   58

Selling Short   60

After-Hours Trading   61

Summary   61

The ECNs   62

chapter 4
market psychology: not the way the market *should* be,
but the way it is   **69**

Running with the Bulls   71

Earnings Reports   73

Analyst Expectations   74

Buying on the Rumor   78

Stock Splits   79

Analyst Upgrades   80

Expert Recommendations   82

Short Interest   83

Psychology of the News   85

Mass Hysteria   87

Other Factors   89

chapter 5
high-probability trading: using technical analysis to predict
the market   **90**

The 70:30 Trade   91

Technical Analysis versus Fundamental Analysis   91

Technical Indicators   93

Charts and Graphs   102

Broad Market Indicators   123

chapter 6
timing your trade for maximum returns: the trading screen
and how to use it   **127**

The Trading Screen   128

The Price-Volume Windows   131

Nasdaq Level II Market Maker Window 133

The Two-Day, Minute-by-Minute Price-Volume Chart 140

The 200-Day Price-Volume Chart 141

The Time and Sales Window 142

The Price-Change Ticker 143

The Exchange Ticker 143

chapter 7
the trading day and its characteristics: how to pick your
stocks and when to trade them   **144**

Before the Market Opens 144

The Open 151

Midmorning 153

Noon 153

Midafternoon 154

The Close 154

chapter 8
trade and grow rich: styles and strategies of day trading   **155**

The Trading System 155

Trading Strategies 159

Trading Styles 164

Mistakes to Avoid 169

Position Trading 172

chapter 9
many happy returns: the end and the beginning   **175**

Paper Trading: The Psychology of You 175

Novus Ordo Seclorum 177

appendix a **the sector indexes** **179**

appendix b **market maker list** **189**

appendix c **setting up the trading screen** **193**

x   contents

glossary   201

about LearnTradingOnline.net   207

about brokersaurus   209

index   211

about the authors   219

preface

Day Trading Defined

We hear more and more these days about "day trading," whatever that is. It's getting to the point where every time you turn on a business TV or radio program, there is a segment or series about something that the reporters call *day trading*. After listening for a few moments, it becomes clear that few of those reporting on this new phenomenon have little more than the vaguest concept of what they are talking about. Fewer still are members of the audience who do. These segments run the gamut from calm and evenhanded to frantic apocalyptical warnings about looming financial disaster should you dare to touch, much less eat, the forbidden fruit of day trading.

Perhaps you have picked up this book with a certain preconceived notion about what day trading is, probably based on reports you may have seen, heard, or read. Of course, under the loosest, broadest definition possible, day trading means simply that you buy and sell stock on the same day, no matter how the purchase or sale is accomplished. Unfortunately, because trading electronically, by whatever means, is so new, it is also widely misunderstood. Media reports on day trading provide little in the way of making the vastly important distinctions between the three primary venues, electronic, online, and broker-assisted, by which day trading can be accomplished. Instead, by lumping together a conglomeration of these diametrically opposed means of day trading, they throw the whole matter into hopeless confusion, and the term *day trading* effectively becomes meaningless. Their general philosophy is like that of the Mad Hatter, "When we talk about day trading, it means exactly what we want it to mean. No more and no less." We, however, should respond as Plato would: "If you wish to converse with us, define your terms!"

Let's therefore summarize the major differences between the three types of so-called day trading so that the advantages of electronic direct-access trading (what our book is about) may become clear by contrast. When you trade through a broker, you (1) pay commissions ranging from moderate to very high, (2) have no access to real-time data, (3) have

EDITOR'S NOTE: "THIS COUPLE HAD CLOTHES ON BEFORE THEY MET HIM."

very slow execution time, resulting in poor fills because stock prices can change between the time you talk to your broker and when the trade is executed, and (4) lose the *spread* (difference between the bid and ask price) because your broker buys, say, at 25¼ per share (*bid*) and sells to you at 25½ (*ask*). That's $250 on a 1,000-share trade! The very slow execution time results because the broker has to send the order to the firm's trading desk, the trading desk then routes the order to a *market maker,* and, finally, the market maker makes the trade. Someone who calls himself a day trader, yet is trading via a broker, is like a mechanic whose tool set consists of a screwdriver and a pair of pliers.

When you trade through an online broker, you (1) pay commissions ranging from low to moderate, (2) sometimes have access to real-time data, but no one tells you what to do with it or how to use it, (3) still have very slow execution time, resulting in poor fills because stock prices can change between the time you push the button to enter your trade and when the trade is executed, and (4) lose the spread because your online brokerage buys, say, at 25¼ per share and sells to you at 25½. The very slow execution time results because you push a button that sends the order to the firm's trading desk, the trading desk then routes the order to a market maker, and, finally, the market maker makes the trade. Thus, the only real differences between broker trading and online trading are that, in doing the latter, there is no broker to ask what in the world is going on when the trade goes awry, and sometimes you save a few bucks on commissions. Someone who calls herself a day trader, yet is trading online in this manner, is like a mechanic whose tool set consists of a screwdriver, a pair of pliers, and a hammer.

By contrast, with electronic direct-access trading, when your day trading is tied directly into the markets, as we will discuss in detail, you (1) pay moderate commissions, (2) have access to real-time data and know how to use it, (3) have instantaneous executions, resulting in good fills because stock prices change little between the time you enter your trade and seconds later when the trade is executed, and (4) have the ability to buy on the bid (25¼, in our example) and sell on the ask (25½). Your rapid fills are possible because you are bypassing not just the broker, but the trading desk and, often, even the market maker. The advantages of electronic direct-access trading are overwhelming, as you will see. Someone who is day trading with direct market access is like a mechanic whose tool set consists of a five-foot-tall red toolbox on wheels, with 30 drawers and hundreds of specialized tools for any contingency. Which way, then, do you want to trade?

Let's think of it this way. Trading in any manner, day or otherwise, through a broker is analogous to having a 1,200-baud modem and using it to communicate with someone else who also has a 1,200-baud modem. Moving "up" to online trading is like getting a 14.4K modem and using it to communicate with someone who has a 1,200-baud modem. Trading with direct access to the markets is like having a cable modem and using it to communicate with someone who also has a cable modem. As you can see, no matter how fast a modem you might have, 56K, cable, or whatever, it makes no difference at all as long as the person on the other end is still using a 1,200-baud one! This is why the typical online trading is nearly as outmoded in every respect as regular call-your-broker trading, and why so few are making any money doing either. If the term *market order* characterizes much of your previous trading history, then, unquestionably, our book is for you!

What This Book Will Do For You

By studying our book, aspiring day traders will learn the details of day trading stocks with direct market access. We will cover how all of this is possible, a brief history of SOES, the Nasdaq marketplace, compliance with applicable Nasdaq and SEC regulations, the various order-entry systems, the psychology of trading, news and its impact on the marketplace, technical analysis, computer trading screen setup, the trading day, and, lastly, several of the numerous trading strategies and styles that you will want to consider and take advantage of as a day trader. Upon completion of our book, aspiring day traders will have a firm foundation in and understanding of the dynamic processes working within the securities marketplace. By using the knowledge so gained, aspiring day traders may embark on a rewarding and potentially quite lucrative career day trading equities on the stock exchanges.

Finally, whenever we introduce important new terms, we will give an explanation of them and italicize them to indicate that these words appear in the glossary. As you progress through our book, you will encounter these words from place to place, and you can refer to the glossary if you need a reminder about their meaning. The index will give the page numbers on which a given term appears throughout our book, so that you may use our book as a ready reference and can refer back to specific concepts to refresh your understanding. Using a PC, a modem, a phone line, and specialized software, you can now trade securities directly on the stock exchanges instantly, with a simple click of the computer mouse. The purpose of our book is to show you how.

An old Chinese proverb tells us that when the student is ready, a teacher appears. Think about this for a moment. It makes good sense. The idea is that the means to reach your goals have always been available, but went unnoticed until you wanted something badly enough or were at the point where you were able to recognize and utilize them—just like Dorothy in the Land of Oz. She could have returned to Kansas any time she pleased, but she just had to learn it for herself. So do we all. Persistence, diligence, and a willingness to become a student of the marketplace are prerequisites of being a successful electronic day trader. In reading this book, you are already taking the big first step.

So, if you're ready to be a day trader, roll up your sleeves, and let's go!

Bob Baird
Craig McBurney

acknowledgments

Putting together our book, trading to not only make money, but to also generate ideas to pass on to our readers, takes significant time away from other responsibilities to family, clients, and community. We would like to thank our families and friends, who have not seen as much of us as they should have, for putting up with even more absences than usual.

To help drive some of our points home, we have commissioned freelance cartoonist, Bill Frauhiger, of Fort Wayne, Indiana, as illustrator for the Brokersaurus cartoon series. We want to thank Bill for the great job he did. For over 15 years, Bill has been providing quality illustration, cartoons, comic strips, logos, and caricatures for clients nationwide. Anyone wishing to contact Bill for his services can call him at his studio at (219) 497-9600, or e-mail him at billfrog@concentric.net. You may also view his online portfolio on the World Wide Web at www.concentric.net/~billfrog/.

Many thanks also go to Pamela van Giessen, our editor at John Wiley & Sons, for having the vision to help us see this project to completion.

introduction

Getting In on the Ground Floor

In the movie *Forrest Gump,* Forrest tells his benchmate at the bus stop that his partner, Lieutenant Dan, had invested all of their funds in a fruit company called Apple. It just so happened that this Apple was Apple Computer, and the duo's ground-floor investment had made Forrest and Lieutenant Dan multimillionaires.

In *Back to the Future, Part II,* the villain, Biff, gets hold of a sports record book, goes back in time before any of the games are played, and becomes wealthy by consistently betting on the winners, no matter how long the supposed odds. If you have the book, it's not hard to do.

Because hindsight is 20/20, it would be an easy job to fill up our book and many others simply by reciting examples of where you would have been today *if* you had simply made the right investment at the right time. But *if* is always the problem. Wouldn't it be nice, just for once, if you could get in on the ground floor of something new and cutting edge *before* it took off and everyone else was also clamoring to get in?

Well, congratulations, those aspiring to day trade today are in on just such a ground floor. Although day trading per se isn't new, what is new is that the quantum leaps in computer technology, telecommunications, and the Internet together make it possible to bring the stock exchanges literally right into your lap (-top computer) in the privacy of your own home. That's not just new; that's revolutionary!

The Price of Ignorance

An early-1999 *Washington Post* article,* "In Bull Market, the Urge to Gamble Is Rising," started out like this:

> Brenda Richardson wanted to squeeze a quick bundle out of the bull market to help put her daughter through college. So in late 1996, the Texas pharmacist plunked down her entire savings of $10,000 to open an account at a Houston securities firm, starting a journey that would take her deep into the addictive world of day trading.
>
> Richardson was given the secret code to a room full of men staring zombie-like at computer screens flickering with stock symbols. She sat at her assigned terminal and, without any investment experience, started buying and selling shares for herself. "I had no idea what I was doing," she said, "I sort of looked around to see what other people are doing."
>
> What she witnessed was a form of high-tech gambling—traders darting in and out of stocks in minutes, sometimes seconds, usually selling all their shares before the day's closing bell.
>
> Richardson said she quickly got into debt and handed over control of her account to a sweet-talking fellow trader. He moved her account to another firm where he was able, through excessive borrowing and wild buying and selling of shares, to trade more than $35 million worth of stock in her name over three months. Richardson said she ultimately lost $60,000. . . .

And so on. You get the picture. We have here exactly what the article said: a woman who had nary the slightest hint of what she was doing and who, moreover, was foolish enough to turn her account over to a stranger in the next chair. Duh! Although the general public stands aghast at such a horror story and runs immediately back to the loving arms of their brokers, is there any other arena of life anywhere on the face of this earth where a similar scenario would not have similarly led to disaster? Of course not!

The lesson here is simple. There just aren't any easy get-rich-quick schemes that work (except for the huckster selling them!). If it sounds too good to be true, it probably is. And we are not touting day trading as either. What we are saying is that electronic direct-access day trading is

---

* Washington Post, 2/1/99, p. 1.

BROKERSAURUS By Bob Baird and Craig McBurney

Contact us or send us your idea for a cartoon at brokersaurus.com

Artistry by Bill Frankiger

a great way to make a *living,* and a lucrative one at that. If it does anything at all, the *Post* article underscores one central, overriding point: that you must know what you are doing in order to profitably day trade. And that, dear reader, is exactly what our book is about. And you're reading it. Perhaps Brenda Richardson will, too. But at least *you* will have the necessary knowledge to avoid being the next Brenda Richardson.

Freedom Is the Goal

But, isn't buy-and-hold investing and isn't day trading gambling? Not at all. Buy-and-hold may be investing, but day trading is not gambling; it is market making. Market makers, as we have mentioned and will discuss in more detail later on, come to work each day and attempt to set stock prices at levels where buying and selling take place. As an electronic direct-access day trader, you are also a market maker, albeit one working out of your own home or from a trading room instead of out of a plush brokerage office. As with any market maker, because you have provided liquidity to the market, because you have taken on the risk associated with purchasing stock, and because you have done all of this as a result of one win-win situation after another, you are entitled to your profits. You have earned them no less honorably than anyone else engaged in any other legal pursuit.

What, then, is the bottom line for trading? Certainly, many may respond that they want to become rich. But simply being rich is meaningless in and of itself. One pursuit is paramount, and all others are secondary by comparison. We are, of course, speaking of *freedom*. Freedom, plain and simple, is the goal. Our finances combined with our own priorities determine whether freedom is ever achieved. Freedom is nothing less than the complete ability to set your own schedule and agenda.

Think about this. There are many wealthy people who are not free by any stretch of the imagination. They rise early to join the rat race and then compete fiercely all day long and well into the night. They can hardly get to sleep from all the day's activities and tomorrow's demands dancing in their heads. And when they do sleep, it is troubled and fitful, and they rise feeling more tired than when they had gone to bed. They certainly have provided "well" for their families, assuming that provision of material goods, instead of themselves, is the measure of providing well. Such folks are not free because they cannot or will not set their own agendas, for whatever reason. Their agendas control them and every aspect of their lives. One of the great industrialists in the early 1900s was once asked how much is enough. His reply? "Just a little bit more." Clearly, such a person is driven by the game itself, and the means becomes the end.

On the other hand, others who would never be considered wealthy may yet be entirely free. Those who own their own small homes and have enough investment income to enable them to spend most of their time traveling may not be wealthy, but they are certainly rich. And the missionary doctor who spends her life in a distant third-world country is definitely poor by almost any standard, yet is undoubtedly rich.

We believe that the freedom to truly prioritize worthy goals is the highest aim: when you can take the day, or even the week, off and go to the mountains or the beach on the spur of the moment; when you can be home with your family at dinnertime; when you can attend or even coach your kids' soccer games; when your cup runneth over to the extent that you can help others who are truly in need through no fault of their own. This is what day trading is all about.

Where to Trade: Trading Room or Home?

One avenue to get started is to begin your trading in one of the many *trading rooms* now opening that cater to the day trader. Trading in a trading room allows you to come in and work on a computer that already has some sort of trading screen set up. You'll have to learn how to use the trading screen, and after that you can trade. The problem is that in this situation you really have no idea why the trading screen is the way it is or whether those who set it up even know. Important features may not even be there, and if you're not familiar with setting up a trading screen, you'll never know what you're missing, and you'll either lose money or make less. A benefit is that you and the other traders there can all learn together or at least be confused together. (A quick note of warning: Don't turn your account over to the novice in the next chair!)

On the subject of trading rooms, it should be noted that you should be very cautious about opening an account and beginning to trade. One reason for this is the wide divergence in quality. Some trading rooms are owned by brokerages that effectively franchise them out to anyone who can come up with the necessary funds, regardless of his actual knowledge of trading. Many trading rooms offer "training," if it can be called that, for new traders. As with the trading rooms themselves, the quality and expertise of the trainers varies greatly. The reason for this is because there are relatively few true electronic (direct-access) day traders at this time, and thus a limited pool from which to draw someone who has successfully traded, is willing to quit working or trading to teach instead, and can form a complete, coherent sentence when she trains you.

In the absence of successful traders for training, the next best thing is to find someone who can pitch a good line, perhaps a salesperson from the used-car lot down the street. As a result, new traders, seldom correct but never in doubt, trade confidently in a near vacuum of knowledge that they do not even recognize, draining their accounts and thus eliminating the customer base for the trading room, which then closes. Then where do you go, assuming yours was not one of the accounts that was drained away? If you trade at a trading room, your best strategy is to have a good enough idea of what you are doing well before you set foot in the place, that is, read our book. At least then, if you do take their training, you'll be able to tell whether the instructor knows what she is talking about.

Trading at home is the most convenient way to trade. For one thing, the commute is short. You can get the same services, and probably more, that a trading room has, but once the software is installed, you'll have to customize the trading screen yourself. That's just one of the many things we'll discuss in detail in our book, because we've already set up the trading screen for you. Our trading screen has been developed by trial and error or, perhaps to say it more accurately, profit and loss! You won't find anything like it anywhere else.

The trading screen won't be just another black box; we'll walk you through the entire process of using it and explain why each data window on the trading screen is there. It's not difficult; you just have to know what to do. If you think of electronic direct-access day trading as attempting to open a safe full of money, the trading screen is the combination. Just as a combination lock is not difficult to open if you know the combination, so also is day trading easy if you trade by the combination. In our book, we'll give you the day trading "combination."

Whether you want to trade at home, at your office, or at a trading room, our book will teach you everything you need to know to get you up and running and trading on the trading scree... Even if you elect not to trade at home, you'll be armed with the information necessary to judge between one trading room and another.

Who Are Day Traders?

Day traders come from all walks of life, and like stockbrokers, need no specialized background, knowledge, or education to get started. Day trading is for all those who are tired of watching the stock market zoom past them, yet don't want to climb onto the bandwagon just before it plummets over a cliff. Anyone with a couple of extra hours once or twice a week can become an effective electronic direct-access day trader.

Despite their diversity, day traders have one thing in common. They have come to the realization that they cannot look to their jobs to bring the success they seek. They have tired of looking to the next promotion to do it. And they are certainly not depending on their horoscope, luck, a winning lottery ticket, or a new government program to do it. No, they resolutely understand that if success is to be theirs, if freedom is to be achieved, they must do it themselves. They look neither to the left nor to the right, but only straight ahead . . . into the mirror. In a speech once, Robert Kennedy made the statement, "Others look at the way things are, and ask, 'Why?' I look at the way things could be, and ask, 'Why not?' " The next time you're in front of a mirror, look into it and ask yourself, "Why not?"

Thus, the following kinds of folks will particularly profit from our book:

- *Current electronic day traders.* As we learned in our preface, not all day trading is created equal. Not by a long shot! Those currently day trading, by whatever means, can particularly profit from the insights we offer because they are in the unique position of being able to put these principles immediately into practice.

- *All online traders.* Investors who are already trading online, but not day trading, will benefit from the expanded opportunities afforded them by the information herein. This market is large and heading even larger. Some 10 million of you are currently trading online. Your ranks are expected to grow exponentially over the coming few years. On a reality note, if you are online trading through a broker, you have undoubtedly found that this is far from the panacea that you envisioned. Recall all of the problems you've ever had with timely execution, along with everything else. Now imagine all that disappearing, because it will all be gone with electronic direct-access day trading.

- *Professionals.* Doctors, dentists, lawyers, and others who can arrange the times that they see patients or clients will benefit because they'll be able to spend some time at their computers during the trading day.

- *Full-timers.* Those who work full-time, but work part of the weekend and thus have a weekday (when the market is open) off, will benefit.

- *Part-timers.* Anyone who has a weekday (when the market is open) off is a good candidate.

- *Investment club members.* Most clubs are always looking for new and better ideas, and our book is just what you've been looking for. The challenge, of course, is to beat the Beardstown Ladies! The gauntlet has just been thrown down. Are you up to it?

- *Those in dead-end careers.* Just because people work full-time doesn't mean that they are either gainfully or meaningfully employed. Many of you are cramped with inflexible work hours that put a strain on more important personal commitments. Our goal is to put you well on the way to a new, profitable, and exciting career opportunity.

- *The downsized.* In our day of reorganization, restructuring, consolidating, merging, downsizing, rightsizing, and other tired euphemisms for layoffs and firings, a lot of folks are finding themselves out on the street at ages too young to retire. For you, as well as for all those wise enough to plan ahead for such a contingency, our book offers the opportunity to continue productive work on your own terms—a better alternative for middle-aged, midlevel managers than temping or competing for positions with 25-year-olds!

- *Early retirees.* Three million men and women have taken early retirement over the past few years. Many of you have gone out with a sizable financial buyout or severance package, which you may parlay into complete financial independence given the right knowledge and training. Electronic direct-access day trading offers exactly this.

- *Regular retirees.* After two or three years of fishing or sitting around the house, too many retirees are either bored stiff or *are* stiffs. For the former, we offer you a road map to a second career and continued productivity.

- *Women.* Probably the largest single group that can most profit from the principles we teach in our book is women! Today's woman is finding it harder and harder to balance the responsibilities of both family and career. Yet the costs of home and family, coupled with a high tax burden, virtually demand two incomes, although family responsibilities and children brought up in day care can be losers in this deal. What is the way out of this quandary? We offer women who would like to stay home and raise their children, as well as those who already are full-time homemakers, the opportunity to do so with a new career that offers the potential of higher income than they could ever have earned away from home.

- *Baby boomers.* A broad group, including many of those already mentioned and more, is the baby boom generation, a segment of our population nearly 50 million strong. You and your peers are roughly in your mid-30s to mid-50s, and the realization of the necessity to save and plan for retirement is only now dawning on you. In order to have an adequate retirement, for instance, a middle boomer, someone in their early 40s, needs to invest around $1,500 per month. This realization, unfortunately, comes about the same time as the one about how much money will be necessary for your children's college educations. Few have the financial wherewithal to accommodate all of these expenses at once and live satisfactorily at the same time. This makes it crucial for boomers to invest shrewdly, effectively, and immediately if they are to survive financially. With this much at stake, you can hardly afford to put all of your hopes and dreams into the hands of a broker, or even a mutual fund manager. Instead, you must take the reins of your own destiny. Our book offers the tools and knowledge to enable you to do so.

Whether you are keeping your day job and just day trading part-time or are pursuing day trading full-time, you need to treat day trading as your new business, because that's just what it is. The beauty of this business venture, however, is that electronic direct-access day trading is one of the few fields in which anyone can begin a new career without having to go back to school or sit for a job interview. But this can also be a double-edged sword. The ease of entry can entice you to let down your guard and begin to believe that performance as a day trader will be just as easy as entering into it.

You, dear reader, will not fall for this false allure, which is why you are reading our book. Read carefully. Learn all you can. Read as many books about the market as you can. Never stop learning. All worthwhile pursuits require that you continue learning if you are to stay successful. This one is no different. And keep in mind that those who have truly stopped learning are pushing up daisies instead.

As with any other new business, you need to have realistic expectations and give your new endeavor time to succeed. Your goal as a beginning trader is not to become independently wealthy in the first few weeks. Even if it is, you won't. Instead, it is to hold on for dear life and preserve as much of your trading capital as possible *one day at a time.* First, you will be happy to simply limit your losses and write them off as good learning experiences as you pursue an advanced degree from the College of Hard Knocks. Then you will progress to breaking even. Next comes small, and ever so rarely, large, profits. Finally, your knowledge will have increased and your skills improved to the point where you can wring consistent good profits from the market. But if

you blow your whole wad starting up, you're out of the game. Remember, Rome wasn't built in a day.

Direct-Access Day Trading: Your New Business
- You will have start-up costs.
- You have to plan for taxes.
- The object is to maximize profits and limit expenses.
- You will need to keep records and books.
- You will have operating expenses (tax-deductible).
- You do not have trading losses, only the cost of doing business, which you will seek to minimize.

The invention of the computer chip to replace thousands of vacuum tubes and miles of wiring brought computers out of the headquarters of only the largest corporations and into the homes of average Americans. Likewise, the introduction of the Small Order Execution System (SOES), which we will discuss in Chapter 2, is what now enables true market participation for the average investor: you. Chapter 1 will review the benefits of direct-access day trading and some stock market basics to get you started off on the right foot.

Market Knowledge Quiz

Before we proceed, however, let's take a moment to test your current knowledge of the state of the market with our surefire, guaranteed Market Knowledge Quiz:

Q: What do the following all have in common: brontosaurus, tyrannosaurus rex, stegosaurus, mastodon, woolly mammoth, saber-toothed tiger, three-toed ground sloth, broker, discount broker, deep-discount broker, NYSE, AMEX.

If you can answer this question correctly, you already know more than 99 percent of market participants. But don't worry if this question is a bit too tough for you right now. If you can't answer it, come back and try again after you've finished our book.

chapter 1

enter the day trader

the markets, and where
the day trader fits in

Technologically speaking, our ancestors of only 130 years ago had more in common with those living at the time of Christ or with the ancient Egyptians than with us. Theirs was a time of no electricity, no running water, chamber pots, outdoor privies, the weekly Saturday night bath (whether needed or not), heating by burning wood or coal, and no air-conditioning. After dark, candles and lanterns supplied minimal lighting for chores or, rarely, reading. Everyday items were still largely made by hand, and most tasks were performed by human or animal power. Horses and buggies and, occasionally, trains, took folks where they wanted to go. Many had never ventured farther than 10 miles from home. And the floor of the New York Stock Exchange was filled with brokers shouting, making signs to one another, and throwing bits and pieces of paper all over the place.

Only two or three decades later, by the end of the nineteenth century, all of this was radically changing. Brute force was being replaced by machinery. Mass production made articles previously available only to the privileged common household items. Waterworks and electric companies were springing up in the cities. Electric power provided lighting, fans, and a whole host of appliances and conveniences to average folks. The telephone allowed instantaneous communication with those far away. And the phonograph allowed the ever increasing leisure time fostered by these advancements to be filled with music. The automobile was the newcomer on the block, despite the lack of paved roads, and the airplane was just around the corner. The invention of the ticker tape allowed those who followed the nation's business and commerce to stay up-to-date. And the floor of the New York Stock Exchange was filled with brokers shouting, making signs to one another, and throwing bits and pieces of paper all over the place.

Those who stood at the brink of the twentieth century could only look back with amazement upon all the technological marvels wrought in so short a time. And when they looked ahead, they knew that a century of promise lay before them, but they had no way to comprehend just how far and how fast technology and invention would take them. They "saw through a glass darkly," as it were.

In like manner, we live within the portals not just of a new century, but of a new millennium. As with them, we need make no pretense of having any foresight into the new innovations that lie ahead,

BROKERSAURUS   By Bob Baird and Craig McBurney

Contact us or send us your idea for a cartoon at brokersaurus.com

Artistry by Bill Frankiger

for though our hindsight is 20/20, our vision of the future is just as dim. Yet we do know that whatever changes come will be for the betterment of all.

Still, there were those at the close of the last century who clung to the past and resisted change, dismissing new inventions and innovations as so much faddish amusement and newfangled novelty that would not stand the test of time. For them, the horse and buggy were to be preferred over the automobile. Unlike technology, human nature undergoes virtually no change with the passage of time, so it is not surprising that there are those in our own day who also resist change. Just one example is the floor of the modern New York Stock Exchange, where brokers, as did their brethren of the nineteenth century, still transact business by shouting, making signs to one another, and throwing bits and pieces of paper all over the place. Their buggy whips stand ever poised and ready. The old ways were good enough for pappy and grandpappy and, by cracky, they're good enough for the NYSE!

Just as the last 20 to 30 years of the nineteenth century were a time of great tumult and change, so were the last 10 to 15 years of the twentieth century an era of massive transformation in the way transactions in the stock market are made. The Nasdaq Stock Exchange has stood in the forefront of these technological changes that have made the markets, once the unassailable private domain of the privileged few, available to the average person in the privacy of their own home or office in the form of the electronic or virtual marketplace.

Although there are many little Dutch boys with all 20 fingers and toes stuck here and there in the myriad holes in the technological dike, and others are trying with all their might to scoop back the tide, the shift to the virtual marketplace, and its opening up to the average person new vistas never before imagined or available, is now inevitable. In fact, it has already happened, and the death knell of the past has even now occurred. Although we have automobiles, we still ride horses for enjoyment. This will not be the case, however, with live-auction markets such as the NYSE and AMEX. These avenues of trading will be as useless in the not-too-distant future as is bloodletting to rid oneself of "bad blood." Thus, those of you who are reading our book will be positioned on the leading edge of market technology and will be ready for whatever comes. Exactly what will this entail? No one knows. But we can be sure that the next bend in the road will reveal changes to come even more astounding than those that awaited the entrants into the twentieth century.

BROKERSAURUS By Bob Baird and Craig McBurney
Contact us or send us your idea for a cartoon at brokersaurus.com

Artistry by Bill Frauhiger

Day Trading Benefits

Day traders, by definition, trade only within the confines of a single trading day. Unlike the buy-and-holders, who hope a company will be doing well 5, 10, or 20 years out, electronic direct-access day traders are most interested in what a given stock is going to do during the next few minutes or hours within the confines of a single trading day. Whether the company is the next Microsoft or bankrupt in five years, or even tomorrow, is completely irrelevant. The day trader thus takes no thought concerning tomorrow, but lets tomorrow take care of itself.

Although in our book we will teach you how to use information sources to do better trading, the beauty of direct-access day trading is that the day trader really needs no information about a company at all to be a successful trader. You may never even have heard of the company you are buying and selling, much less know what the company does. You certainly aren't concerned about its long-term prospects or what the quarterly earnings report will be, except how this information affects the stock on the very day you are looking at it.

Because of the intraday time frame during which day trading takes place, it is the safest and least-risky type of trading. This is because of a number of factors.

Protection from Overnight Price Drops

For one, stock prices can change overnight. And when they do, it is usually dramatic. Unless they follow the market closely, typical investors who simply call their broker for a quote and then buy or sell do not realize this. As we will discuss in detail later, adjusting prices of stocks is the job of the market maker. If bad news comes out overnight, the market maker adjusts the next opening price accordingly, and there is nothing you can do but watch. Not even a previously set stop-loss will help you because the stock never traded at the level you picked.

For instance, let's say that you buy 1,000 shares of XYZ Company at 25⅛ just before the 4:00 P.M. closing at the same price. At 4:30 that afternoon, a news flash indicates that the CEO of XYZ has been arrested for embezzlement and that the previously glowing earnings reports had been falsified to cover this up. If the market maker were to simply open XYZ the next morning at 25⅛, there would be many sellers in addition to yourself trying to dump XYZ at 25⅛, but there would be zero takers and thus no market. To do her job, the market maker typically sets the opening price at a level where previous buying and selling had taken place, usually at a low point over the past several months.

Thus, even if the opening price had not been adjusted by the market maker, you still would not have been able to get out of XYZ that morning at the price you would have liked. This is just one example of the dangers of the *buy-and-hold* strategy. If you asked your broker about this, you were told to not worry because you were "investing for the long term." Of course, your broker never waited for the "long term" for his yacht!

Investors who buy in to this philosophy pacify themselves that the stock will go back up "over the long run," which may or may not be so, but at least this makes them feel better. Electronic direct-access day traders, however, are not satisfied to buy at 25⅛ and hold for months after a drop, waiting for the stock to simply tunnel its way back to the surface again way on down the line. Instead, they are concerned with the *time value* of their money and insist that it be hard at work for them *the whole while.*

Protection from Overnight Price Increases

Not only can stock prices fall overnight, they can rise as well. And, as with drops, when they rise it is often dramatic as well. Now, you may ask, who would need protection from an overnight price increase? Isn't that exactly what you want? Well, it depends on whether you own the stock the day before the rise. If you happen to own the stock already, then any increase will make you happy. However, stocks usually rise dramatically after a bit of unexpected good news comes out. Average investors may catch this good news in the evening after work from the newspaper or the evening news. They may log on to their on-line brokerages and place a *market order,* that is, an order to buy at the prevailing price when the order is received. Thus, millions of average investors dutifully jump on the bandwagon at the same time. All of these orders received by hundreds of brokerages around the country cause the price to rise the next day.

Let's say that the stock closed at 45½ the day an average investor got the news and entered a market buy order. The next day, the investor goes to work as usual. That evening, as she leisurely logs on to his online brokerage, she is dumfounded to discover that the stock she wanted was purchased all right, but at 55½, and that it closed for the day at 52⅜. Thus, not only did the average investor pay $10 per share more than she thought she would, but the stock is now worth less than the high price she paid for it. If our average investor had simply entered a *limit order* instead, that is, an order with a not-to-exceed price, the purchase would not have been made at all. But by not trading, you may not lose money but you won't make any, either.

Day Trading versus Buy and Hold

Even if there is no bad news per se, *position traders,* that is, those who buy and hold stocks for periods ranging from days to years, are still gambling that they "know" what a given stock is going to do over the long haul. Further, because the typical position trader is not aware of the day-to-day price fluctuations of his stock, he may buy XYZ at 25⅛ and be happy to sell it three years later at 45⅛. What he may miss in doing this, however, is that perhaps XYZ hit 45⅛ over a one- to two-day *rally* six months after he bought it, but subsequently went back down and eventually rose back up over the ensuing 2½ years. Had he sold at that time, his 80 percent gain over three years would have occurred in only six months, for an annualized gain of more like 160 percent instead of the 27 percent he was happy with. Thus, he has lost the time value of

2½ years, never knew what hit him, and was fat, dumb, and happy the whole while!

The day trader realizes that no one knows where a stock is going to be years out. That the great majority of mutual fund managers, who are touted as the foremost experts in their respective fields, fail to even match the overall market return, much less surpass it (as evidenced by the rise in popularity of index funds), provides irrefutable testimony to this. Clearly, making money by position trading isn't quite as easy as you might think. If the experts rarely do it, how can the average investor expect to?

Market "Corrections"

Other factors indicating the relative safety of day trading are those nasty "corrections" that occur in the markets from time to time. Certainly, so far anyway, corrections in the past have had their effects eventually erased by market movement as a whole, but, again, why sit for weeks or months with your money doing nothing except trying to find its way back to square one?

By contrast, a *correction* (defined as a pullback of less than 20 percent from previous market highs) provides one of the most profitable opportunities possible for the electronic direct-access day trader. For standard buy-and-holders, it has long been said that "the trend is your friend." For the day trader, it can equally be said, "*volatility* is your friend." What frightens the average investor most is the type of trading climate in which the day trader thrives. The day trader, of course, is safely in cash during any market decline. As she perceives any given stock hit by the correction to be bottoming out, or even experiencing a short-lived rally, she can move in as *bargain hunters* and others begin to drive up prices of individual stocks.

Think about what your investments did during the declines of October 1997 or late summer and fall of 1998. Now consider what might have happened to day traders' investments then. First, they didn't lose any money due to unexpected declines because they weren't in any stocks so as to be able to. Second, because they watch the markets on a daily basis, they were able to find shorting opportunities during the many weeks of decline, and then to go long over the recovery period. That's why volatility, that is, market declines and uncertainty like this, is the day trader's best friend.

The day trader's only problem is not being able to take advantage of the plethora of opportunities that corrections afford. So many stocks, so little time. By employing this strategy in times of market corrections, the day trader can make the same amount of money that the buy-and-holders lose. Think about it: *Someone always wins.* Why not you? Note that the day trading strategy is not at all the same as the *market timing* as employed by many position traders and contrarian investors.

> In times of market corrections, the day trader can make the same amount of money that the buy-and-holders lose. Think about it: *Someone always wins.* Why not you?

Even day trading, however, is not without risk. To limit their risk, electronic direct-access day traders *must* trade by a system. They buy a stock and then watch to see what it will do. If it goes down by a predetermined amount, they sell. If it goes up, they ride the gains and sell when the stock price turns around by a predetermined amount or at the end of the trading day. We'll discuss all of this and more in detail in later chapters.

Day Trading versus Buying Mutual Funds

Anyone who has ever bought or sold real estate knows the three primary factors in determining the value of a property: (1) location, (2) location, and (3) location. Similarly, there are three primary reasons that stock brokers exist: (1) to generate sales, (2) to generate sales, and (3) to generate sales. There is another term for *broker: salesperson.*

Most of the time, all but the suckers and the gullible hang up when a salesperson calls. Why, then, do many not only hang on every word of their broker, but often initiate the calls themselves? (See previous sentence for answer). Their problem is that they suffer from "heard" instinct (i.e., they *heard* it from their broker).

> Their problem, like that of many others, is that they suffer from "heard" instinct (i.e., they *heard* it from their broker).

There are two types of people: those who have time to actively administer their own trading and those who do not. Those who can manage their own accounts should be electronic direct-access day traders. Period. Just a couple of the advantages are nearly instantaneous execution of trades (i.e., before the price moves) and no intermediary, thus saving on the spreads.

There are almost no good advertisements on television. That makes the few that are stand out all the more. One particularly entertaining one shows a well-dressed couple walking up to and entering a large, spacious house with manicured lawn and fine landscaping. As they walk, the narrator says, "Your investments helped pay for this dream house. . . . Unfortunately, it belongs to your *broker!*" The couple then look at you with a smirk and shut the door in your face. The advertisement works because you are led to imagine that it is your house, and then comes the twist. It's funny, too, because it contains a large kernel of truth, as all good humor must.

Those without the time to actively work their own accounts often fall into the trap of using a broker. Not only are they getting into and out of trades at a snail's pace and losing the spreads, they are also acting on the advice of those who are not even remotely close to being top experts in the field. A broker is rarely a market expert, but, as we have noted, is always a salesperson. Think about it, if brokers really were experts, why would they be dealing with the hassles of working with

BROKERSAURUS   By Bob Baird and Craig McBurney

Contact us or send us your idea for a cartoon at brokersaurus.com

Artistry by Bill Frankiger

**DECIDING HOW TO TRADE ISN'T ALL THAT HARD.
YOU JUST HAVE TO LOOK A LITTLE BELOW THE SURFACE.**

you and dozens of others like you? Because they are selfless, altruistic philanthropists? Hardly.

If the broker were really the expert you think he is, he would be trading his own account and setting his own schedule, just as you will be able to do as a day trader, and he wouldn't be a broker at all! If your broker really fancies himself an expert, then he should charge you a commission when he makes gains for your account and he should pay you the commission when he loses your money on a trade. After all, if he's still learning with your money, he owes you the tuition. But, of course, this will never happen. The broker will make commissions going in and coming out, whether your account is drained to zero in the process or not. You take the losses, but your broker is completely insulated.

If a broker truly is a market expert, then he definitely won't be *your* broker unless you have a huge account from which to mine commissions and the spreads. The best you can hope for is that the actual

---

BROKERSAURUS   By Bob Baird and Craig McBurney

Contact us or send us your idea for a cartoon at brokersaurus.com

Artistry by Bill Frankiger

HOW MUCH EXPERIENCE DOES YOUR BROKER *REALLY* HAVE!

broker you work with will get a hot tip from the true expert somewhere way, way up the line. So, if you don't have time to direct your own trading, why not go to the source and get the services of a real expert at the lowest possible price, which is what you get when you buy a mutual fund? After all, who would you rather have picking your stocks for you, Peter Lynch or Horace Schmutt? The real choice, therefore, is not between day trading and using a broker, but between day trading and buying mutual funds, as we have appropriately titled this section. And, of course, you must know full well why a broker is called a broker—because after he's finished with you, you are!

> **And, of course, you must know full well why a broker is
> called a broker—because when he's finished with you,
> you are!**

Using a broker for your trading is therefore, to put it bluntly, akin to using a pencil for everything you write. Using a "discount" broker, even a so-called online one and even one who discounts to zero, is similar to trading up to a manual typewriter. Mutual fund investing is analogous to sitting down to the fabled IBM Selectric. Day trading, by contrast, is like using a modern word processing program on a state-of-the-art microcomputer, and every time you turn around, the technology not only gets better, but cheaper to boot. We believe you'll agree with us, once you've read our book, that direct-access day trading is far and away the superior method of trading for virtually everyone. But if you do choose to go the mutual fund route, don't go from the frying pan into the fire by using a broker to pick them for you. Simply go to a list of the best funds, as often given in *Money* magazine and others, pick them yourself, and avoid the broker commissions and management fees.

In order to profit as a day trader, it is necessary to have an understanding of the marketplace and all of the players. Before we discuss the individuals and institutions who comprise the markets, however, let's review some stock market basics.

The Basics

In the *securities* markets of the world, people buy and sell stocks, bonds, and other investment vehicles daily in the hope of profiting from properly anticipating future movements in the market. This is the goal and wish of every market participant. Because our book focuses only on investing in the stock market, and particularly the Nasdaq, we will confine our discussion principally to those topics that relate specifically to this arena of trading.

For decades seemingly without end, the investor's only option for getting into the market was a full-service, full-commission broker. In those days, most folks were content to keep their money in a 5¼ percent passbook savings account at their local bank (and many wish they could get these rates today!). Eventually, discount brokers, such as Schwab and others, came onto the scene and began to offer the small investor a small break on commissions. Due to free-market competition, the commissions of so-called discount brokers continued to decline. The ability of the average investor to be in the market has since made a quantum leap from the discount-broker era, but this is a little-known fact.

After the end of World War II, some Japanese sailors were left marooned on desert islands and didn't know that the war was over and a new age had come. They lived in their own worlds and continued fighting the war for years afterward. No doubt, each morning as they looked upon the rising sun, they must have imagined that the empire was in like manner spreading over the face of the whole earth. Like these sailors, all too many investors today are still living in the age of the discount broker, unaware that a new paradigm has come. Many discount-broker adherents may have even dared to venture onto the Internet to trade. Nirvana, these investors believe, has now been achieved. What else could they ask for in this the best-of-all-possible trading worlds? If you learn nothing else, you will learn well the answer to that question in our book.

Equity versus Debt

Stock, also known as *equity,* represents ownership in a company, just as equity in your home represents the part of it you own. It is impossible to put a concrete value on assets that include many intangible and ever changing factors, such as the risk and fluctuating price values associated with the purchase and sale of securities. Instead, market participants, or traders, establish these prices on a moment-by-moment basis within the framework of one of two types of marketplaces: an auction exchange or a dealer exchange. This is the free market at its best.

Bid-Ask and the Spread

Whatever price someone is willing to purchase stock for is a *bid* price for that issue. Similarly, any price at which someone is willing to sell stock is an *ask* or *offer* price. The highest price bid (*inside bid*) for a stock and the lowest price asked (*inside ask,* or *inside offer*) for a stock together constitute the *quote;* the difference between the two prices is the *spread.* These two best prices are also known as the *inside market* for the stock. The bid-ask information from Nasdaq is the lowest ranking of information and is known as *Level I* data. Consider the following quote for XYZ Corporation:

$$XYZ\ 25\ (bid) \times 25\frac{1}{4}\ (ask)$$

In this example, the inside market or quote is constituted by a bid to purchase XYZ at 25 and an offer to sell it at 25¼. This Level I quote is what the typical investor receives when calling a broker. The ¼ difference between the two is the spread.

Using Electronic Communication Networks (ECNs), available to the public just since 1997, however, the investor is now able to bypass the brokers and market maker intermediary and directly buy shares at the bid and to sell them at the ask, thus eliminating the spread both going in and coming out and saving slippage costs that must otherwise be made up by favorable changes in the stock price.

Market Participants

NYSE/AMEX (Auction Market)

The *auction market* is what most folks think of when they consider how the stock market operates—much like the futures trading floor seen in the classic, *Trading Places,* with Eddie Murphy and Dan Akroyd. Best exemplified by the New York Stock Exchange (*NYSE*) trading floor, this type of auction functions like a double auction system. In other words, unlike a conventional auction with one auctioneer and many buyers, here we have many buyers bidding for various securities and many sellers offering them. As in any auction, prices are established by competitive bidding between traders acting as agents for buyers and sellers. It is important to note that an auction market operates in a single physical place. To participate directly, you or your firm must have a seat on the exchange and must physically be there.

Although there may be many buyers and sellers of a given stock, all transactions must take place through a single trader known as a *specialist.* There may be multiple stocks per specialist, but not multiple specialists per stock. Stocks bought and sold on the auction market are known as *listed stocks,* that is, they are listed on the exchange. Specialists function as auctioneers for their stocks and are charged with matching buy and sell orders and maintaining an orderly market in them. To accomplish this, the specialist adjusts the price of each stock to balance supply and demand. In return, the specialist receives the spread on all orders. As an employee of one of the large brokerage houses, the specialist may also buy or sell the stock out of the brokerage's inventory.

Specialists have a powerful advantage that no one else has. They are in charge of the limit order book, which lists all of the buy and sell orders and the prices that traders are willing to pay or sell for. Thus, specialists know before anyone else the direction that the stock is trending, and may sell from their inventory when they sense a downturn or purchase before the stock price begins rising. Knowledge of order flow that is unavailable to anyone else places specialists in an extremely lucrative position. When they have a large pile of buy orders and only a small pile of sell orders, specialists obviously know which way the market is headed, and they make purchases accordingly. When they begin to execute buy orders, the price can only go up to coax additional sellers into the market. Once specialists begin to have sell orders pile up, they sell their own positions first, reaping huge profits, and then begin to execute the rest of the orders. You may be wondering what the difference is between insider trading and what a specialist does. There is only one difference: specialist trading is legal.

Because of the specialists' knowledge of the book, it is difficult for any trader to directly compete against them. In exchange for the privilege of serving on the exchange, however, the specialist must be the buyer or seller of last resort. If there are buyers, but no sellers, the specialist must become the seller, and if there are sellers, but no buyers, the specialist must become the buyer. Thus, the specialist helps maintain liquidity for a given issue.

Several trading rules ensure that the system functions in an orderly fashion:

1. The first bid or ask (offer) at a given price has priority over any other bid or offer at the same price (i.e., first come, first served).

2. The high bid and low offer "have the floor."

3. A new auction begins whenever all the bids or offers at a given price are exhausted.

4. Secret transactions are prohibited.

5. Bids and offers must be made in an audible voice.

Effective day trading on the NYSE or other auction exchanges is not easy. Because a single specialist is in charge of the stock, trading for a given issue may not begin until as late as 11:00 A.M. Further, stocks may be stopped from trading if they drop far enough. A 50-point change puts a stop on program trading. If you've bought in, your ride may stop. Worse, the NYSE may stop trading on a stock and later open it $5 lower. This is the kiss of death for the day trader. On a typical trade of 1,000 shares, this represents an instant $5,000 loss. It's also hard to day trade on the NYSE because of the difficulty of getting timely executions. This exchange, then, is best for the position trader, as the true bid-ask numbers are posted and you can get a feel for the actual momentum of a stock.

The future of the auction exchange is dim. Already, the prices of seats on the various exchanges have reached highs from which they are declining with no end in sight. Even the American Stock Exchange (*AMEX*) has seen the writing on the wall and has merged with the Nasdaq. The growth of the *virtual market* is rendering the auction exchange more and more irrelevant with every passing day. Due to the ability of specialists in their privileged positions both to pocket the entire spread and to have knowledge of order flow, you can expect the large, powerful brokerages that profit from this arrangement to fight tooth and nail to preserve it and to resort to whatever means necessary to do so. Remember, the steps of even the last dinosaur to walk the earth still caused the earth to shake . . . until it died. Ultimately, however, the only real remaining question is what words should be engraved on their memorial.

Nasdaq (Dealer Market)

Contrast the actual single trading floor of the live-auction market to the *Nasdaq* (National Association of Securities Dealers Automated Quotations system) *dealer market* wherein transactions are conducted through a telephone and computer network connecting the various dealers, making the Nasdaq into a virtual market with as many "trading floors" as there are computer terminals (including yours!) with the actual single trading floor of an auction market. In the dealer market, *market makers* place bids and offers through a network of computers that display quotations to all participants. In contrast to the auction market, this type of system is also known as an *over-the-counter (OTC)* market. With this brief summary of how the market works, let's now discuss some of the players and their roles.

Market Makers.   The market maker is typically a representative of a brokerage firm responsible for setting the price of a specific stock. Unlike the auction market specialist, there is no single market maker assigned to a particular stock. Instead, as many or as few as wish may elect to participate. To do so, however, they are required to make a *two-sided market,* that is, they must establish two prices, one price at which they are willing to sell stock and one at which they are willing to buy. One or both of these prices may be at the inside market, but neither need be. For example, take a look at the Level II window for Intel Corporation in Figure 1.1. The inside market is

$$\textit{Intel 109}^{7}\!/\!_{16}\ \textit{(bid)} \times \textit{109}^{1}\!/\!_{2}\ \textit{(ask)}$$

Note that GSCO (Goldman Sachs, Appendix B) is one price level below the inside bid at 109⅜, but at the third level below the inside ask at 109¾, and so is not at the inside market at all. On the bid side, GSCO is probably waiting to get in at a better price. Being so far down on the ask side, however, GSCO is likely not really expecting to sell any stock, but is instead simply fulfilling the obligation to make a two-sided market. Thus, the market maker may bid and ask at any price desired to fulfill this obligation, not just at the inside market.

The job of those who do choose to participate is to *make a market* for a given stock and ideally find a price at which the stock volume balances between buying and selling. Thus, the market maker provides *liquidity* at all times in the marketplace. If the price is too high, there will be few buyers. Conversely, if the price is too low, there will be few sellers. If no buying or selling is taking place, no market is made, and the stock is not *liquid,* that is, it cannot be easily traded or exchanged.

In the instance where a stock is moving slowly, the market maker must probe the market, that is, adjust the price until she finds the level at which buying and selling occur. At this point, the market for that stock has been made. The market maker does this by placing bids and

Figure 1.1   Level II window for Intel
Corporation

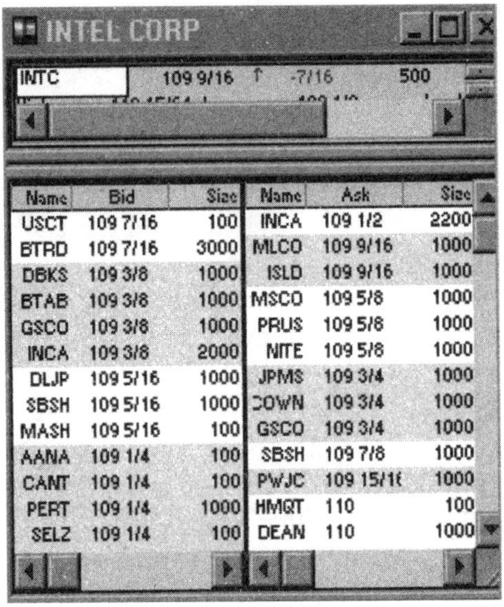

Name	Bid	Size	Name	Ask	Size
USCT	109 7/16	100	INCA	109 1/2	2200
BTRD	109 7/16	3000	MLCO	109 9/16	1000
DBKS	109 3/8	1000	ISLD	109 9/16	1000
BTAB	109 3/8	1000	MSCO	109 5/8	1000
GSCO	109 3/8	1000	PRUS	109 5/8	1000
INCA	109 3/8	2000	NITE	109 5/8	1000
DLJP	109 5/16	1000	JPMS	109 3/4	1000
SBSH	109 5/16	1000	COWN	109 3/4	1000
MASH	109 5/16	100	GSCO	109 3/4	1000
AANA	109 1/4	100	SBSH	109 7/8	1000
CANT	109 1/4	100	PWJC	109 15/16	1000
PERT	109 1/4	1000	HMQT	110	100
SELZ	109 1/4	100	DEAN	110	1000

Reprinted with permission of Townsend Analytics, Ltd.

offers in the stock in which she is responsible for making a market. Often, the market maker has no real idea at what price a market will be made, so she may encourage trading simply by adjusting the stock's opening price to a previous low or high at which buying and selling were taking place.

In exchange for providing liquidity to the market, the market maker receives the spread on trades. To understand this, think of the market maker as a casino. Consider the brokerage clients as customers of the casino. For the casino to profit, it must have a slight advantage in all games. Although the advantage is slight, the casino realizes that over time it will profit from this disparity. The role of the market maker is little different than the role played by a casino. The market maker may both bid and ask. As bidder, she is able to purchase Intel at the bid price of 109$\frac{7}{16}$. She then turns around and, as seller, offers it to you for the ask price of 109$\frac{1}{2}$, thus making the $\frac{1}{16}$ spread—but out of your pocket!

Here's how it works: When you trade through a broker, he simply takes your order to buy or sell stock and sends it on to a market maker trader. If you wish to purchase 1,000 shares of Intel, the market maker is willing to sell them to you at 109½, for a total purchase price to you of $109,500.00, plus broker commissions. Let's assume you decide to sell that same stock immediately, although there has been no change in the inside market price. The market maker is now willing to buy back that stock from you at the bid price of 109⁷⁄₁₆. Therefore, you receive proceeds from the sale in the amount of $109,437.50, less any commissions.

As you can see from this example, you lost a quick $62.50, not including two commissions, due to the spread in Intel. Note further that the spread in this example is a small ¹⁄₁₆. Spreads can commonly be ⅛ ($125.00) or even ¼ ($250.00), costing you a lot of money. Now compare this to discount brokerage commissions of $18, $14, $8, $5, or even zero.

The majority of average investors place *market orders* for their stock purchases, that is, they pay whatever *ask* price is prevailing at the moment. Never forget that the words "market order" are to your broker what "open sesame" was to Ali Baba. This is because brokers, whether traditional, discount, "deep-discount," or commission-free, all make most of their money in one of two ways. The first is by execution of the trade itself, either by having the firm's own market maker execute the trade or by sending the trade on to another firm that does.

> **Never forget that the words "market order" are to your broker what "open sesame" was to Ali Baba.**

If the brokerage has a market maker in the stock of interest, it simply sends the order on to him. He buys at the bid price, which is lower, and sells to the customer at the ask price, which is higher, thus pocketing the difference, or *making the spread,* for the company. However, because the customer buys at the market ask, the stock can rise in price between the time that the broker buys it and the time that he sells it to his customer, thus enhancing broker profits even further. (Close your eyes and try to envision the market maker, having bought on the bid, frantically scrambling to complete the sale to you *before* the ask price increases. Now open your eyes to the real world.) Not surprisingly, brokerage houses that have market makers in a particular stock will have their army of salespeople (brokers) touting trading in that stock to all their customers.

Usually, the broker's firm does not have a market maker in the stock of interest. After all, few firms can have a market maker for all the stocks on the Nasdaq. In this instance, he sends it on to a particular market maker with whom the firm has made a prior, shall we say, "agreement." The market maker transacts the order as outlined previously and gives a kickback to the broker's company. This bribe, er, token of appreciation, is known as *payment for order flow*. And, of course, if you know nothing else, you certainly know that when people pay others to have your business directed to them, it is always your best interests that they have at heart.

The second way that brokerages make money is by acting similarly to banks. Your account balance can be used to generate profits for the brokerage much the same as your bank balance generates profits for the bank. Thus, making the spread and payment for order flow and generating profits from your account balance explain how many brokerages, working with the market makers, can now claim to charge low or no commissions. How do they do it? Now you know. Who do those discount brokers think they're kidding!

Market makers are just like anyone else playing the markets: They are trying to make a profit. The way in which they go about accomplishing this, however, is somewhat different than methods typically used by the brokerage's clients. In order to truly understand both the mind-set of the market maker and the differences between market makers and their customers, it is important to place the market maker's method of trading into perspective.

The placement of the market maker's bids and offers is anything but random. The market maker is analyzing the *tape,* that is, a listing of volumes of stock sold and the price at which each volume sold, and reviewing charts in the same way as any trader does. The market makers will strategically place bids or offers out at a price where they feel they can profit with little risk. There are circumstances in which market makers will aggressively buy or sell stock if they are negotiating a customer order or accumulating a *position,* that is, ownership of a certain amount of stock, but by and large they profit by adjusting the bids and asks and pocketing the spreads.

Market makers also have advantages over the small investor. Being, as they typically are, employees of the big brokerage houses, the market maker may know from the morning meeting that her firm is poised to upgrade its rating of a particular stock. Thus, prior to the announcement, she may purchase shares of the stock. Thus, when the rating increase is announced, the market maker is poised to become a seller, raking in huge profits for her firm. The same thing can happen if a downgrade is planned, and the market maker can either unload inventory prior to the announcement or get in and sell short just before the slide starts.

By now, you're probably wondering how you can ever compete on a level playing field when the system is rigged from the start in the market maker's favor. Recall, however, that unlike the auction-exchange specialist, who has his book with all the buy and sell orders for his eyes only, each Nasdaq issue may have many market makers. Because all of these market makers can be seen on the Level II window (see Figure 1.1), the window is to the trader what the book is to the specialist. With it, you have as much information as any of the major broker-dealers in the market, which is vastly more than the average Joe who still does regular online trading.

Take a look at the Intel Level II window in Figure 1.1. The typical online trader sees only the top line of the chart, the inside bid-ask prices only, minus the buyer/seller symbols and minus the number of shares offered. A few online brokerages are beginning to offer Level II data, which is an improvement, but, even so, losing the spread and painfully slow execution times while the price is moving away from where it was when you wanted to trade make the online broker path to wealth very tenuous. If you have an online broker, you may not have realized what you have just learned about losing the spread, but you certainly know, only too well, about the problems of timely order execution at the price you wanted.

Of course, because Level II data is available to anyone who works in the market or to those knowledgeable enough to request it, you are not the only one who sees the order flow. But this is as good as it gets, and it is more than enough. If you want more, simply purchase a seat on the NYSE once you've built up your account through day trading. Further, although a given market maker or trading participant may individually know something that you don't, no one else does, either. Neither are your own plans known to any of the other Nasdaq participants. Thus, the playing field in the Nasdaq market is about as level as it can be expected to be.

Fortunately, as we will discuss in detail over the next several chapters, the technology now exists to allow electronic direct-access day traders to themselves be market makers and to make markets from their own homes or office computers. In such an instance, the day trader, as market maker, is also entitled to take his or her own share of the spread, which brings us to our next section.

Why Market Makers Despise Day Traders   Day traders are now coming along and challenging the market makers in a domain that was long theirs and theirs alone. Although this is certainly no longer the case, they still believe it to be true. Like the buggy whip manufacturers of yesteryear, the old-guard trading establishment refuses to accept that a new day has arrived. Thus they are defensive and resentful when it comes to day traders, and even accuse the day traders of coming in and ripping off the average investor in an attempt to turn public (particularly SEC) opinion against day traders. This is why you will rarely hear day trading presented in a positive light in stock news reports, so don't be surprised. But, let's examine this allegation in closer detail.

We now have three players in the trading game, the day trader, the market maker, and the average investor. The goal of the former two is to get a piece of the spread. Let's see how this works. Consider the following quote:

$$XYZ\ 25 \times 25^{1}\!/_{4}$$

Before direct-access day trading came onto the scene, the unwary investor would call his broker. He sells XYZ at 25 and the market maker, often a brokerage employee, turns around and sells it for 25¼ to another unsuspecting investor, or else the investor is sold stock at 25¼ for which the market maker paid 25. Let's say that 1,000 shares change hands. Either way, the market maker pockets $250 (1,000 shares times the ¼ spread).

With the advent of computer technology, the direct-access day trader can function just as a market maker does. In order to place her bid at the top of the stack, the day trader may look at the 25 bid and instead offer 25⅟₁₆, making the quote

$$XYZ\ 25^{1}\!/_{16} \times 25^{1}\!/_{4}$$

Because the day trader's bid is now the highest one in the market, the investor who wishes to sell now gets 25⅟₁₆, or $62.50 *more* than he would have without the day trader's involvement. To make her money, the day trader now enters an offer to sell, again beating the previous price by ⅟₁₆, making the market

$$XYZ\ 25^{1}\!/_{16} \times 25^{3}\!/_{16}$$

Again, the day trader's ask is lower than the previous 25¼ and is purchased by yet another investor. As before, that investor also comes out ⅟₁₆, or $62.50, ahead. Thus, for providing extra liquidity in the market, plus the fact that she was willing to take on the added risk of offering better prices than anyone else was willing to, the day trader earns her own spread of 25³⁄₁₆ − 25⅟₁₆ = ⅛, or $125. In the meantime, the market maker lost $250 (25¼ − 25) because the rascally day trader came and invaded what he wanted to keep as his private domain.

In effect, the day trader and the investor hooked up directly, bypassed the market maker intermediary entirely, and each side of this bargain was $125 better off for having done so. So, it is easy to see why the market makers (i.e., the large brokerages) have a vested interest in trying to disseminate false propaganda to discourage new day traders from entering the market: The brokerages prefer to keep making inflated spreads. They do not like having their previous astronomical salaries reduced to only stratospheric, and they will say anything necessary to prevent anyone from becoming a day trader. This process of eliminating the intermediary, or *disintermediation,* made possible by the advent of the Internet, will change all marketplaces, as we now know them, beyond recognition. Brokerages are only the first of many dominoes yet to fall.

We see, therefore, that direct-access day trading is not simply a one-way street whereby the day trader comes in and takes without giving anything back. To the contrary, day traders benefit the market and many of its participants by providing extra liquidity (remember, for every purchase there's a seller and vice versa) and oftentimes a better price to market participants on transactions than they would have gotten otherwise.

So don't be concerned about the grumblings of the market makers. If there really were anything fundamentally bad about the average person day trading and market making, the SEC wouldn't have allowed it in the first place, and a growing number of firms wouldn't be offering it to their customers. This is a tide that will not be turned back.

Because brokers have a blatant vested interest in trashing day trading, we cannot emphasize enough that when you do hear news about so-called day trading, you should take careful note of what is meant by day trading. If by day trading, they mean the typical investors attempting to clumsily day trade using an online broker and losing all their money in the process, then what you hear is probably true, and more besides. If by day trading, they mean the day traders competing directly on the Nasdaq against the market makers and taking all *their* money in the process, then what you hear is probably nothing more than big-brokerage bellyaching.

Remember, if, as news reports portray to the glee of brokerage firms, day traders really were losing all their money by getting into such a "risky" endeavor, do you actually think those taking it away from them would be complaining!

Other Participants

Institutional Clients

Institutional clients are banks, savings and loans, insurance companies, investment advisors, or any other entity with total assets under management of at least $50 million. On the surface, there is no difference between an institutional client and a retail client. Yet closer review of the facts reveals significant differences.

Because of finances they bring to the table, the institutional clients receive the direct services of the market maker or head trader through the broker-dealer where they execute their trades. The market maker has experience on his side. In order to become a market maker at an established broker-dealer, the aspiring trader must usually apprentice as a junior trader for a number of years. Even then, experience alone is not enough to guarantee a position as a market maker. Junior traders must display a keen aptitude for trading before they are given any opportunity to trade large sums of money for the firm. Competition is fierce for these positions because a successful market maker earns more than almost any other employee of the broker-dealer. So it stands to reason that the institutional client receives the services of some of Wall Street's finest traders, while the retail client is relegated to seeking assistance from a salesperson many levels removed from where the real knowledge and action is.

Additionally, and equally as important, the market maker has knowledge of *order flow*. Order flow can best be defined as knowledge on a moment-to-moment basis of all incoming buy and sell orders received by the broker-dealer. (Remember, a market maker has knowledge of order flow for his firm only; a specialist has this knowledge for the entire market for a given stock.) If more buy orders are coming in, the market maker knows the stock may *rally*, that is, rapidly increase in price; if more sell orders are received, a *sell-off*, that is, a rapid drop in price, may ensue. Knowledge of order flow greatly assists the market maker in getting the best price possible for the institutional client because buying and selling of customer positions can be tailored to coincide with market rallies and sell-offs.

Finally, the market maker has relations with other market makers and traders at other broker-dealers and is in daily contact with them in order to negotiate larger customer orders. This frequent interaction allows the market maker to speculate with a high degree of probability on the needs of market makers from other broker-dealers for a given security and to thus receive the most favorable pricing for the institutional client.

Retail Clients

The *retail client* is the individual investor (i.e., most of us). Lowest on the totem pole, this investor usually does her own homework and has no interaction with the professional traders and market makers. After all, from the perspective of a professional trader, which client should get first priority, one with at least $50 million in assets under management, or one with an account most likely in the range of $100,000? Although the game appears to be rigged in favor of market makers and institutional clients, the day trader, if astute, can profit handsomely by riding the coattails of her larger colleagues.

Being a retail client can be advantageous, however. This is because the day trader has so little in the way of assets that she can move in and invest her money stealthily and quickly without moving (affecting) the markets. If the day trader sees an opportunity in the market, all that is needed is one or a few pushes of a button and she is in on the move. This agility allows the retail client to profit where a larger client would be unable to do so.

Economic and Political Factors: Overview

A number of factors foster the growth and development of the securities markets. During periods of controlled economic expansion, investor sentiment is at its highest. It is generally understood that if monetary policy allows for steady expansion of the economy, the stock market will appreciate (a *bull market*). Such policy requires a balancing act wherein neither rapid growth nor a slowdown in economic productivity occurs. To achieve this end, it is necessary to regulate the availability and flow of money through the banking system. Central to the role of balancing the availability of funds flowing to the private sector is the *Fed.*

The Fed

The Federal Reserve System, often referred to simply as "the Fed," was formed in 1917 in response to an earlier crash in the securities markets known as the "rich man's panic of 1907." The original role of the Fed was to guarantee the soundness of American banks by holding a reserve of capital against all deposits in the U.S. banking system. Since that time, though, the role of the Fed has evolved. Today, the Fed has six functions, as follows:

1. Commercial and investment banker for the U.S. Treasury

2. Dealer-manager for portfolios of securities owned by a special list of investors (primarily government trust funds and dollar holdings of foreign central banks)

3. Administrator and regulator of the U.S. government securities market

4. Protector of U.S. currency against unwarranted devaluation

5. Guardian of the national banking system

6. Implementor of national monetary policy

Whereas each of these functions is meaningful, here we will address only the matter of monetary policy and its effects on the securities markets. The role of the Fed is to monitor the growth of the U.S. economy with an eye toward controlled expansion. When the economy is left to expand or contract at will, the securities markets suffer. The Fed, by tightening or loosening the availability of funds to the U.S. banking system, controls the economy so that sustained economic expansion can occur. Discussed subsequently are two possible scenarios of unbalanced economic conditions.

During periods of uncontrolled economic expansion, increased availability of credit from the Fed to banks leads to more liberal extension of credit from the banks to the private sector. This allows the private sector to ramp up growth. Higher levels of corporate earnings growth stimulate greater demand for labor. Increased demand for labor from a limited supply forces the private sector to bid up the price of wages. Upward-spiraling wage pressures contribute directly to increases in the cost of goods and services. Thus, the prices of goods and services increase. During an expansionary economic cycle as just described, such a chain of events is inflationary.

Conversely, during recessionary periods, money is scarce. As a result of the increasing difficulty for the private sector to obtain credit, growth is subdued. Consequently, firms put expansion projects on hold until the cost of borrowing money from lending institutions is lower. During periods of anemic growth, demand for labor is reduced. As jobs become scarce, the supply of labor increases. The resulting larger pool of labor places a cap on wage pressures. Therefore, the cost of goods and services remains unchanged. During periods of extreme recession, deflation may occur, and the cost of goods and services may actually be reduced. In order to prevent either of these scenarios from happening, it is the role of the Fed to stimulate controlled expansion of the U.S. economy. During periods when the general public perceives economic expansion to be steady, the securities markets thrive.

In evaluating the state of the market, it is essential for the day trader to understand and assess the role of the Fed. Failing to properly understand the impact of the Fed on the securities markets will prove costly. In addition to economic factors, political events also play a large role in the daily fluctuations of the securities markets.

Political Factors
Political events affect the securities markets significantly. Investors fear the unknown. It is for this reason alone that political events jar the markets so. As investors feel a loss of control, they tend to shift their investments into cash. Political uncertainties contribute to this fear perhaps greater than any other event. Conversely, certainty gives the investor a level of comfort. Witness the reelection in 1996 of Bill Clinton to office. Upon his reelection, the Nasdaq composite rallied some 15 percent from the 1,200 range to 1,400 in little more than two months. This rally was less of an indication that the market approved of Clinton's policies than that those policies were a known quantity, ending the months of uncertainty engendered by a long campaign season. This is but one of many examples of the effect that political events have on the securities markets. In other words, for the markets, for better or for worse, the devil you know is better than the devil you don't know.

It is of utmost importance for the day trader to quickly and properly decipher the significance of political events on the market. A day trader who fails to understand the impact of market-altering events will pay dearly when trading.

With the foregoing foundation, let's move on to Chapter 2, where we will discuss what started it all: the introduction of SOES, the Small Order Execution System.

chapter 2

what makes it all possible

the small order execution system (soes)

A Short History of SOES

The need for greater efficiency of the order-execution process in the over-the-counter (OTC) National Association of Securities Dealers Automated Quotations system (*Nasdaq*) market became apparent during the surge in trading volume that began in the fall of 1982, coinciding with one of the longest bull markets in history. As a result of this volume increase, the handling of routine small orders became more and more burdensome for market makers.

Consequently, the National Association of Securities Dealers (NASD), an association of securities broker-dealers, implemented the initial phase of an automated system known as the Small Order Execution System (*SOES*). SOES became operational in January 1985 to assist market makers in their daily trading activities and, presumably, to aid small investors in getting their orders executed during times of low trading volume and diminished liquidity.

SOES allowed traders to automatically execute small orders (up to a maximum of 1,000 shares of any number of stocks) at the inside market (bid-ask quote), thus freeing up their time for trades larger in size that required negotiation. The system worked efficiently until October

1987. What transpired during the market crash of that month forever changed the Nasdaq stock market and led to the creation and evolution of a cottage industry known as "SOES trading."

Mandatory Order Execution

When the market crashed on "Black Monday" in October 1987, average investors, as usual, panicked at the news and rushed to sell and get whatever they could for stocks they were convinced would soon be worthless. Regardless of the legitimacy of this selling, they faced two problems. First, at that time, small investors were limited to using the telephone to contact their brokers. Because a broker can talk to only one person at a time, most were not able to even get through. This wasn't because other small investors had contacted the brokers first. Most likely, the brokers were talking to their best customers, the big institutional clients, (i.e., mutual fund and pension plan managers) and executing their orders.

Second, until that time, SOES had not been a mandatory order-execution system. As a result, the liquidity, or ability to find buyers or sellers of stocks at a given price, of the OTC market was reduced dramatically because market makers withdrew from Nasdaq and SOES, thereby exacerbating the effects of the sell-off. Thus, when the market maker received an order to sell, he felt no obligation to do so and didn't. This means that the small investor would not have been able to sell her stock anyway even if she had been able to talk to her broker, at least not near any price that she may have wanted. That market makers were unwilling to buy stock in a general market decline was understandable. However, this left the great majority of small investors on the sidelines, unable to buy or sell, watching the value of their holdings dwindle away, as institutional clients got out because of their inside track with the market makers.

In the wake of this crisis, the NASD made participation in SOES mandatory for all market makers in Nasdaq National Market Stocks (NMS) securities as of June 30, 1988. Market makers are responsible for the state of the market. All market makers making a market (i.e., buying or selling a given stock) were now required to execute any SOES order directed to them within a certain time frame or pass it on to another market maker. To enforce this, penalties were imposed on market makers who withdrew from Nasdaq or SOES without a permissible excuse. Although this took care of the execution per se of the small investors' orders, it would be several more years before technology advanced to the point where investors could bypass telephoning their brokers to enter the order in the first place.

As a result of this rule change, market makers were further required to commit to execution in SOES for a minimum of two times the maximum order size (usually 1,000 shares × 2, for a total of 2,000 shares) in every security for which they made a market if their quotes were at the inside bid or offer (quote) or if orders were sent specifically to, or *preferenced* to, them. Were the market makers to be so "hit," and thus required to trade, their trading exposure was limited to the 2,000 shares.

Further, mandatory order execution required that market makers honor their quotes that were in effect when the order was placed. Prior to mandatory order execution, market makers would post a given quote and then would decide whether they really wanted to honor it once an order arrived. If it appeared that the stock was moving in price, they filled the order, but at a different price than the buyer expected; thus both buyers and sellers were constantly plagued with unfavorable executions. But try to guess, if you can, who made all of the money performing the transactions and came out smelling like a rose.

To understand the severe disadvantage at which these unfair practices placed the small investor, imagine calling a catalog sales desk and ordering an item that was priced in the catalog at $1,000 and receiving a bill for $1,200. When you inquire, you are told that this is because the company decided to raise the price, not before, but *after* your order was received. Or consider that you have just filled your car with gas at $0.899 per gallon. When you are ready to pay, you find that the price has gone up to $1.199 in the time it took you to put your gas cap on and walk into the store. These examples are clearly absurd, because such a sham would not even be tried more than once, but the identical sort of thing was an unending fact of life to the small investor prior to the advent of mandatory order execution.

An important point to remember is that market makers are not some nameless, faceless entity out there somewhere whom no one can control. No, they are representatives of the major brokerage houses who were carrying out the anti-small-investor policies of those firms. These firms, of course, are the same ones you probably have accounts with right now, and whom you trust to look out for your best interests. Remember, these policies and many similar ones were freely adopted by the market makers' firms and would still be in effect as of this writing if it weren't for SEC intervention! Think about that the next time you feel the desire to call one of them and place an order.

With the advent of mandatory order execution, the market makers were no longer able to sidestep their responsibilities to provide the proper liquidity to the marketplace for all investors. In requiring this, however, the NASD unwittingly provided the impetus for a new and fertile trading environment: SOES trading. SOES trading was the natural by-product of the automatic order-execution system. The early pioneers of SOES trading quickly recognized its power. As long as they closely monitored the markets, they were able to enter into the market at the start of a given move and exit the market once the trend subsided. At that time, however, few people recognized how easily money could be made in this way.

Using SOES and its mandatory order execution, market makers began getting hit with SOES orders that they were now required to fill; they were basically blindsided. Previously, they had entered whatever quote they wanted to and then, once an order was received, decided whether to fill it or not at that price. In effect, they had gotten fat and lazy. When they entered $25 per share ask for a certain stock, they really meant $27.50, yet when they were *SOESed,* as it were, the stock went for the price publicized, *as is expected in any other type of market on earth,* and they didn't like it one bit. The market makers suddenly had to pay attention to what they were advertising because now they might actually have to trade at that price. They complained that they really intended to change their quotes, but just didn't have enough time. The poor dears! In their rage, they coined the term *SOES bandit* for those shameless day traders who actually *took the market makers at their word.* Please put your book down and join us in a moment of silence for the pitiable market makers for so terribly having been taken advantage of. After all, the market makers are only the employees of the biggest and most powerful brokerage firms on Wall Street. Why don't those mean old day traders go pick on somebody their own size!

Note, however, that although market makers are required to trade the volume of shares advertised at the price advertised, they are not required to post the total amount of shares they may actually have for sale. Thus, a market maker who posts 1,000 shares may be simply fulfilling his obligation to make a market in a given stock, or he may actually have 20,000 shares to trade, but doesn't want to let on and cause the price to change accordingly. A market maker who keeps showing up again at the quote with more shares after selling those previously advertised may be doing just this. Keep a lookout for this. A corollary of this is that SOES offers no privacy or anonymity to a market maker posting orders. His company's name is there for all to see, and thus to attempt, and possibly to succeed, to figure out what the market maker may be doing.

Because the technique of being able to force market makers to sell as advertised was so little known, the early SOES traders were able to profit from a system that, at the time, took relatively little skill compared to that required in today's markets. This easy money was short-lived, however, as the monied interests in Wall Street (i.e., your broker) soon realized that someone else was getting a portion of their previously protected profits.

The NASD, the most influential members of which were the market makers and their respective brokerage firms, began to respond to the grumbling about day traders. In August 1988, in a blatant effort to curb the activities of the SOES traders, the NASD implemented the first of many rules to come designed to stamp out the SOES trading community. At that time, the NASD set forth a variety of interpretations of the SOES rules in Notice-To-Members (NTM) 88-61. Even to this day, NTM 88-61 serves as the definitive guide for many of the curtailing rules still imposed upon SOES trading. Central to the interpretations outlined in the NTM 88-61 is the 1,000-share rule.

The 1,000-Share Rule

Prior to the implementation of these regulations, SOES traders and SOES order-entry firms found two ways to enter orders on SOES in excess of the 1,000-share order limit if they perceived a stock to be trending in one direction or another. One was to simultaneously place several 1,000-share orders for a given stock piecemeal in a single account. The other was to submit several orders for a stock at the 1,000-share limit in numerous accounts, often in multiple accounts for the same client. Traders were also opening multiple corporate accounts for their benefit and executing orders simultaneously, thereby circumventing the intent of the rule.

The NASD policy, that SOES was created to allow public customers to enter orders of limited size into the Nasdaq system for immediate execution at the best available price, was being thwarted. Consequently, the NASD clarified their long-standing position. The process of entering multiple orders at the 1,000-share limit, known as *batching*, was made illegal, and has remained so ever since in an attempt to maintain the integrity of SOES as an automatic execution system for the small investor. Regarding the 1,000-share rule, the NASD stated, "Where a single investment decision has been made involving the purchase or sale of more than the maximum order size, the order cannot be executed through SOES."

In addition, the NASD defined the usage of SOES to exclude registered representatives of a securities dealer and members of their immediate families. Implicit in this interpretation was a prohibition on the trading activities of customers who controlled several accounts. These initial restrictions, however, were only the start of a long series of battles for the SOES community.

Professional Trader Rules

Although these measures served to dampen the activities of some forms of SOES trading, the SOES industry overall was growing rapidly as word spread of a new and potentially profitable way for the average investor to trade in the markets. Not surprisingly, the market makers demanded still more regulations to further restrict the activities of the SOES trader.

In September 1988, to cripple this new and growing industry, the NASD again adopted new rules for approval by the Securities and Exchange Commission (*SEC*). Not satisfied with the restrictive measures already placed regarding batching and registered representatives, this time the market makers sought to exert their influence to expand the definition of "professional trader" to include *any* account in which five or more "day trades" had been executed through SOES during any trading day, or where a "professional trading pattern" in SOES was exhibited.

A professional trading pattern was deemed to be demonstrated by (1) the existence of a consistent pattern or practice of executing day trades, (2) the execution of a high proportion of day trades in relation to the total transactions in the account, or (3) the execution of a high volume of day trades in relation to the amount and value of securities held in the account. Basically, the rules boil down to making anyone who day trades and has access to Level II data or who has the ability to use SOES a professional trader subject to all the rules and restrictions thereof.

The defining of a "professional trader" in such nebulous terms illustrates a policy the NASD has used for years to search out and destroy any activity that ran counter to the market makers' own best interests. To this day, you will find restrictions throughout the NASD manual that are purposely left vague in nature to allow the association unfettered and subjective enforcement of its rules. These restrictive rules were again expanded upon in May 1991, but this time were met in short order by stiff opposition.

SOES activists and SOES order-entry firms were finally gaining power. By late 1991, the NASD was met with a backlash of opposition from the growing SOES community regarding SEC approval of the "professional trader" rule. SOES activists argued that the NASD was erecting a protective barrier in favor of market makers and thus restricting competitive forces. They asserted that if this rule were approved, market makers would have little motivation to update their quotes, spreads would widen, and because trading would be inhibited, liquidity would be reduced. They further argued that approval of these amendments was tantamount to allowing the Nasdaq stock market to revert to its state prior to the implementation of the mandatory SOES order execution. In other words, market makers would again be able to protect themselves from fair competition by excluding one class of traders.

The SOES trading community also appealed the SEC's approval of other aspects of these rules to the U.S. Court of Appeals for the District of Columbia Circuit, which remanded the matter to the SEC in 1993 to consider, among other things, whether the professional trading account rules were unacceptably vague, thereby allowing the NASD to enforce the "professional trader" rule in an arbitrary and capricious manner favoring market makers. Thankfully, the decision was rendered in favor of the SOES community, and so marked the turning point in the SOES industry. In October 1993, the NASD repealed the "professional trading account" rules. In addition, the NASD withdrew its definitions of "day trade" and "day trading." In so doing, one more step was taken toward the achievement and maintenance of a free and open market.

The Five-Minute Rule

The five-minute rule dovetails the 1,000-share-limit rule. In light of certain order aggregation practices of registered representatives and seasoned traders who maintained power of attorney over several accounts, the NASD adopted the five-minute rule. This rule was established to prevent traders from entering multiple 1,000-share orders in rapid-fire succession under the pretense that each order was based on a new investment decision. The five-minute rule states very simply "that any trades entered within any five-minute period in accounts controlled by an associated person or customer will be presumed to be based on a single investment decision." Such an interpretation prevents anyone hoping to batch orders in a manner inconsistent with the intent of the rule.

In sum, the following rules for using SOES apply:

- SOES can be used to purchase or sell short any size lot of stock from 1 to 1,000 shares within a five-minute period beginning with the initial purchase of a given stock.
- There are no time restrictions on long selling using SOES.
- Several small purchases, sales, and repurchases of a given stock can be made within a five-minute period as long as the 1,000-share limit within the five-minute period is not exceeded.
- The five-minute rule and 1,000-share limit apply only to a single stock. Many different stocks may be purchased at once as long as purchases of each adhere to the SOES rules.

The intent of the rule is to prevent the trader from owning more than 1,000 shares of stock purchased using SOES within any given five-minute period. Thus, there should be no problem with buying 1,000 shares, selling them, and buying 1,000 shares again as many times as may be possible within five minutes, because at no time is the 1,000-share rule violated. However, different order-entry firms interpret this point in different ways. Some tend to the restrictive side and will not allow you to repurchase the same stock within a five-minute period even if you make a sale of the previous purchase first. Because buying, selling, and repeating is a very valuable strategy for those who wish to engage in one-stock trading, as we will detail in Chapter 8, "Trade and Grow Rich," you will want to ask any potential order-entry firms about their interpretation of this rule prior to opening an account.

The Short-Sale Rule

Another important regulation pertinent to SOES trading is the short-sale rule. Prior to explaining the short-sale rule, let's first clarify that there are two important types of sales used in trading: long and short. *Long sales* are what we normally think of when we think of selling, that is, sales of securities owned by the seller prior to the placement of the sell order. Of course, anyone is permitted to sell securities they already own (long), regardless of which way the market is heading.

Short sales are sales of securities *borrowed* by the customer from the broker-dealer where the customer trading account resides. You may be wondering, "Why would someone ever *borrow* securities from a broker-dealer?" Oftentimes, a trader may feel that a given security is overpriced, and thus poised to drop in price. At this point, you would like to sell any such shares you own, and, if you don't own them, then you wish you did so you could sell them. A short sale is just as good. To profit from this belief, a trader will borrow shares from the broker-dealer and immediately sell those shares at the prevailing market price. The trader hopes the price of the stock will then plummet so that the stock can be repurchased at a lower price and she can keep the difference. Instead of adhering to the axiom, "buy low, sell high," this trader has reversed the mind-set: "Sell high now, buy low later."

For example, using technical and other indicators that we will discuss in Chapter 5, "High-Probability Trading," you decide that a stock selling at 25⅛ is headed down and not up. You sell 1,000 shares short and $25,125 is added to your account. You must now replace the stock you borrowed. As predicted, the stock sells off and the price moves down to 15⅛. You purchase the 1,000 shares at $15,125 and replace the stock you borrowed. In the bargain, you pocket the difference between the amount you received for selling the borrowed stock and your cost of replacing it, for a profit of $10,000.

If instead of falling, the price began to rally, your cost of replacing the borrowed shares would be more than you got for the short sale. For example, if the price rallied to 35⅛, you would have to replace the shares at a cost of $35,125. Subtracting the short sale proceeds of $25,125 from this would put you in the hole for $10,000. This prospect is what frightens many investors away from short selling. However, if you had gone long at 25⅛ and the price dropped to 15⅛, you would also have lost $10,000, but going long seems more natural to people, especially considering that over the long term, the stock market has been up more times than down.

Happily, the day trader would never lose $10,000 on such a trade in the first place. This is because trading rules set *prior* to beginning trading would mandate a certain stop-loss, at which point the day trader sells to cut losses. We'll have more on setting trading rules later.

Although the stock market is up more often than down, another factor comes into play regarding short sales that may compensate for this and thus makes the risks of short and long selling just about a wash. Due to the panic factor, as we will explore further in Chapter 4,

"Market Psychology," stocks in general fall much faster and farther than they rise. It's similar to building a glacier. Glaciers and polar ice caps form slowly because it takes thousands of seasons of snow and ice buildup to form them. But once the temperatures rise sufficiently, all of it can melt away in a relatively short time period.

The market is primarily driven by fear and greed. But fear is the stronger of the two. The fear of loss is a more powerful drive for people than is the greed for gain. People who will sometimes do very little to make an extra dollar will often go to great lengths to save one. The ironic thing is that the fear of loss is itself all too often what causes the loss. This is why bear markets last from one-third to one-half the time that bull markets do, but the drop occurs twice to three times as fast. The majority of people, of course, do little to either make an extra dollar or to keep from losing one, as all honest salespeople marketing a good product surely know. In any event, however, because stocks fall more quickly than they rise, more money can actually be made by an astute trader selling short than by going long.

When many traders all begin selling a stock short, however, the resulting increase in the number of shares becoming available at the same time triggers a self-fulfilling prophecy based on the law of supply and demand: When more of something is offered for sale, the price falls. Prior to 1994, it was rock-'n'-roll time on free-falling Nasdaq stocks, and a lot of folks made a lot of money selling short.

To forestall such a possible snowball effect, the Nasdaq in January 1994 prohibited all short selling on SOES. By September of that year, another rule had been formulated, and became effective in January 1995, at which time shorting using SOES was allowed to resume. Nasdaq's short-sale rule now prohibits short sales in Nasdaq securities at or below the inside bid when the current inside bid is below the previous inside bid. This rule forbids anyone from selling borrowed shares (short) on a *downbid* or a *zero downbid,* that is when the bid price is either falling or remaining steady after a previous fall. Short sales can be executed only on an *upbid* or a *zero-plus upbid,* that is, when the bid price is either rising or remaining steady after a previous rise. In plain English, all of this simply means that no stock can be sold short unless the last *change* in its bid was upward. Moreover, the upbid must be a minimum of $\frac{1}{16}$ of a point, or a *teenie.* This disallows anyone from selling a stock short on a free fall and thus profiting on the way down.

Once even a single upbid has occurred, however, short sales can be executed until another downbid takes place. Plus, it's very easy to tell if a stock is shortable. Your Level II Market Maker window, as we will discuss in detail in Chapter 6, "Timing Your Trade Using RealTick III™," has either a green upbid arrow or a red downbid arrow next to the current bid price, depending on which way the stock is moving. So, if you've got a green light, then it's full speed ahead. Take a look at the Intel Level II window in Chapter 1, Figure 1.1. Near the top, to the right of the INTC symbol in the white box, is the last sale price of 109%6. To the right of that is a small up arrow. This is the green upbid arrow we are speaking of.

The Nasdaq short-sale rule is similar to that of the NYSE. The NYSE rules are basically the same, except that they apply to up*ticks* and not upbids. A tick, of course, represents an actual sale, whereas a bid is simply an offer to buy. The NYSE bases its rule on an uptick because a single specialist oversees each stock and so can enter the sales in the order in which they occur. By contrast, the Nasdaq has many market makers for each stock. Each market maker has 90 seconds to report the sale. Thus, it is entirely possible, if not altogether likely, that sales of Nasdaq stocks may not appear in the order in which they actually took place, making an uptick rule unreliable. Thus, the Nasdaq rule is more effectively based on what someone is willing to pay rather than on what has been paid.

Affirmative Determination

As noted, anyone can sell on a downbid if they already own the stock they are selling. This is known as a *long sale*. However, in an effort to evade the short-sale rule, some traders began to place sell orders for stock they did not own (short) as though they did own the stock and the sale was long. This was possible because many order-entry systems weren't sophisticated enough to distinguish between traders selling their own stock and traders selling stock they didn't own. This failing allows traders to sell stock on a downbid even though the trader has no position, because the order-entry system interprets the sale as a long sale, which can be legally executed on a downbid. To combat this abuse, the NASD placed the onus of responsibility on the order-entry firm to watch all of its customers.

As a matter of policy, the NASD requires all broker-dealers to make a notation on the order ticket at the time the order is taken that reflects the conversation with the customer regarding the present location of the securities in question. If such securities are in good deliverable form and the customer is able to deliver the securities within the prescribed time requirement, then the sale is considered a long sale. In any other instance, the sale must be considered a short sale.

This requirement, of course, presupposes that all trades are placed through brokers prior to execution and that all trades are written up on order tickets. Whereas such a scenario may be the case for the typical investor, SOES traders place orders without prior consultation, and they do so in a ticketless environment. It is, therefore, incumbent upon the trader to monitor any errors that may take place.

Regarding affirmative determination, such a transgression on the part of the trader is not taken lightly by the order-entry firm. Whereas mistakes are made and forgiven, especially with new traders, any such error made on a regular basis by an experienced trader is usually interpreted as willful disregard for the rule. If such a pattern is noted, the order-entry firm will ask the trader to close out his account rather than jeopardize the good standing of the firm.

Order-Handling Rules

In addition to all their other shady dealings, market makers frequently failed to display quotes and limit orders received that were priced better than the one at which the market maker wanted to trade the stock. In other instances, the market maker waited to report certain transactions after the market closed to prevent anyone from finding out at what price a trade took place until it was too late to act on it. The result was years of artificially high spreads while the market makers and the big brokerage houses took untold millions of dollars out of the hide of the small investor.

Here's how this worked. You would call your broker and place a market order. He would either place the order with his firm's market maker or with another brokerage's market maker who funneled to your broker's firm a kickback (payment for order flow) for the order. The market maker has a display of 25¼ for the stock, but he also has received an order to sell stock for 25⅛. Instead of selling the stock to you at the best price, he sells it to you for 25¼, and you have been instantly ripped off for ⅛, or $125 on a 1,000-share order. Regardless of what sellers and buyers actually were willing to trade their stocks for, there was an informal agreement (read collusion and conspiracy) among the market makers to keep the spreads unfairly high. Before political correctness came into vogue, we would call that highway robbery, and in the old days we would hang someone for less!

This is worse than the blind leading the blind. When a blind person leads another blind person, at least the leader has a strong incentive not to fall into a pit. When you are led by your broker and the entrenched Wall Street trading establishment, you are blind and being led directly into the pit by those with 20/20 vision who know exactly where they are taking you! Never forget that however much your broker may tell you that all of this is in the past, it was your broker's firm and others that set up these unfair trading practices to cheat you out of your money in the first place, and none of them instituted any change until absolutely forced to do so by the SEC. These and many other fraudulent practices of the Wall Street brokerage establishment are the antithesis of a free market such as we discussed in our introduction.

In response, independent traders again filed charges against the big brokerage houses in 1994, initiating a Justice Department and SEC probe. In 1996, the Justice Department launched an antitrust probe

BROKERSAURUS   By Bob Baird and Craig McBurney

Contact us or send us your idea for a cartoon at brokersaurus.com

Artistry by Bill Frankiger

against the market makers. In their continuing charge to bring a level playing field into the markets, despite having to fight your broker's firm and others tooth and nail to do it, the SEC mandated new order-handling rules effective in January 1997 that required market makers to always display the best price at which a given issue was available. As if someone really had to tell them! As a result, by the end of 1997, spreads had seen a 25 to 33 percent reduction.

It should be noted, however, that even with the new rules, *block orders,* that is, orders greater than 10,000 shares or over $250,000 in value, are still not required to be displayed. Though these come along more infrequently than regular market maker orders, when they do, they cause the biggest price movements, and so are the very ones you would like to know about! Clearly, more work still remains to be done in opening this market, but we have made amazing gains nonetheless.

We have already touched upon the ability of the day trader to make markets by buying and selling between the spread. This allowed the day trader to make money, while at the same time giving the small investor a better deal. This strategy was easy to employ when the spreads were ½ or even ¼. Now, with lower spreads since 1997, this is a somewhat less lucrative method of trading. Buying and selling between the spread is not possible using SOES, but can be done via Electronic Communications Networks, which we will discuss in Chapter 3.

The Actual-Size Rule

The actual-size rule is but the latest example of market maker and NASD clout with the SEC in their continuing war against the day trader. In July 1998, the SEC approved a new rule that, in some instances, reduces the number of shares that market makers must post in order to make a market from 1,000 to only 100 shares. The new rule applies to market makers entering a customer limit order. The rationale for this was that market makers may not always actually have orders for 1,000 shares, and that it is unfair to make them responsible for trading additional shares themselves that they actually had no orders for. Therefore, they now may post the "actual size" of a customer limit order down to a minimum required of 100 shares as opposed to the previously required 1,000 shares. When market makers are entering the market in a stock for themselves, the 1,000-share minimum still applies.

At first blush, this would appear to be bad news for the day trader. One of the premier advantages of day trading has been the ability to hit or "SOES" all market makers for 1,000 shares and get out in the event that a trade suddenly moves against you. For the day trader to trade in 100-share units means that she would have to do 10 trades to make the same gross as she would have in a single trade previously. Subtract from that 20 commissions for getting in and out of 10 trades, and suddenly day trading ceases to be a profitable proposition.

Thankfully, however, the practical effect of the actual-size rule is that virtually nothing has changed at all. Day trading has been little affected by the rule, and a new day trader would be hard-pressed to figure out that this rule was in effect were he not to read about it. In a sense, the actual-size rule actually benefits day traders. Prior to the rule, all Level II windows were filled with 1,000-share bids and offers. A low-liquidity, low-interest issue would have 1,000-share bids and offers posted, and, because market makers were not required to post more than 1,000 shares, high-interest stocks having market makers with many more than 1,000 shares to trade also were filled with 1,000-share posts. Thus, there was no immediate way to discriminate between them on this basis.

Now it is easier to tell at a glance where the real interest lies. When the day trader pulls up a Level II window filled with many 100-share posts, she simply moves on. Although it is still not directly possible to determine whether 1,000-share posts are the tip of a 10,000-share (or more) iceberg, at least real interest is signified. Thus the day trader can trade with more confidence than ever before!

SOES Today

As you can easily surmise from the many recent dates of SOES rule changes, the broad avenues of trading now afforded to the aspiring day trader are nearly brand-new. As we discussed in the introduction, this is not something that has been going on for a long time and you're joining in after everything has been wrung out of it. You are truly in on the ground floor of one of the greatest technological breakthroughs of all time, and an exploding industry in its infancy. Think of it as having bought stock in a company the day before it announced it was adding a dot com to the end of its name. Day trading is gonna be big. Really big!

SOES today is the backbone of low-risk day trading. Because of the ability to obtain virtually instantaneous execution of a trade, the day trader can take greater risks on entering a trade. If she finds shortly thereafter that the trade is moving against her, she simply enters an order on SOES to exit that trade and she is out within seconds. This instantaneous execution feature allows day trading to be far safer than any other kind of trading.

If a stock's price is making a strong move against the trader, SOES will likely be the only market allowing for prompt exit from the trade. The other Electronic Communications Networks (ECNs), as we will discuss in Chapter 3, are frequently one-sided. If a stock in one of these is trending forcefully against them, participants will simply cancel their orders, thus avoiding this powerful wave of momentum, but diminishing the liquidity of the stock. This is because traders in these markets have no obligation to make a market. Keep in mind that this works in your favor, because you are one of these traders.

By contrast, market makers in SOES have the duty to make fair and orderly markets. Rarely will a market maker in SOES lift his bid or offer during an unforeseen move. To do so regularly would risk close scrutiny by the NASD, with accompanying sanctions levied if the NASD concluded the market maker was failing to honor that specific market.

Because of the various before-and-after changes we have discussed in the previous section, let's summarize the current, pertinent SOES trading rules here to avoid any confusion.

SOES Trading

When trading stocks using SOES, you have only two choices regarding price. If you want to trade the stock at the current inside market quote and *only* at that price, you enter a *market limit order.* For example, you are watching your Nasdaq Level II market maker window, and there are two market makers offering at the inside market of 25⅛. Others are offering at 25¼ and higher. You enter your SOES market limit order for 25⅛. But because there are other traders out there watching the same stock, two or more of them decided to buy on SOES before you did. Thus, they SOES the two market makers at the inside quote, meaning that no stock is available at 25⅛. This happens because SOES works on a first-come, first-served basis. Your order is not filled.

If you want the stock at the current inside market quote, but are willing to have a little less favorable execution in the event that you really, really, cross-your-heart-and-hope-to-die want the stock, you simply enter a *market order.* Use caution here because this practice is known as *chasing the trade* if the stock is already moving, which can be dangerous, as we will discuss later. In this instance, the same scenario as outlined previously would transpire, but instead of your order not being filled, it would be filled at the next-best price of 25¼.

In both of these instances, the best the trader can do is to purchase at the inside market ask price and so lose the spread. At worst, using a market order, the trader has lost the spread and bought at a higher price than originally planned. It is not possible using SOES to purchase at the bid or between the bid and ask. SOES can be used only to purchase at the ask or sell at the bid. Because of these limitations, SOES is most useful to the day trader as an *exit strategy* when a trade is going against him. Exiting a bad trade will always be done at market, and you'll be glad to get it.

SOES Summary

SOES today is a complex field. Gone are the days when a trader simply watched and waited for the market in a given security to move. Due to acceptance of SOES as a legitimate form of trading that is here to stay, market makers have responded by adroitly manipulating their purchases and sales to achieve their objectives in spite of SOES traders. Now, market makers have resorted to trading strategies known as *head-fakes, wiggles and jiggles,* and *fading the trend* in order to make SOES traders think that the trend is moving in one direction when it is actually moving in another, and so to outmaneuver them. As a matter of policy, these trading techniques are perfectly acceptable. Given the fact that, as market makers, they provide for the operation of fair and orderly markets, they are entitled to a profit if they are adept traders. But the day trader is just as entitled if he or she is just as adept.

With this in mind, the goal of the SOES trader today must be to have vision. By understanding not only the minute-to-minute fluctuations occurring in the markets, but also the greater overall trends, SOES traders are able to capitalize on movements arising daily in the Nasdaq marketplace. In this way, the astute trader can potentially profit far more than would be possible by employing the traditional buy-and-hold strategy.

In sum, SOES benefits day traders in many ways:

- Routing of the order electronically to the market maker quoting the best price
- Automatic execution at the best quoted price (provided there are no orders ahead of that order)
- Reporting of the trade to the Nasdaq system
- Comparison, matching, clearing, settlement, and confirmation of small orders

- Real-time display of all SOES executions
- Executions of limit orders
- And most important, protection for the small investor during periods of heavy volume and market activity by guaranteed order execution

The following SOES rules apply:

- *Mandatory order execution.* Regardless of whether market makers are posting 100 or 1,000 shares, they are required to execute a trade for that amount whenever they receive a SOES order.
- *1,000-share/five-minute rule.* The day trader cannot purchase in excess of 1,000 shares during any five-minute period using SOES.
- *Professional trader rules.* The typical day trader, trading from home, office, or trading room, is not considered a professional trader and is not subject to professional trader rules.
- *Short-sale rule/affirmative determination.* The day trader cannot sell shares short unless the last *change* in the bid price was upward.
- *Order-handling rules.* Market makers are required to post the best bids they have and honor the bids they post.
- *Actual-size rule.* Market makers must post the maximum SOES limit of 1,000, 500, or 200 shares if they are making a market in the stock. The exception is if the market maker is entering a customer limit order, in which case the market maker may post as few as 100 shares.

SOES Tomorrow

As we have learned, market makers and the big brokerage houses (probably *your* broker) they work for are not at all pleased with the day trader invasion into their self-proclaimed private territory. We can expect them to continue their war, but with far less effect. Day traders are one of the fastest-growing segments of the already-burgeoning, online trading community. All it takes to convert an online trader to a true electronic day trader is knowledge—such as we are providing in this book. New ECNs, order-entry firms, and trading rooms are cropping up everywhere to cater to the needs of the day trader. We day traders are too numerous, along with all the new companies and businesses that work on our behalf, to be brushed aside or silenced by a new rule. And you, as a new or aspiring day trader, are further strengthening our ranks. Welcome!

The Nasdaq market is a dynamic trading environment. Accordingly, modifications in the rules will inevitably continue in order to meet ever varying market needs. Although change can be frightening, one thing is certain: Day trading will flourish in the twenty-first century, and all aspiring day traders can confidently begin their careers secure in the knowledge that day trading will be an honorable vocation for years to come.

In Chapter 3, we will learn about the various Electronic Communications Networks (ECNs) that, combined with SOES, make profitable day trading possible as never before.

chapter 3

entering the market

electronic communications networks and how they operate

Prior to January 1997, quote and size were not publicly posted on Electronic Communications Networks (*ECNs*). At that time, Nasdaq added ECNs to their automated quotations system. This is the primary sea change that makes effective day trading possible. If you are just starting to day trade, you can compare getting in this close to the ground floor to purchasing a one- or two-year-old vehicle: It's really better than it was when it was new because all of the bugs have been worked out by someone else before you came along, and that person took the biggest depreciation hit as well. If Nasdaq will build it, you will come. Well, they built it, and here you are!

Using ECNs

ECNs are services you can use to place both buy and sell orders. They offer ease and flexibility of order entry. Unlike with SOES, by using ECNs, you can actually make markets, just as the market makers do. You can enter an order at any price that you wish, whether it be between the spread, at the inside bid or ask, lower than the inside bid, or higher than the inside ask. For instance, if there appears to be some momentum, a trader might be able to *fade the trend* and receive a better price than that of the inside market. Using the example of Company ABCD, where the inside market (quote) is 25 (bid) × 25⅛ (offer), let's assume that the stock is trending up. Although the inside market is currently 25 × 25⅛, by all appearances the stock seems to be headed to 25⅛ × 25¼. In this situation, it is possible for the trader to sell the stock to someone at the offer (25⅛) because other investors also perceive the price to be moving higher. Whereas the stock price may never actually move up to 25⅛ × 25¼, the trader has been able to sell the stock on the offer. Such a scenario is not possible with SOES. However, there is no requirement for anyone to sell or buy your shares at your posted price should you need to exit a bad trade. It's best to stick with trades no larger than the mandatory order-execution size limit (usually 1,000 shares) so you can always use SOES to get out.

SOES, as we have noted, offers no anonymity or privacy to the market maker, who, if he is doing serious trading, most definitely has a strategy and does not want to tip his hand to the trading world. Although he can sell in small blocks over and over, it is only a matter of time before this approach is discovered. In this instance, the market maker may elect to use an ECN. The number of shares at a given price posted on an ECN is the true sum total of everyone using that ECN to trade, and any given trader's bids and asks are diluted among all the rest. Because of this, and because the ECN symbol is all that is displayed, complete anonymity for anyone using an ECN is assured.

On most Nasdaq stocks in which the day trader will be interested, the market maker is typically required to make a market for 1,000 shares. Market makers will rarely post larger trades, lest this tip off other traders to what they are wanting to do and so possibly affect the price adversely. Thus, on SOES, market makers with 10,000 shares to sell may post only 1,000 or 2,000 at selected prices to try to keep the price from moving against them too quickly. On the other hand, market makers who are not serious at the moment about the stock, but want to be in it just in case, can enter their 1,000 shares and then keep adjusting their price so as to never really have to trade much. Thus, SOES does not allow direct determination of what a given market maker is actually doing at a given moment.

By contrast, ECNs allow more insight into the actual interest in a given issue. One major advantage of ECNs is that, because the number of shares displayed is the aggregate of everyone's entries into that ECN, the posted shares-to-trade number is a much more reliable indicator of the actual interest in the stock than are the individual market maker bids and asks. This can be a valuable indicator for what direction the market in that stock is actually headed. For example, if 5,000 shares are being bid for on an ECN and only 750 on the ask, it just might indicate real interest, and the price may be headed up.

A *headfake* can occur on SOES when a market maker quickly posts shares at a price better than the current inside market to create the perception that the market is moving in the opposite direction than it really is. The market maker hopes to remove it before anyone actually attempts to trade it. Were the market maker to be "hit," and thus required to trade, his loss would not be too great.

The day trader thus realizes that a big order on an ECN is likely a valid order and not a headfake as may be the case on SOES. There is a reason for this conviction. In order to fake out traders on an ECN, the individual or firm usually must put out a fairly sizable order, say 5,000 to 10,000 shares or more, to catch the attention of the astute day trader. That such a headfake could backfire and end up being costly to the institution initiating such a trade is evident. This is because any trader on an ECN, seeing a trade of that size, has the freedom to hit such a bid or offer in its entirety should she so desire. Therefore, a headfake of this magnitude takes on a far greater degree of risk than is associated with a similar type of play on SOES, and so is less likely to occur.

Certain trading firms have adapted programs to allow retail clientele to combine into one list all of the stocks considered tradeworthy. In addition, the list provides detailed information regarding volume and price movement. For instance, it might provide the inside bid and offer as well as whether that inside bid or offer is locking or crossing the inside market. A *locked market* is when the bid and ask are identical, and a *crossed market* is when the bid is higher than the ask. Armed with this knowledge, the day trader can step in quickly when a trade imbalance such as this is perceived, having the confidence of knowing the "smart" money has a big order to fill, which might propel a little order (such as hers) a level or two.

Selling Short

You will recall from our last chapter that short selling on SOES first required an upbid to occur. Of course, an upbid in a falling stock is not as likely to occur as we may wish, and we are thus often prevented from selling short on SOES because of this, which is exactly what Nasdaq wanted. However, because the day trader can make markets using an ECN and can enter in any price she wishes, it is possible for her to create her own upbid by simply offering to buy a small lot of shares for $\frac{1}{16}$ higher than the going price. That makes the day trader's ask the best inside market quote, and, particularly in a falling market, it won't be long until someone picks it up. This sale, then, is by definition its own upbid. Immediately following, you may enter your short sale order. Of course, you can also include the small lot you just bought. If the stock is really headed down, the extra $\frac{1}{16}$ you pay to be able to sell it short is a bargain. In fact, you could say that it's "teenie" in comparison to your potential for profit.

After-Hours Trading

Many times, we hear news that breaks after the stock markets close (usually by design) that would be anticipated to cause a given stock to begin to move. And we wish that we could trade the stock at that time in order to take advantage of the move. An advantage of ECNs over SOES is the ability to do after-hours trading just like this. Remember, the Nasdaq is a virtual market. Whereas the NYSE folks may leave promptly for the golf course at 4:00 P.M., leaving only piles of confetti for the janitor to sweep up, the Nasdaq is open as long as there are any two traders sitting at their computer terminals. Of course, most Nasdaq traders also quit at 4:00, so the liquidity of most issues falls dramatically. And because there is no SOES trading after hours, you cannot SOES your way out of a bad trade. Nevertheless, in times of after-hours news, the day trader can take full advantage, if desired. But with extended trading hours just around the corner, and round-the-clock, round-the-world trading sure to follow, the whole concept of "after hours" will soon cease to exist.

Summary

As you can see, ECNs offer much more flexibility than SOES. However, they also carry commensurately more risk if not used properly in conjunction with SOES. This is because of the nonguarantee of anyone either buying from you or selling to you at your posted price. SOES is your only guaranteed exit mechanism, so your use of ECNs should always be guided by the requirements of SOES. Although you can purchase over 1,000 shares on an ECN, in practice you will not because you can sell only up to 1,000 shares on SOES every five minutes. Although you can trade after hours using ECNs, in practice you will not because (for now) there is no SOES after hours.

In sum, ECNs will be your primary means of buying, selling, or selling short when you are actually making markets. Only when the market begins to turn against you will you sell quickly on SOES. It is the guarantee of being able to SOES your way out of a trade gone awry that will allow you to confidently ride out your many profitable trades and have an exit strategy for the bad ones. Don't adopt any trading practices that will jeopardize this.

The ECNs

There are several ECNs, such as SelectNet, Instinet, the Island, and Archipelago, through which you can trade via your order-entry firm. Each ECN has its pros and cons, its unique characteristics, and its advantages and disadvantages, which we will discuss here. For your convenience and reference, Table 3.1 summarizes and compares the pertinent features of SOES and the various ECNs.

SelectNet

SelectNet is Nasdaq's ECN. It is the primary method market makers use to trade share volumes in excess of those allowed on SOES, but, of course, orders of any size, small or large, are eligible. SelectNet offers traders the ability to automate negotiation and execution of trades. SelectNet provides fast, low-cost, and efficient service, thus eliminating the need for verbal contact between trading desks. SelectNet offers automated trading for both market makers and order-entry firms. Order-entry firms can program their Nasdaq Level 2 workstations to view orders from market makers. Moreover, market makers can interact with orders from order-entry firms. After negotiation and execution, transactions are automatically reported to Nasdaq for public dissemination and sent to a clearing corporation for comparison and settlement.

SelectNet offers traders both flexibility and control. The flexibility of SelectNet allows Level 2 (order-entry firms) or Level 3 (market makers) Nasdaq subscribers to *preference* (to specified market makers) or *broadcast* (to all market makers) orders in Nasdaq securities. Preferencing means that you can select or "hit" a particular market maker advertising the number of shares that you want. However, this requires

Table 3.1 SOES and Electronic Communication Networks Comparison Chart

Features	SOES	SelectNet	Instinet	Island	Archipelago
Guaranteed order execution/small investor protection	100, 200, 500, 1,000 shares	No	No	No	No
Market makers required to make a market	Yes	No	No	No	No
Automatic submission of order to market maker with best price	Yes	No	No	No	No
Preferencing—ability to select specific market maker	No	Yes	No	No	Yes
Price improvement—ability to get better price than quote	No	Yes	Yes	Yes	Yes
Always posts true bid/ask volumes	No	Yes	Yes	Yes	Yes
Maximum order size	1,000	None	None	None	None
Stop or limit orders	At inside market price only	Between spread only	At any price	At any price	At any price
Short selling	On down-bid only	On down-bid or bid $+\frac{1}{16}$	On down-bid or bid $+\frac{1}{16}$	On down-bid or bid $+\frac{1}{16}$	On down-bid or bid $+\frac{1}{16}$
Partial fills	Yes	No	No	No	No
Ability for trader to make a market	No	Yes	Yes	Yes	Yes
Before- and after-hours trading	No	Yes	Yes	Yes	Yes
Market liquidity/ significant order flow	High	High	High	Medium	Low
Additional fee for use	No	Low	High	Low	Lowest

that you pay whatever price she is advertising, usually the inside market. Broadcasting is what you do when you want to make a market by setting your own price, but (for SelectNet) only between the spread. SelectNet also identifies incoming and outgoing orders and allows traders to see subsequent messages and negotiation results.

The advantages over SOES are substantial. Yet the trader must be cautioned about two significant shortcomings with this service. First, SelectNet does not allow traders to place stop orders or limit orders outside the inside market. Stop and limit orders are important for any trader using technical analysis charts or programs that identify good entry and exit points. The ability to place orders outside the market is quite important in that it allows traders to reserve their place as far to the front of the line as possible should the stock ever trade at the desired level.

Second, SelectNet operates primarily for the benefit of market makers. Market makers comprise the lion's share of all volume traded on SelectNet. What this means is that the day trader placing orders on SelectNet is matching wits against the best traders on Wall Street. Such a situation is not nearly as likely on the other proprietary exchanges (ECNs)—namely, Instinet, the Island, and Archipelago.

In sum, the pros and cons of SelectNet are as follows:

Pros

- Fast trade execution and reporting
- The ability to preference market makers
- Price improvement
- Eligibility of any-size order
- A proprietary market with significant order flow
- Availability of before- and after-hours trading (9:00 to 9:30 A.M. and 4:00 to 5:15 P.M. ET)

Cons

- No stop or limit orders outside the inside market
- Service primarily for the use of market makers

Finally, there is a fee associated with supplementary services like SelectNet. For each SelectNet order, Nasdaq charges the order-entry firm providing order execution and clearing an additional $2.50. Cancellation of an order also entails a fee. These charges are passed along to the customer.

Instinet

Instinet is a private market operated by Reuters, a British firm. It was first introduced in 1969 for institution-to-institution trading, but was later expanded to include brokers. Like SelectNet, Instinet is also mainly for the use of market makers.

A closer review of the primary advantages related to Instinet— order flow and the ability to place orders outside the inside market— will help explain the circumstances under which Instinet can be most beneficial. Perhaps the most significant of the advantages of Instinet is its acceptance of orders placed outside the inside market. Each bid or ask at a given price level is placed in sequence as received. This feature allows traders to *queue up* well in advance of an anticipated market move to the desired trading level. By having one's order placed in advance, frequently a trader is able to buy on the bid or sell on the offer when a stock initially begins to trade at those levels. This advantage is enormous because it eliminates the spread and, in effect, affords the trader all of the benefits generally reserved only for the market makers.

As the most established ECN, Instinet is the largest and most liquid. It has the most extensive order flow from market makers, institutions, and retail clients of all the private securities markets. Order flow, of course, is vital to prompt order execution. With more traders viewing this ECN than any other private market, execution of a given order would be more likely to take place here than on any other.

Because Instinet is a proprietary marketplace utilized by professional traders and institutions, the trading that takes place in this market is generally considered "smart" trading, which simply means that those individuals and institutions, placing a large portion of their order flow through Instinet, trade for a living and have been doing so for years. With this in mind, the trading activities that take place through this ECN provide invaluable signals from which the astute trader can benefit. Pertinent to this order flow are the trades from both institutional and retail clientele. Because of the inclusion of a good percentage of retail clients, it can be said that the level of participant expertise is somewhat less sophisticated than that found on SelectNet.

In addition, trade reporting is less efficient than in other markets. Whereas order execution for Instinet is every bit as efficient as the other markets, trade entry and trade reporting are manually handled, which places the day trader at a disadvantage. Frequently, a fill will not be reported to the day trader for as long as a minute, whereas effective day trading can require confirmation within seconds. During this time, the market can be moving. If a day trader isn't sure that a fill has been recorded, his hands are tied until fill of the trade is reported. Such a flaw can cost the trader a great deal of money. If you receive no confirmation in a couple of minutes, it is best to simply cancel your order. If a stock is moving rapidly, you don't want to end up finding that the price you entered and traded at is not as good as what the stock is trading at by the time you receive order confirmation.

There is, however, one way to reasonably determine whether your order has been filled even before your confirmation has arrived. If an order is logged early enough, the trader's will be the first order placed at that level. If the security trades at that level, and the trader notes that the Instinet order flow changes by an amount that corresponds to the volume the trader entered, it is likely the trader's order has been filled. With that in mind, the trader can make decisions based on a presumed fill. Fortunately, other private markets such as the Island do not have this uncertainty-of-fill shortcoming.

The pros and cons of Instinet are as follows:

Pros

- Fast order execution
- Price improvement
- Stop and limit orders
- Eligibility of any-size order
- A proprietary market with significant order flow
- Availability of before- and after-hours trading

Cons

- Slow trade reporting
- Service primarily for the use of market makers

As the most established private market, Instinet charges a large premium over the other markets for its products and services. Each Instinet order costs the order-entry firm between $4.00 and $15.00, depending on the level of activity. As you know, this expense is passed along to the customer.

The Island
The Island, a proprietary ECN operated by Datek Securities of New York, was added to the Nasdaq in January 1997. It has numerous features that make it an attractive alternative to the other private markets as a means of maximizing gains from trades. Of great importance is the speed of order execution and trade reporting. Execution and trade reporting for orders initiated through the Island can be nearly instantaneous, much like SOES or SelectNet. Should there be a corresponding trade contra to the one the trader has entered, provided there are no other trades queued up in front of the trade, the orders will typically be matched, and execution will be swift.

Perhaps the most significant advantage of the Island is the nature of the order flow, which consists primarily of retail clientele. As a whole, this customer base is the least sophisticated of all the ECN markets and, as a logical consequence, most susceptible to poor interpretation of market conditions. This offers the astute trader a windfall opportunity to benefit from the inexperience of others.

A visit to the Island offers the following:

- Fast execution and trade reporting
- Price improvement
- Stop and limit orders
- Eligibility of any-size order
- Availability of before- and after-hours trading

Another advantage of trading on the Island is its modest cost structure, similar to SelectNet. The order-entry firm passes along a fee of $1.00 for all customer trades effected through the Island.

Archipelago
Archipelago is another proprietary electronic communications network. It is among the newest of the private marketplaces and has a number of features, some of which set it ahead of the others. As with the other ECNs, Archipelago offers automated negotiation and trading. These features make order execution fast and eliminate the necessity

for verbal contact between order-entry firms. Due to its speed of execution and trade reporting, it can be preferable to Instinet, where uncertainty handicaps the trader.

Traders also have the ability to preference orders in Archipelago. The ability to direct orders can be beneficial if particular market makers are slow in refreshing their quotes, allowing you to hit them at a better price if the other market makers have begun adjusting their quotes. Additionally, Archipelago offers price improvement. Price improvement is a primary feature that makes it an attractive alternative to other markets under certain circumstances.

Archipelago allows traders to place orders outside the inside market. As has been previously mentioned, this feature allows the trader to queue up early at a trading level where momentum is perceived to be developing. As with the other ECNs, Archipelago allows orders of any size to be placed into its system. Such flexibility allows traders to enter into or unwind larger positions than would be possible under SOES.

In brief, Archipelago offers traders the following:

- Fast execution and trade reporting
- The ability to preference market makers
- Price improvement
- Stop and limit orders
- Eligibility of any-size order
- Availability of before- and after-hours trading

Furthermore, the pricing structure of Archipelago is very attractive. Pricewise, the $0.50 premium per 1,000 shares makes it the least-expensive option of all the ECNs.

In Chapter 4, we will get into the nitty-gritty of market psychology and how big movements in a stock are primarily driven by one of two forces: fear or greed.

chapter 4

market psychology

not the way the market *should* be, but the way it *is*

To say that our day is the information age would be a massive understatement. Innumerable newspapers, magazines, books (other than this one), radio, television, and now thousands upon thousands of Web sites on the Internet are all part of the daily deluge of information that comes our way. It's fairly easy to make a first cut and weed out all of the superfluous information. This leaves only the information that is relevant to what we are interested in at any given time. For us, this means information on investing and the markets.

The problem is that even though we have narrowed our focus to only media that are pertinent, the information left is still completely overwhelming. Remember the good old essay test at school? You sit down, and the first question is: "Explain in detail the history of the universe and man's part in it." You write half a page. Are you done? You write a couple more pages. Is that enough? No matter how much you write, there's no real way to determine when you're done—other than getting into the professor's mind, where the answer lies.

Compiling information for investing is the same way. There is simply no end to the amount of data you could assimilate, if you had the time, and there is no way to tell when, if ever, you have assimilated enough. The only way to tell is to get into the mind of the market, that is, into what makes the thousands of investors out there do what they do.

To do this, the day trader maintains a keen awareness of how market news may affect the psychology of the market. Despite great fundamentals, such as a company's management team, market share, and so forth, a bit of negative news might drive down the price of stock of a very good company. A *fundamentalist*, one who keeps tabs on the fundamentals of a company, may worry that there is no rational reason for this. The day trader fully agrees with this, but instead of moping, she is buying at the bottom of the market and getting ready for when all of the *bargain hunters* come in and drive the price back up.

On the other hand, good news or expectations about a stock or industry sector may cause prices of a stock to career wildly upward, such as Internet stocks that can trade at prices several hundred times earnings, that is, if there are earnings at all. Fundamentalists can do nothing but pound their fists on the table when things that shouldn't happen happen anyway, while the day trader is more than happy to be not only among the first on the bandwagon (which, by the way, is the only way to be on a bandwagon), but also among the first out. In summary, the day trader buys and sells on his expectations of market psychology.

In fact, betting on the ability of advertising to sway the public can be a great way to pick stocks to trade. For instance, there are a lot of good Internet service providers out there with competitive rates for unlimited access. A couple of years or so ago, America Online began barraging the nation by sending out their $22 per month CD-ROM Internet connection kits like they were going out of style. If your mailbox wasn't stuffed with them, there they were falling out when you opened your Sunday newspaper! Because this advertising campaign literally brought the company's product to the consumer's lap via the CD, the average person who received one ran, not walked, directly to his computer, put it in, signed up, and began sending in his money. Anyone betting that droves would choose to be online this way would have cleaned up on AOL stock.

Another of many possible examples is Charles Schwab, which became one of the first so-called discount brokers by offering investors a tiny price break in commissions. Now there is a veritable flood of discounters, with commissions as low as zero, as we have previously discussed. What was once a high commission rate at Schwab, but still better than you could find most anywhere else, has changed relatively little, so that now Schwab is among the highest-priced "discount" brokers. Logic would dictate that Schwab would have been washed away and lost at sea in the face of this deluge. Not so! Investors are theoretically trading to make money, yet they have clung to Schwab to such an extent that Schwab consistently has great earnings and a high stock price.

With typical investors so oblivious to where their money is going, it is not surprising that most of them don't make a nickel in the market and trade only out of an altruistic compulsion to transfer their funds to someone who has a greater need for them—like you and me! Anyone with a modicum of common sense can run circles around those who refuse to change even when it is to their benefit.

The fact that people are as unpredictable as they are means that you want to be a fair-weather trader. It's just like fair-weather friends, who are around as long as things are going well with you and they need something. This is the way you want to treat your stocks. As long as things are going well with your stocks and you are getting something from them, continue to trade them. But when the stock settles down into a listless trading range, don't hang around out of nostalgia over better days. Drop the stock like a hot potato and find another. And don't shed a tear over it.

Running with the Bulls

The current bull market has been raging for nearly two decades, notwithstanding minor corrections such as those in 1987 and 1998. This is a result of the combination of many factors, such as the reduction of bank savings account interest rates and the markets opening up to the average investor through direct stock purchases, but especially through the increasing popularity of mutual funds. And there is no sign of the bull slowing down.

Behind the investment boom is another sort of "boom," that is, the baby boomers, those born between 1946 and 1964. The baby boomers are in their peak earning years and, even with the so-called low investment rates of Americans, are investing more than ever before. Most of this money is pouring into the stock market via mutual funds. We are now to the point where $25 billion *per month* is becoming routine! That comes to some $4 trillion by the time the first baby boomers begin to retire in 2011! This is why the bull is not likely to be corralled for a long time to come. Privately held companies will be forced to go public for no other reason than to take up some of the avalanche of money to keep the rest of us from smothering in it.

Some have expressed concerns that the markets will collapse when these retirements come, as a result of boomers ceasing to put money in and beginning to take money out. We must not forget, however, that boomer retirements in 2011 will be gradual and will not come as an abrupt change from previous years. There were, after all, folks born in 1945 and earlier who will be retiring in 2010 and before. Even more important, boomers will not be closing out their accounts altogether; instead, they will be making small withdrawals relative to a large volume of funds that have built up over decades. More than likely, the yield of the remaining funds will outpace the withdrawals, so the overall balances will continue to grow, and the majority of those monies will stay invested and at work in the market.

Moreover, hot on the tails of the boomers is another boom in its own right, that of the Generation Xers, most of whom are children of the baby boomers. The baby-boom generation has thus replaced itself with another generation of greater investors than themselves! There seems to be no end in sight. As many are saying, we may be at the dawn of a whole new paradigm in investing. No one can say for sure, but we do know this: The fundamentals are better now than they have been at any other point in history. And, for all this, we aren't even counting the billions of people in developing countries who will all be assuming their rightful places in revving up the global economy.

As a result of the cash blizzard, mutual fund managers find themselves with millions and millions of dollars being added to their accounts each and every month. They have the choice of either remaining in cash while the market whizzes by them or to making the increasingly difficult investment decisions of finding good companies for the long haul. Inevitably, this cannot help but result in an overall lowering of the quality of stocks in any given mutual fund. There are two reasons for this: One is that extensive purchases of traditional blue-chip companies by a multiplicity of fund managers drives the price-to-earnings ratio to greater and greater heights. This is the so-called flight to quality that occurs every couple of weeks when the market slightly dips and fund managers double up on their blue-chip purchases. No company under these circumstances can be expected to have earnings that can possibly keep pace with its ever increasing stock price. Low P/Es may just become a thing of the past.

The other is that the only alternative to so-called quality stocks is the purchase of more and more marginal and riskier companies to simply get the cash flow invested. It's sort of like going into a restaurant and seeing the maximum occupancy sign. The sign tells you the maximum number of people that the local fire marshal has determined can die in a fire there. In like manner, the fire marshals are now having to post signs at mutual fund companies prohibiting a given fund manager from having more than so much cash money on hand before she is required to burn it.

Though this may or may not present a problem for position investors some day down the line, it provides great opportunity for the day trader. In a bull market, it is almost impossible to keep any stock down for long. Many investors are tiring of purchasing stocks on the rise and look to any opportunity to buy them "on sale," that is, when their prices have been knocked down for some reason. Accordingly, the day trader has only a limited window of opportunity to get in on these stocks before bargain hunters start driving the prices back up again to levels more lofty than before. On the positive side, once the day trader is in, profits may be quickly made during increasingly more rapid and steeper rises.

The moral to this story is that, although there may be occasions when the day trader can profit by selling stocks short, an overall rising market necessitates that most gains be made by going *long*. The rest of this chapter will examine some of the various events and circumstances that can change a stock's price, mostly in the downward direction, from which the day trader may expect to profit.

Earnings Reports

Yes, there is a need for information, and we'll talk about some of the places to look for it in Chapter 7, "The Trading Day and Its Characteristics." But more important than the raw information is the psychology of the market response to it. For instance, in the spring of 1998, analysts estimated that the quarterly earnings of Kimberly-Clark Corporation would be 63 cents per share. Kimberly-Clark reported that it expected earnings in the 54 to 58 cents per share range. Thus, it had not "met" analysts' expectations. In response to this 7 to 9 cents per share difference, stock in the company dropped in value $6⅞ per share!

Why is this? Was there anything fundamentally wrong with

Kimberly-Clark? Maybe. Maybe not. Although most people would say that the company dropped nearly $7 per share in value because of a lower-than-expected earnings report, this is not the case at all. Kimberly-Clark dropped nearly $7 a share because of the *perception* (psychology) that missing some analyst's guess of 63 cents by 7 to 9 cents is somehow negative, which is not necessarily the case.

But looking out at the market and lamenting the hoopla over 7 to 9 cents is like explaining to someone why red should be their favorite color instead of green. The market will go the way the market will go, and few of us, save for the occasional Warren Buffett or Bill Gates, can have any effect on it whatsoever, even if we were to sell off our entire stake. Our purpose is to instead teach you some guidelines on *anticipating* the market direction so that you can have it work for you and not against you.

So, as part of your preparation to trade, check announcements of earnings reports to see which are coming up. Just before the actual release, check the chart trends of the stock to see whether it has been drifting up or down in the few weeks prior. This will allow you to determine what the insiders are doing. If the report is likely to beat *street* expectations, insiders, their families, and friends may be buying in anticipation of a jump in the stock's price right after the report. If the report is likely to fall short of expectations, this same group may be selling in anticipation of a drop in the stock's price. By careful analysis, day traders can position themselves among the first on the outside to profit from the earnings report.

Remember, insider buying for any ostensible reason is bullish. Insider selling may or may not be bearish. After all, anyone might need an extra couple hundred million now and then.

Analyst Expectations

Of course, the whole quarterly hoopla about companies meeting or not meeting analysts' expectations is an exercise in psychology, if not futility, itself, quite separate from the actual response of the public to the earnings announcement. Think about it. A company is going to do what a company is going to do, much the same as it will or will not rain regardless of whether you do a rain dance. It has better access to its own information and data than anyone else, and once that data has been processed and assimilated, an announcement will come forth regarding earnings for the quarter.

On the other side, we have a cadre of people working for various stock brokerages. Well, they have to do *something* when they come into the office. These *analysts* (number crunchers) decide to forecast the earnings of a company using what scanty data they may have, which can obviously never be as good as what the company has. Then, when the company's numbers don't match the analysts', the analysts say the company didn't meet *their* expectations. What gall! That's like learning your multiplication tables in one of today's self-esteem-enhancement math classes that most of the analysts themselves probably attended: The teacher asks you what is 5 times 5. You answer 30. When she tells you 25, you tell her that her answer failed to meet your expectations.

As you may surmise, there is no reason other than blatant manipulation of a stock's price for analysts to go through this charade four times a year. This fact may be illustrated by considering what would happen if analysts always got their predictions correct. If there were no analyst predictions, then a company would come out with an earnings report. If the earnings were higher than previously, then folks might say the company was on the right track and purchase shares. If not, they might sell.

Now enter the analyst who comes out a month ahead of time with a prediction. The analyst would issue his prediction, say 50 cents per share. Then a month later the company comes out with earnings at 50 cents a share. The only difference would be that folks would respond a month earlier based on the analyst's prediction, and not to the later company report. The analyst who could *accurately* predict would effectively have the news a month ahead of time and could act accordingly. Such an analyst, however, would have no incentive to make his estimate public—at least not until after he purchased all the stock he wanted prior to issuing his report early. This, of course, would cause the stock to move following the announcement. Still, the analyst could accomplish the same thing by putting off his purchase another month, until just before the company announced on its own, and he would still make his money. The bottom line is that if analysts could predict earnings to the penny, there would be no overriding reason for them to make their estimates public. But no one can predict earnings to the penny, no matter how good they are, except by sheer luck.

Because the analyst clearly already knows this, the earnings estimate will inevitably be designed to move the stock in a certain desired direction. If the analyst believes the stock has good potential, he has great incentive to come in slightly below what he thinks the company

might earn. Once the earnings report is issued, this has the effect of causing the stock to rally, because it has now "beat street expectations." Conversely, if the analyst believes that the company is not performing well, he may overestimate the earnings. When the actual earnings report "fails to meet street expectations," the price falls. Either way, you can be sure that the analysts and the brokerages they represent are poised to benefit. And you, not having easy access to the type of information the analyst does, have no way of knowing which way the analyst intends to move the stock's price when issuing his prediction.

The one wrench in the works is that the CEO and all her pals on the board also have advance notice along with everyone else of what the analysts are expecting. They have only one goal, and that is to beat street expectations. If the analyst's estimate is low, they are happy, and so is the analyst because everyone knows what is to follow. If the analyst's estimate is high, they are not happy and will do every barely legal accounting trick and manipulation in the book and then some in order to boost their earnings to at least what the street expected. Otherwise, their stock price falls, and the shareholders are doubly upset—both by that and by the poor job management must be doing to have failed to meet street expectations.

If the analyst is intending to cause the price to drop and has done a good job, the company management will not be able to boost the earnings number sufficiently. If the analyst has not placed his expectations high enough though, the company may actually hit the number. In this case, the board is happy, but the sell-off the analyst wanted will not happen. This is what has often happened in those rare instances when the earnings meet street expectations. Of course, management will attempt to exceed expectations if at all possible to cause a rally. Then the board is very happy, but the analysts, whose firms probably sold short, are not.

In sum, analysts' predictions do nothing for the average investor except to cause a lot of completely unnecessary volatility in the market, along with the added uncertainty of whether earnings will meet expectations and the very likely result of having companies fudge their actual earnings in order to beat some arbitrary figure instead of issuing the honest ones. The SEC would do the average investor a favor by banning them. But don't count on this happening anytime soon. Instead, as a day trader, just be aware of what is going on, buy at the beginning of the rally or sell short at the onset of the sell-off and profit from it.

Buying on the Rumor

"Buy on the rumor; sell on the news" and "buy on the cannons; sell on the trumpets" are two renditions of the same trading philosophy. As we discussed previously, a lot of trading takes place in advance of the news as the market anticipates what the news will be. Thus, stock prices begin to move based strictly on the rumor. Of course, some of those trading know what the news will be in advance, so they are also numbered with those trading in advance. Regarding the latter, known as *insider trading*, it is a no-no. What, then, does an insider do with news that is potentially worth a whole lot of money? If she herself cannot trade, she will tell a few trusted associates at other corporations, who will reciprocate in due season. Either way, very few with a true hot tip will fail to capitalize on it in some way.

During the brief, and all but forgotten (except by astute day traders who were numbered among the beneficiaries of all the losses being sustained by average investors), bear market of 1998, a *bear market* being defined as a 20 percent decline in the market, Fed Chairman Alan Greenspan stepped forward to save the day with three interest rate cuts. The first one actually caused the market to fall, which is the opposite of what logic would dictate. Many of us feel that the U.S. economy is capable of sustaining more growth than the Fed is willing to allow, and thus would like to have seen more and greater interest rate cuts much earlier. By the time the Fed finally came around to this opinion, everyone else was already there waiting for them. Because of where we were in the slump, there was just about no way that the Fed was going to meet again and fail to lower rates.

Since this view of the coming Fed action was becoming widely accepted, most traders felt confident enough about it to act on it in their trading. Thus, when a quarter-point cut actually came, it was ho-hum. No big deal. The market had already acted upon the expectation, and thus no rally occurred when the announcement actually came. In fact, the market fell, because, although everyone expected that the rate would be cut by a quarter point, they knew that it *should* have been cut by at least a half point.

Thus, a half-point cut would have generated a rally; the quarter point generated malaise and a small drop; whereas no cut would have probably resulted in a sell-off, as market participants attempted to take their profits on stocks that had risen in anticipation of something that failed to materialize.

When the United States engages in a military action, the uncertainty generally causes a drop in stock prices as nervous traders are reluctant to hold large positions that may fall in the wake of a long and protracted affair or an unexpected result. This is the "cannons." If we are confident that the United States will prevail and perhaps do so quickly, we can buy on the cannons after everyone else has sold, and ride the gains back up when the trumpets sound. Of course, sometimes this can result in the proverbial boy-that-cried-wolf syndrome. At the end of 1998, when Bill Clinton reluctantly decided to bomb Iraq, the market hardly sneezed. After all, the previous 38 times hadn't caused any market consequences; why should this one?

Stock Splits

A *stock split* occurs when the board of directors at a company decides that the price of its company's stock has risen to the point where it *appears* expensive in the eyes of potential purchasers and so authorizes a stock split, which decreases the price per share while, at the same time, commensurately increases the number of shares outstanding. Such appearances never bothered Warren Buffett of Berkshire Hathaway fame, however, whose stock has never split, and now a single share is worth more than most folks make in a year!

Announcements of stock splits typically offer two opportunities for the day trader to get in on the ground floor of a rise in a stock's price. This is because roughly two out of three stocks rise following an announcement of a stock split, as well as following the actual split itself. The reason for the former rise is that many investors are aware of this, and so they purchase the stock to take advantage of the rise. The process of these investors purchasing in anticipation of a rise is, of course, what causes the rise, and thus the rise becomes a self-fulfilling prophecy. Since there is little in the way of fundamental reasons for the rise to be sustained, it may pull back shortly thereafter. But who cares? The day trader, in the meantime, will have ridden the rise and sold at the top.

The explanation for a rise following a stock split is psychological. Investors looking at a $120 stock think that it is a bit too pricey. The company's board of directors may authorize a three-for-one split, that is, the price per share will be reduced to one-third of what it had been (in this case, to $40), while the number of outstanding shares triples. Thus someone who owned 100 shares at $120, for a market value of

$12,000, now owns 300 shares at $40, for the same market value of $12,000. Thus no change other than in appearance alone has happened.

That's when the psychology takes hold. Investors who liked the stock, but thought it was too expensive at $120, now think they are getting a bargain at $40. So, the fact that the ostensibly lower price is bringing in new shareholders again drives up the share price. Thus, the discerning day trader will profit by paying close attention both to stock-split announcements and to the actual splits themselves.

Analyst Upgrades

Analyst upgrades can be useful to the informed day trader, although they can be nearly worthless to everyone else. Worse, they can be less than worthless, in that acting on some upgrades the way the issuing analyst hopes may be a losing proposition. This is one of the benefits of always examining the recent trend charts of the stock before responding to news of upgrades. No one gets sued for upgrading a stock, so upgrades such as "buy" or "strong buy" are obvious in their meaning. However, fearing repercussions from a company for causing a sell-off of a stock, the downgrades are purposely ambiguous, such as a downgrade from "buy" to "accumulate." Of course, we all know there is no difference between buy and accumulate, but the latter basically means "hold" or don't do anything. A downgrade from "accumulate" to "hold" may actually mean "sell." Thus, if an analyst actually ever says "sell," you'd better liquidate your holdings and be happy to get a penny a share!

Analyst upgrades often provide little information that the chart doesn't already tell you. If an analyst upgrades a stock and the price is riding at the top of a long string of highs, what have you really learned from the upgrade? The fact that the stock is way up indicates to even the greenest novice investor that people like it. Anyone can upgrade the stock at the top of its recent price range. Yet these are exactly the kind of "hot" stock tips that most investors get from their brokers. When your broker sees a bandwagon careening past his window, the speed-dial button to you is usually pushed.

So, what exactly does an upgrade mean when it comes after a run-up of the stock price? We must understand that analysts work for the big brokerages who are also the market makers. The big brokerages often hold large positions in the stock they have upgraded, or perhaps they have received a large-block sell order from a preferred client.

When a stock has run up for whatever reason, that means a lot of people are already on the buying bandwagon. Most of those who want to own the stock have already purchased it.

Unfortunately, then, an analyst upgrade on a stock already riding high may mean that the brokerage for which the analyst works realizes that the stock has little further upside and may want to dump the stock and realize the gains. If the brokerage did this with no upgrade, there would be little interest and few buyers; the appearance of a large amount of the stock for sale on the market would drive the price down; and the brokerage's profits on it would suffer. On the other hand, if the upgrade causes a spurt of interest (greed) in the stock and brings in the last remaining buyers for it, the brokerage can sell off its position to these buyers, and the price may even rise at the same time! The brokerage has thus served itself or a favored client well, but pity those who bought the stock on analyst hype at the top of the market.

The same thing can work in reverse. If a brokerage sees great upside potential in a stock that is near its bottom, an analyst may downgrade the stock. This brings in sellers who want to get out before the stock goes even lower (panic). The brokerage may then buy from these sellers without incurring a price increase and perhaps even as the price falls.

It may look bad for one brokerage with a large position in a stock to do the actual upgrading or downgrading itself. In this case, rumor of a stock's potential may go out over the insider grapevine, or one brokerage may speak discreetly to other brokerages about their upgrading the stock instead. Of course, the favor will be repaid when these other brokerages have something to move or buy. Due to herd (or *heard*) instinct, it is rare for one analyst to want to stick out like a sore thumb and be the only one changing her recommendation for a stock. This is why once a change is announced, many others will follow suit. There is safety in numbers, so when an upgrade, for instance, comes, and the stock price rallies but later falls, analysts can point to all their colleagues who made the same mistake, too.

So, how does the day trader figure out which way the analysts actually want the stock to move once the company issues its earnings report? Well, for the typical investor, this is not possible, although upgrades at peaks and downgrades at bottoms may partially tell the tale. The day trader with access to Level II Nasdaq data can actually see which market makers are buying and selling the stock. If the brokerage that upgraded the stock is selling it, that may be a good time to buy at the bottom of a brief rally and then look for an opportunity to sell the stock short at the turnaround. If the brokerage that down-graded the stock is in the buying column, you may want to sell short on the brief sell-off and be poised to purchase at the turnaround. Access to this type of information is invaluable to both the day trader and the position trader.

Expert Recommendations

Closely related to, but ranking below (with respect to their ability to move a stock's price) analyst upgrades are expert recommendations. These experts are usually fund managers who make the talk-show cir-cuit. They are typically chosen because their funds have been up over a certain recent time frame. Regarding fund rankings, never forget that no matter what fund managers are doing, one of them has to be first. And with only so many stocks to choose from, some of them have to go up.

"So tell us, Mortimer, what stocks would you be recommending to our viewing audience, today?"

"Well, Lou, EFG has just reorganized and it appears like they're positioned to take an increased market share. And XYZ has beat earn-ings expectations for two quarters in a row, with little increase in the stock price. It looks like a sleeper that's primed for a big move."

"Mortimer, do you own these stocks in your own fund?"

"Of course, Lou."

That Mortimer has these stocks in the fund he manages is some-how supposed to legitimize his recommendation. After all, Mortimer would be a bit hypocritical if he went around recommending stocks that he wouldn't buy himself. But why doesn't someone ever ask, "Mor-timer, are you recommending these stocks so that investors will go out and buy them, thus driving up their prices and, consequently, that of your own fund, which will, in turn, guarantee you a fat bonus this year?" Why indeed.

In the old days, such a recommendation could have an effect on a stock's price. That was when you could go into the restaurant and whisper, "My broker is E. F. Hutton," and everyone would get quiet and try to overhear E. F. Hutton's recommendations. Today, you could go into a restaurant and say E. F. Hutton all you wanted, and most people would likely respond, "Hey, Buddy! Who you huntin' for?" This is because there are so many funds and fund managers now that, if you had time to listen to them all, virtually every stock there is would eventually be recommended. In that case, you'd be back to square one.

Keep in mind also that many fund managers often buy limited volumes of hot stocks at the end of the year. This is no indication of their bullishness toward a particular issue, however. Rather, it usually means that they have missed out on the big run of that stock. For instance, XYZ traded between $20 and $40 per share for many years. Then one day, the company changed its name to XYZ.com, and the price began a rally to $350 per share. When owners and potential buyers of the fund look at the prospectus and see that XYZ is missing from the list of stocks owned, they will doubt the foresight of the fund manager. To counter this, a fund manager will purchase a few shares of XYZ.com at the end of the year so it can be listed on the prospectus. Then readers will rest assured. Few will ever do the math.

Short Interest

Short-interest lists in the newspapers typically give the statistics on stocks that have been sold short. Reviewing a list of stocks that more folks are betting against than any other can provide a potential winners list for the day trader. As we have learned by examining market psychology, many of these companies are up strictly because of market hype. As long as such news continues, the price may remain high. Eventually, the bubble may burst and send the price plummeting, as the short sellers are hoping.

It must be noted that a certain amount of short interest today represents hedge fund selling and not necessarily the belief that the stock is actually poised to drop. But this is good for the day trader. If a company really were on the brink of collapse, and everyone knew this, there might be a good reason to be shorting it. In this instance, the stock will probably eventually move down, vindicating the short sellers. However, if short interest includes a lot of hedging, or if shorting occurs simply because many traders can't bring themselves to believe that the stock can possibly go up another dollar, then the stock may well surprise them, as with Internet stocks, which give everyone vertigo when gazing at their lofty heights and then proceed to go up another $100. And, as we have learned, there doesn't have to be a rational reason for the stock to continue going up. Hype and greed are all that are often necessary.

Selling a stock short means that all the short sellers stand to lose if the stock begins to rise. They will hold on for a while, but once it becomes obvious that the stock rise is not slowing, they must purchase the stock to *cover their shorts.* This situation is known as a *short squeeze.* The greater the short interest, the greater the flood of purchasers covering their shorts. Add these buyers to those already in the market, and the stock may experience a pretty good rally.

Of course, it could be that, for whatever reason, the short sellers are right. In this case, the stock may well decline. But, even so, in order for the short sellers to profit, they must eventually repurchase the shares to cover their shorts. To determine at what price to unload, they will turn to technical analysis, as we will detail in Chapter 5, "High-Probability Trading," to find a good support level (i.e., a price that previously generated a lot of buying when it was reached). If a stock trend chart shows that significant buying took place at $67, few short sellers will try to hold out for $65, because if a previous rally occurred at $67, it is likely to occur there again.

Thus, the day trader's strategy is to also watch for a stock that was sold short to fall to a previous support level. She may wish to sell short herself as the drop begins. If the stock has not reached $67 by the end of the trading day, she repurchases the shares at whatever price they have reached, thus covering her short. But she also keeps her eyes on the $67 target price. Once it reaches that target, the stock will rally as short sellers cover (purchase) at $67 with a maximum profit, and the day trader will be a buyer, assuming the technicals (which we will discuss in Chapter 5, "High-Probability Trading") are in place.

Thus, it pays for the day trader to keep a list of the greatest short-interest stocks handy to check in the event that one of the stocks she is monitoring looks poised to move upward. Monthly short-interest sections, with lists of the stocks with the greatest short interest, are found in most financial publications, including *Investor's Business Daily,* the *Wall Street Journal,* and *Barron's.*

These stocks are the ones to keep an eye on day to day. At one time, Compaq Computer was number one on the short-interest list, that is, more investors thought this stock was going down than any other stock on the market. The main problems at Compaq at the time were slow sales and a buildup of excess inventory, both of which are temporary, although painful. Unless there are serious structural problems with a company or it is going bankrupt, investors will eventually see a bargain in the price and begin buying it. When this happens to a stock, you want to be able to get in at the bottom. With a list of short-interest stocks, it is a good time to check the 200-day price chart and see if support levels during that time frame are now being hit or broken.

Psychology of the News

In early 1998, talk was of the world being awash in oil. Oil-sector stocks fell. All looked dead. Shortly thereafter, it was announced that oil-producing countries would cut world production by 2 million barrels per day, a literal drop in the bucket. In response, the oil sector stock prices spiked up much more than would logically be expected on such a minor bit of good news. Of course, nothing had fundamentally changed regarding the supply of oil. But we're not talking about logic here. We're talking about investor psychology. Amid all the gloom and doom, even this glimmer of hope was enough to cause an overreaction and enrich the pockets of those who held oil stocks and were wise enough to sell into the rally. Curiously, a gradual rise in prices of these stocks had already begun a few days before this news. Could it be that there were some who knew about this *before* the street did?

Trading on the news is almost always a losing proposition for position traders, or at minimum a risky one. This is one advantage the day trader has over the position trader. It is best to keep in mind that by the time we hear the news, most of the big money, the insiders, and who knows who else have already heard it—and have accordingly factored it into the stock price. The report you hear may cause enough of a blip to allow the day trader to profit, however, before the final public buyers get into the stock on this "news."

It is always wise to check the charts first to see if the stock has been gradually rising/falling for a week or two already as those who are really in the know and their friends and families have responded. Enough movement in a stock prior to the "news" may limit movement potential afterward. Sometimes, the stock may actually fall. Remember, it is psychology at work here, and humans are quite the unpredictable animal.

Of course, there may be a few times when you and everyone else hear the news at the same time, such as a report that Saddam Hussein has begun bombing Saudi Arabian oil fields. This will probably have quite an effect on oil stock prices, and you can seek to take advantage of it. But even then, you never know if Saddam and his buddies have themselves already been buying oil futures and calls on oil stocks!

Another instance occurred in early 1999 when Brazil devalued its currency. This earth-shattering news is not unlike learning that Swaziland has abruptly fired its trade minister. Brazil, of course, has a gross domestic product similar to that of one of our rural counties. Yet in response to this news, the Dow almost immediately dropped well over 200 points, and Nasdaq fell commensurately. At the time, the market had reached new highs after the brief bear market of the previous late summer and fall. Many investors were skittish about these highs and used the news as an excuse to take some profits. Nevertheless, action by Brazil was quite a flimsy reason for stocks to make such a broad dip. That the reason for the drop was insubstantial creates an opportunity for the day trader to move in, buy into a couple of issues, and ride them up as everyone begins to ask what in the world they have done. A review of the charts indicates that almost every stock that fell on the Nasdaq recovered within a few hours to higher prices than before the announcement. Thus, virtually any purchase that morning would have made money.

The day trader must not overlook other trading opportunities afforded by sympathetic movement in related stocks when one particular stock begins moving on the news. For instance, when Pfizer announced its new impotence drug, Viagra, not only did Pfizer move, but so did the stock of some other companies that made related impotence drugs. When Warren Buffett announced that Berkshire Hathaway had purchased almost $1 billion in silver, the stock of not just silver, but silver-mining companies as well, went up. And when Entremed was in the news regarding a possible advance in the war against cancer, both it and related stocks in the biotechnology sector moved. And, believe it or not, shares of Ray-Ban soared following release of the popular movie, *Men in Black*. And airline stocks took off when oil prices dropped. The list goes on and on.

The reason for sympathetic movement in related stocks is because there are many investors out there who are figuring that if one stock is hot, then other stocks in the same or corresponding market sectors will follow. Of course, this is but a self-fulfilling prophecy, but it is there nevertheless. The shrewd day trader will thus not only seek to profit on the company in the news, but also on those affected by that same news.

The Standard & Poor's 500 Index is a capitalization-weighted index of 500 stocks from a broad range of industries. This index is designed to measure performance of the broad domestic economy through changes in the aggregate market value of 500 stocks representing all major industries in approximately the same proportion to their representation on the New York Stock Exchange. The index was developed with a benchmark value of 10 based on aggregate stock values between 1941 and 1943.

Because the S&P represents the blue-chip corporations covering a wide range of sectors, it is a great way to keep track of sector movement and is perhaps the single best indicator of minute-to-minute market movements. In many instances, the S&P serves as a leading indicator to stock market activity. For this reason, the S&P must be watched closely throughout the trading day.

For your convenience, we have listed the stocks that make up the various Standard & Poor's Sector Indexes in Appendix A. We have also highlighted the ones that trade on the Nasdaq, the exchange most used by the day trader.

Mass Hysteria

Regardless of what initiates a move in a particular stock, reports on the increase in the price of the stock can themselves cause further increases in its price as a result of positive synergy. This generally happens in three stages. In stage 1, thinking people (that's us) get in. In stage 2, folks who didn't initially get in (i.e., average investors) kick themselves because of missing the first move, but vow not to be left behind. Thus, they jump onto the bandwagon in an attempt to ride it to fortune, convinced that the stock must have unlimited potential. Depending on when they jump on, they may or may not see the price increase further. Stage 3 comes after everyone who is inclined to ride bandwagons has done so, and there is no one left to buy the stock and drive its price any higher.

Left in the precarious position of owning stock with a very high price and little in the way of company fundamentals to support it, a round of *profit taking* is likely to soon follow. Those who were first on board do pretty well, as long as they know when to get out. Even if they sell after the price begins to fall, they still profit. Those who do not watch the moment-by-moment moves of their stocks after buying, as is the case with most *position traders* (i.e., the average investors), end up with a lot of stock that is worth far less than they paid. But hey, most of the time they never even realize it, and you know that ignorance is bliss. For those who do, their only choices are to stay in and wish upon a star to break even if the stock eventually goes back up or to get out anyway and hope to find a better investment somewhere else. Neither of these alternatives offers much in the way of a decent rate of return.

As we have noted, the day trader, on the other hand, doesn't mind being on a bandwagon, that is, as long as she is the first one on board. Doing this is not out of the question because she has the tools to identify which way a stock is trending. This being the case, she will also be one of the first to disembark at the other end of the line. We'll discuss these tools in detail in Chapter 5, "High-Probability Trading."

Keep in mind that mass hysteria is just that. It doesn't have to make any sense at all and, accordingly, rarely does. Whether the trend has any real merit is of no consequence; if enough people believe it, they will make it happen, and that's all you want. Though some trends reflect reality, others reflect belief alone. A line from the old *Rawhide* TV series theme song goes: "Don't try to understand 'em, just rope, throw, and brand 'em." In like manner, you needn't try to understand why the crowds do as they do, just trade and grow rich.

There is one thing crowds can always be counted on to do, and that is to repeat their errors time and time again. This is because crowds have only short-term memories. Experience is never a factor in making a decision about the future. The previous 167 times mean nothing. This time is different. For example, what if someone you know fairly well is killed in an automobile accident? You drive supercautiously for about a week and then gradually sink back into your old ways. As they say, time heals all wounds. The problem is that time heals most experience, too.

> **As they say, time heals all wounds. The problem is that time heals most experience, too.**

And so it is with crowds and the latest stock craze. So what if that Internet stock is $250 per share and has no earnings, and thus a P/E of infinity? After all, we're just discounting future earnings. Who cares if it won't be until 2043 before the company can possibly catch up and have a normal P/E ratio? Certainly not the day trader! Remember, however, that a $250 per share stock is not typically tradable. In this instance, the day trader will wait for a stock split to bring the price back under $100 per share.

Of course, it's one thing to sit back in a detached manner and talk theoretically about the mass psychology of others. But when some Internet stock goes up $50 in a single trading day, you will find out just how easy it is to get caught up. In this book, we teach a very conservative method of trading, the initial goal being not to make money per se, but rather simply to not lose money. Our strategy is to help you turn a 50:50 trade into a 70:30 trade using technical and other indicators. We'll discuss technical analysis in Chapter 5, but suffice it to say that there is virtually nothing in the way of technical (and especially fundamental) indicators that will predict which Internet stock is going to rally by $50 per share within a single trading day. This is when the day trader will gain a little insight into his own psychology.

Other Factors

Sometimes stock prices change for strictly mechanical reasons that are more predictable and more of a sure thing than some of the other psychological factors we have touched upon. An example of this occurs when a major index switches a stock out of its index and substitutes another. For instance, in 1998, Pennzoil, just one of many declining oil stocks at the time, was booted out of the S&P 500 and replaced with an upstart called Selectron. What do you suppose this did to the prices of each of these issues, respectively? Of course, there is the psychological factor that Pennzoil must be bad to have gotten the ax, and Selectron must be good to have been chosen as the replacement. This in itself would have driven Pennzoil down and Selectron up.

In this instance, however, there is another and more important reason why Pennzoil dropped and Selectron rose: Because Pennzoil was being eliminated from the S&P 500, all index fund managers were immediately required to dump their Pennzoil and replace it with Selectron. This brought an abundance of Pennzoil onto the market at the same moment that it was cut from the S&P, thus producing a double whammy against the price. On the other hand, the necessity of buying Selectron to replace Pennzoil in index funds pushes Selectron up even more. So keep your eye out for these once-in-a-while opportunities.

As we have alluded to already, in Chapter 5 we will get down to the nitty-gritty of using charts, stock trends, and technical analysis to do some high-probability trading!

chapter 5

high-probability trading

using technical analysis
to predict the market

In this chapter, we'll explain some of the types of graphs and other technical indicators of stock trends you will later learn to pull up on a given stock to help you decide whether to buy or sell. It's truly amazing what you can see once someone points you in the right direction. For example, to most people, a rock is a rock is a rock. But a geologist can look at a rock and read the saga of the earth. A glance at a roadcut while driving down the highway can reveal ancient rivers meandering their way to the sea, rises and falls in sea levels of old, or volcanoes erupting as continents began to split and drift. A geologist sees these things because she has learned to read the testimony of the rocks. In like manner, once we have pointed out the stories that stock trends have to tell, you, too, will be able to see what the untrained eye never does.

Remember, playing the stock markets is a *when-to,* not a how-to, game. How-to is easy. For how-to, all you need do is call your broker and ask if he needs a new boat. If he says yes, send him all your money. That's how-to, and it's just that easy. To be a day trader, you will, however, be concerned with when-to, and that's what technical analysis is all about.

The 70:30 Trade

If you take a dart and throw it at the stock report in your local newspaper, your chances of hitting a winning stock are 50:50, that is, the stock will either go up or go down. What we want to do is introduce you to a few simple concepts that can be used to turn a 50:50 trade into a 70:30 or better trade.

In actuality, the dart method may not even give you odds as great as 50:50. In fact, random picking may be no better than 30:70. This is because there is a third path that the stock can take, and that is to stay level in a listless trading range. If you have bought in and the stock stays level and you sell at the end of the day, you lose the commissions and possibly the spread going in and getting out.

All day trading is not created equal! Some who have attempted day trading before have failed and given up. This leads to the idea that day trading is somehow "riskier" than other types of trading, which is not the case at all. Having the right information at your fingertips, as we will discuss in Chapter 6, "Timing Your Trade Using RealTick III™," and knowing when a trade is a 70:30, as we will discuss in this chapter, are the two keys to success that will help turn a good trade into a great trade. We want to help you put as many factors in your favor as possible before you make the trade.

We're very conservative in the methods we are teaching in this book. That's because it's *your* money. By following our recommendations, you will be out of some trades that could have made money for you. But you'll also be out of a lot of the 50:50 or worse trades on which you would have lost money. Our goal is that you average $1 per share on 7 out of 10 trades, and that you lose no more than 25 cents per share on the other three.

Technical Analysis versus Fundamental Analysis

Most securities firms employ *analysts* who dissect and evaluate companies and stocks every which way to determine whether a given stock is overvalued, undervalued, or about right compared with the potential of the company issuing the stock. Analysts use two methods to evaluate stock prices. One of these is known as *technical analysis;* the other is called *fundamental analysis.* Fundamental analysis is for investing, and technical analysis is for trading. It's just that simple.

Analysts use two methods to evaluate stock prices. One of these is known as *technical analysis;* the other is called *fundamental analysis.* Fundamental analysis is for investing, and technical analysis is for trading. It's just that simple.

As may be discerned from the name, fundamental analysis looks at the fundamentals of a company, that is, such things as price to earnings (P/E), future earnings potential, dividends, income, debt, management, market share, and a whole host of other aspects. Fundamental analysis attempts to determine where a share price *should* be, based on the company's current characteristics and future potential. At first blush, anyone would think that this is the most rational and logical way to look at a company. And it is.

The problem is just that: fundamental analysis is a superb way to look at a *company.* And it is a great way to determine what that company's stock price *should* be. But it is a lousy method when it comes to explaining *why* a stock's price is what it is or in predicting what a stock's price *will* be! In an ideal world, all investors would look at a company in a sensible way and make investment decisions in a detached, analytical manner, and stock prices would show only secular movement, if any, as the days and weeks rolled by. Unfortunately, this is not an ideal world, and investor decisions rarely correspond with the way things *should* be.

Fundamental analysis can be used to accurately assess and predict a stock's price only until a wrench is thrown into the works. What is this wrench? Plainly and simply (and always), *people.* Regardless of what the stock's price should be, 10 different people will interpret the same data in 10 different ways. Or, more likely, most will ignore it altogether. The result, as we learned in Chapter 4, is that their buying decisions will be based on emotions, hype, or what have you—almost anything but careful, reasoned analysis.

This is why the day trader relies on *technical analysis* to assist her in her investment decisions. She is not concerned with where a company will be in five years, or even if it will be bankrupt tomorrow. Instead, she utilizes simple charts and graphs to determine where a particular stock's price is likely to be going today. What she seeks to glean from such charts and graphs is not how well a company is managed, but how likely it is that thousands of other traders looking at the same charts and graphs at the same time will be drawing the same conclusions from them. Even this is psychology. When we use technical analysis, we see the hopes and fears through all the years, the expectations, and the sentiments of thousands or millions of investors at or over any period of time we choose, boiled down into a single chart or graph. It's all right there. The goal of the astute day trader is to draw conclusions just a little ahead of the market, buy in before the crowd, and thus ride a trend to profits.

As we will explain in this chapter, there are a lot of solid reasons that stocks form the trends they do, and this allows us to firmly rely on technical analysis. The very fact that technical analysis is so widely understood and used means that stocks often respond the way they would be predicted to even when there is no actual underlying reason for them to do so. This happens simply because thousands of *technicians,* as those who follow the technical trends of stocks are called, are watching the same trends at the same time you are. When the stock begins to form a trend, all of them respond accordingly, and thus drive the stock in the predicted direction—a self-fulfilling prophecy. But who cares?

If technical analysis the way we are presenting it sounds easy, then we have succeeded in our aim for this chapter. It *is* easy. Oh, there are plenty of more complicated ways to analyze the market, far more in fact than the ways we will discuss. But we want to avoid complexity for a good reason: The simpler a system is, the more people who will understand it and thus use it. And when a lot of people are doing the same thing, it works whether it should or not. When something already works, as technical analysis does, more technical analysts coming on board, such as you, will make it work just that much better.

Technical Indicators

Technical indicators provide clues to broad- and narrow-based trend patterns. The theory of technical analysis is grounded in the notion that price and volume dictate the state of the market. But it is the successful technical analyst who understands that the mass psychology of fear and greed is intertwined with movements of both price and volume.

As you use charts, it will be an easy matter to find all sorts of patterns in just about every one you look at. This is because, as human beings, we are already predisposed to find order of some sort in everything we see, even when only chaos is there. As you lie back on your picnic blanket on a lazy summer afternoon watching all of the big, billowy cumulus clouds wafting by, after a while you being to see things:

a rabbit, perhaps . . . Frosty the Snowman . . . an angel with wings . . .
Santa Claus . . . a cauliflower . . . or pieces of cotton. The point is that
there are no rabbits or people or anything other than fog. Nevertheless, your mind has produced order from chaos. And it's just as easy to
find trends in charts that may not be there, either.

Although you won't be able to do this regularly in your day trading, if you have access to a copy machine and transparency paper (like
you would use on overhead projectors), try making a few copies of
some of the charts you have printed out on transparency paper. Turn
them over so that the trend is reversed and see whether the buy signal
becomes a sell signal or vice versa. If the pattern goes away or is
ambiguous, perhaps it was never there at all. This is a worthwhile exercise, but one rarely used even by experienced traders. If you don't have
transparency paper, just hold the sheet of white paper up to a window
or a light and look at the trend in reverse.

As we will explore in depth, to make a good trade, the day trader
looks for the three Vs: volatility, volume, and velocity. *Volatility* is a
measure of the stock's average daily price range. *Volume* determines
whether there is interest enough in a stock to make it take off in a trend.
Thus, the dynamic combination of volatility and volume produces
velocity, and the stock begins to move. Velocity, of course, is the same
thing as momentum. We use velocity instead because it starts with a V.
"Two Vs and an M" just doesn't have quite the same ring!

Volume

Volume is the first criterion that the day trader uses in selecting which
stocks to purchase. When you go to buy a new house, the real estate
agent tells you that the house you like is priced $20,000 more than sim-
ilar ones because of its location. To the agent, the three most important
factors that determine a home's value are location, location, and location. Similarly, the three most important factors that determine the
tradability of a stock are volume, volume, and volume. Volume is what
confirms the trends you think you see on the charts. Volume tells you
how interested others are in the stock. Ultimately, the success of the
trader hinges on the ability to decipher volume levels associated with
price movement, for it is volume that most accurately expresses the
strength and depth of a trend.

Total volume is important because this directly determines the
liquidity or tradability of the stock. Too little volume means that no one
is interested in the issue, and therefore liquidity is limited. However,

there can also be too much of a good thing. When volume is very high, volatility, as we will discuss shortly, increases commensurately, and you run the risk of getting lost in a rapidly moving market. You want something in between: enough volume to guarantee a liquid stock, but not to the extent that you are always chasing a moving price target.

Changes in volume are also important. Rising volume means that interest in the stock is picking up, and increasing interest means that the price is likely to move. There is no absolute volume to look for, rather simply an increase *relative* to what the stock has been doing. Your trading screen, as we will discuss in detail in Chapter 6, will show real-time volume as well as real-time price ticks. You can sort the Nasdaq exchange by volume, and you can sort your own preselected list by volume. As you keep track of the volume on the exchange, you will occasionally note that a new stock symbol has moved up farther on the list, meaning interest has picked up in this stock for whatever reason. This is a key indicator of a stock that you might want to watch for a while. Your strategy will be to examine the historic price chart of the stock to determine whether the stock is approaching a support or resistance level.

Falling volume is a key indicator also. Your trading screen will show the price-change graph with a bar graph of volume below it. As the volume trails off, the interest in it is going away. Usually, this means that whatever price trend was in effect goes away, too. If you own the stock, falling volume is your cue to sell. Let's discuss some examples that show how important it is to understand the role of volume in your trading. As we'll see, the volume cue works on any time frame the day trader may be viewing.

Take a look at the two-day one-minute chart of Ciena Corporation in Figure 5.1. On January 12, Ciena moved listlessly at around $15 per share. The next day, following a brief drop in the morning, it traded within a small range. At about 12:15, the price began to rise precipitously, accompanied by a distinct increase in volume. Volume tapered off at about 12:45, and the price fell. At about 13:10, an even bigger spike in volume occurred, pushing the price to the high of the day. After the high was reached, volume began to drop off, and price did also. At 14:10 and at 15:15, the volume again showed spikes accompanied by price spikes. And, again, as volume tapered off, so did the price. In view of the fact that volume and price virtually always go hand in hand, it is difficult to overemphasize the importance of volume.

Dell Computer Corp. (DELL) experienced a surge in volume in early September 1996 that served as a leading indicator of price move-

Figure 5.1 Two-day chart showing the relationship between volume and price

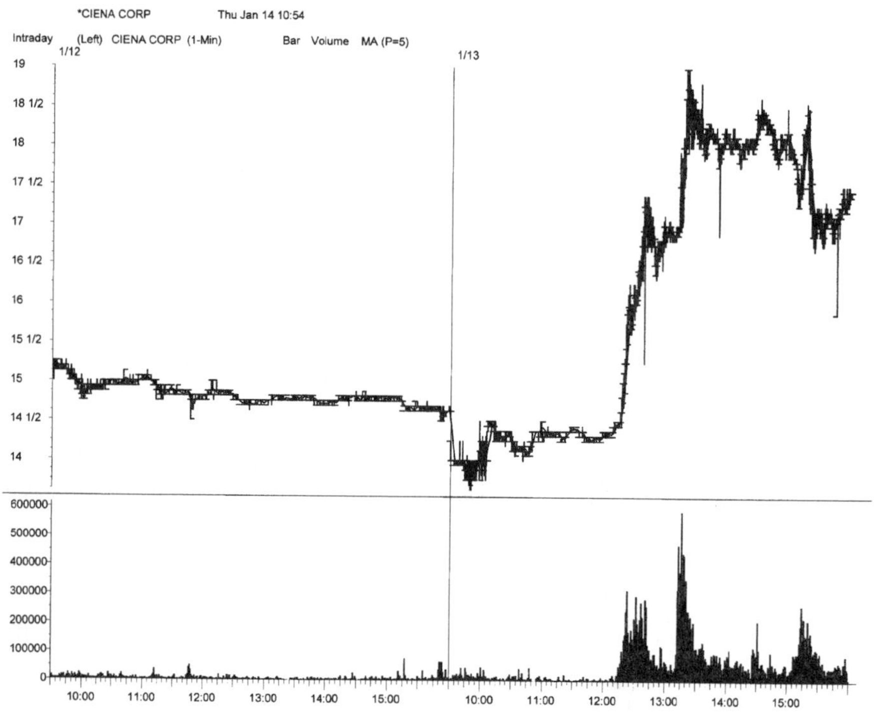

Reprinted with permission of Townsend Analytics, Ltd.

ment. (See Figure 5.2.) Day traders in particular benefit from this knowledge. If the overall trend is upward on a stock that is clearly outperforming the market in terms of price appreciation, it is prudent to be long in the stock when day trading unless the market is experiencing a particularly negative short-term trend. In the nine months following the high volume surge, Dell tripled in price.

In brief, a price rise accompanied by expanding volume is normal market behavior in a stock or index that is in an uptrend.

In the next example (Figure 5.3), a stock that reaches a new price high on expanding volume (March 1997), yet with lower volume than that experienced in the previous market breakout to new highs (January 1997), is suspect in nature. The logic relates to investor psychology. If interest in the stock is waning, such a sentiment is expressed by higher prices on lower volume. When interest in a security subsides completely, a sell-off ensues.

Figure 5.2   Volume as a precursor of price

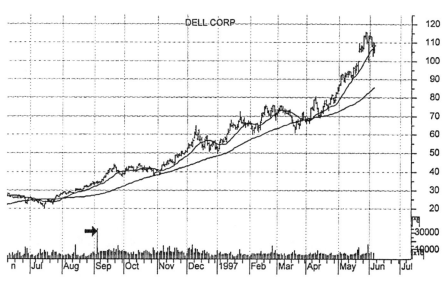

Reprinted with permission of Townsend Analytics, Ltd.

Figure 5.3   Higher prices on decreasing volume signals a downtrend

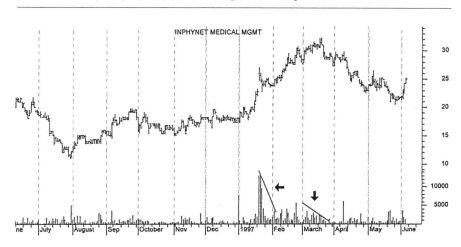

Reprinted with permission of Townsend Analytics, Ltd.

Figure 5.4   A rally that occurs on contracting volume could be a harbinger of a downtrend

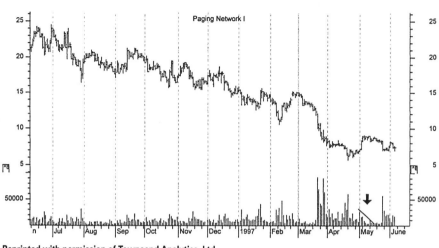

Reprinted with permission of Townsend Analytics, Ltd.

Figure 5.4 shows another example where a rally occurs on contracting volume, which also should be questioned.

In Figure 5.5, it is evident that when price and volume expand slowly and the stock experiences a final price/volume peak with a subsequent decrease in price and volume, the trend is over.

Figure 5.5   The final price/volume peak following slowly expanding price and volume indicates a trend is over

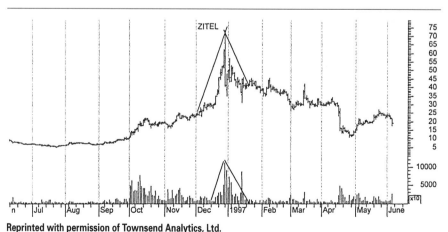

Reprinted with permission of Townsend Analytics, Ltd.

Figure 5.6 A lengthy decline followed by a rally and another decline to the previous low signals the beginning of an uptrend

Reprinted with permission of Townsend Analytics, Ltd.

As shown in Figure 5.6, if, after a lengthy decline and subsequent rally, prices decline again to the approximate level of the first trough on lower volume, this is bullish. This chart pattern signifies few sellers at a level that previously supplied a large supply of anxious sellers.

Similarly, a stock that experiences a double-bottom model (a W formation) with expanding volume at and after the second bottom is a bullish sign, as shown in Figure 5.7. Such a high-volume day in con-

Figure 5.7 A chart that exhibits a W formation is bullish

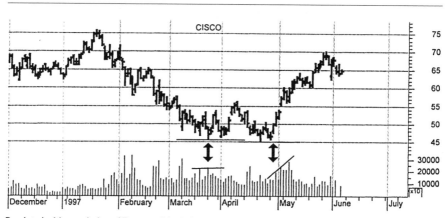

Reprinted with permission of Townsend Analytics, Ltd.

junction with a second bottom indicates investors are willing to buy up as much stock as is offered at the price equal to or slightly below the first bottom.

In the final example (Figure 5.8), price decreases on increasing volume is a confirmation of reversal of the previous uptrend.

Price

Price is another key technical indicator that helps unravel the complexities involved in stock picking and day trading. Whereas most investors and traders (i.e., the fundamentalists) search endlessly for the reasons a company is, or should be, successful, technical analysts concern themselves only with movement of price. One of the price philosophies on Wall Street perpetrated by the fundamentalist crowd is the belief that the market is so efficient that all news and information about a stock is instantaneously reflected in its price, with no lag time. Thus, technical analysis is moot, and studying fundamentals is all that is left.

This is such a preposterous idea that it is difficult to see how anyone could give it any credence at all. If this were true, there would be no predictive value in technical analysis because all trends would also have already been taken into account. Thus, all market psychology also falls by the wayside because the only way such a thing could be possible would be for human beings, with all their foibles, failings, and

Figure 5.8 Price decreases on increasing volume indicates a reversal of the previous uptrend

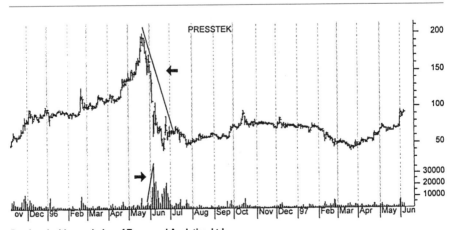

Reprinted with permission of Townsend Analytics, Ltd.

shortcomings, to have no participation in the market. It should not be surprising, then, to find that those who hold to this philosophy are often the same fundamentalists who cannot understand why so few see how right they are when they say a stock trading at $340 per share should actually be $20 per share.

To the contrary, it is the belief of the day trader that many of the fundamental, technical, and psychological factors that relate to a specific company do indeed experience a lag time before being reflected in a stock's price. In this event, those day traders who are most discerning and ingenious can enter the market, identify these trades, take a position, and be there when the rest of the market participants finally notice, act, and thus cause the price to move in favor of the day trader.

Volatility

The rapidity of the changes in the price of a stock are an indication of its volatility. Remember, our goal is to make at least $1 per share on a 1,000-share trade. The likelihood of this depends on the volatility of the stock. The day trader's goal is to find stocks that have just the right amount of volatility to make for successful trading. A stock that moves within a $1 range over the course of a week is not very volatile and thus not profitably tradable.

On the other hand, a stock that moves $1 up and $1 down within the same minute or two is usually too volatile to profitably trade. This is because the actual trend may be unpredictable over such a short time frame. One of our trading rules is to set a certain dollar or percentage maximum loss that you will endure, and then stick with it without fail. With $1,000 at stake with each $1 fluctuation and no guarantee that the stock will not move another dollar or two down the next minute, the day trader cannot trade such a stock without abandoning all of his rules and returning to a reliance on gut feelings. Gut feelings are for the purchasers of lottery tickets, not for the day trader.

In order to select possible stocks to trade that have the right amount of volatility, the day trader resorts to two methods. One of these is to review various stocks' 50-day charts to determine which ones have average daily trading ranges of a dollar or so. Ones that meet this criterion will be added to the day trader's "hot list" of stocks to watch. Note that the actual price of a stock can have a major impact on the success of your trading. Count on the likelihood of about a $1 daily price move for each $40 of share price. For instance, it's a lot easier for an $80 stock to move $2 (2.5 percent change) than a $5 stock to do so

(40 percent change). High-priced stocks can fluctuate from 60 cents to $1 per share simply because such variations are a relatively small percentage of their total value. The other side of the coin, however, is that it takes $80,000 to purchase 1,000 shares of an $80 stock, but only $5,000 for the same amount of a $5 stock. After trading for a while, you will settle into a price range that suits your own personal trading style.

The other method involves selecting stocks each morning that are up or down at least 10 percent from the previous day. This usually indicates that there has been some sort of news and thus a surge in interest in such issues. A 10 percent change often is the precursor of an impending reversal in the stock's price. In other words, an $80 stock that has dropped to $72 may well regain some of the initial losses. If the market feels that the drop has been excessive, bargain hunters will come in and push the price back up. An advance of only a couple of dollars, to $74, would mean $2,000 on a 1,000-share trade.

Don't forget that 10 percent of a $5 stock is only 50 cents. Often, you will look at the sort-by-losers window on your trading screen and see a stock that is down 60 percent. This sounds astounding until you learn that it is a $5 stock that has moved down to $2. This is virtually always attributable to news and is one reason that very low priced stocks are hard to trade.

Charts and Graphs

The technical use of charts and graphs to determine stock trends and to predict future moves has long been used and has been the subject of numerous books for many decades. Despite the endless abundance of literature detailing all of this, the principles are really very simple. As we have already seen in Figures 5.1 to 5.8, all stock price trends plotted against time form a series of wave-appearing curves or zigzags reflecting the up and down movement of prices over time. Basically, technical analysis involves little more than drawing one line over the peaks of the curves and another beneath the valleys to help predict and define *trends*.

This can be illustrated using the chart of QLT Phototherapeutics in Figure 5.9. The top line forms a ceiling that prices have not been able to overcome over the time frame of interest. The bottom line forms a floor that prices have not been able to drop below during the same time frame. Technical analysis is part art and part science, particularly when it comes to which peaks and valleys to draw the *trendlines* along. But there are some basic guidelines to follow that will make this easy.

Figure 5.9 Drawing trendlines along price peaks and valleys over a time frame of interest

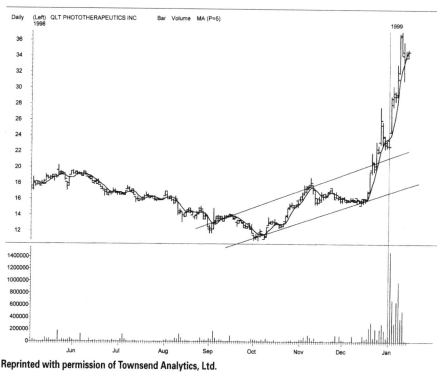

Reprinted with permission of Townsend Analytics, Ltd.

First, the diagram shows a gradual decline in prices between June and October 1998. October, of course, was the bottom of the brief 1998 bear market. Between October and January 1999 on the chart, the price recovered and the bull market continued. Thus, we would not want to try connecting peaks and valleys back into June, because that was a different market situation and there would be little in the way of useful predictive value based on it. To do so would have included the market situation both before and during the correction, as well as the recovery since. This would be comparing apples to oranges and would yield little reliability in the way of trend definition. In this instance, the best thing to do is to extend your chart only back to the beginning of the recovery. As a general rule, you want to chart no farther back than the last unusual situation or change in market trends.

We want to do our best to connect peaks and valleys that are truly part of the same trend. This is what we have done in Figure 5.9. Second, although there are minor peaks and valleys between October and January, we want to draw out trendlines over the tops of the highest ones so that the price fluctuates between them. We do this because we want to define a zone that the price has not been able to break out of during the period of interest. Technical analysts refer to these floor and ceiling trendlines as *support* and *resistance* levels, respectively. The zone between the trend lines is known as a *trend channel.* The narrower the trend channel, the weaker the support and resistance; the wider, the stronger they are.

We will use support and resistance levels in two ways: first, to determine when a stock is nearing a support or resistance level and thus a possible turnaround in price; second, to predict when a stock might make a *breakout,* either rallying past the resistance level or falling below the support level. Note that QLT experienced a strong breakout upon testing the upper support trendline in late December. And, as we have attempted to emphasize, pivotal to this technique is what *volume* is doing each time a support or resistance level is approached. Go back and examine what volume was doing as QLT experienced the aforementioned breakout. Now compare that with the volume when the resistance level was approached in September and early November.

As you read, you will note that there are a lot of different indicators (rectangles, flags, etc.) formed by the trendlines, which we will discuss throughout the rest of this chapter. Although all these new terms may seem intimidating at first, you will find that most of them are simply variations of the same theme. All of them involve trendlines. The only differences are simply the angles that the upper and lower trendlines make to each other and to the horizontal. Just as you don't have to know the name of a company to trade it, you don't have to know the technical term for a trend as long as you are able to recognize it.

Support and Resistance

Over any given period of time, a stock can begin to show price support and resistance. This can show on a one- or two-day chart all the way up to multimonth and multiyear charts. The day trader, however, will be most concerned with shorter-term charts, showing trends on a minute-by-minute scale over a couple of days, and daily charts over a few months duration. The longer the time frame, the more durable the support or resistance is likely to be; however, if they hold briefly during the trading day, that is often all the day trader needs.

A 200-day chart is about as long a time frame as you will typically use. This is long enough for a couple of quarters of earnings reports to have come in. In some instances, such as stocks that are seasonal, you may wish to go out to a year on the chart. You don't really want to go out for much longer than a year because factors that pertained in the past may no longer be valid, such as the previously discussed correction and recovery seen in Figure 5.9. Worrying about this is for position traders and investors who concentrate on a few stocks and do massive research on them. Our purpose is to enable you to buy and sell with minimal knowledge of the actual stock you are buying. If you're trading in September, it won't matter if the stock usually rises or falls in March because you will be out by the end of today.

With an appropriate-length chart of stock prices in front of you, you can tell a lot about a stock you are considering buying—and where it may be going. If you see volume (interest) pick up in the stock and the price falls (volatility) toward the support level, buying at the support level may be a good 70:30 trade.

Perhaps a given stock shows rises and falls in typical fashion, but always seems to bottom out at, say, $55. It has done this several times and now is back down to nearly $55. This may be a good time to make a 50:50 trade into a 70:30. The chances are good that the stock will again begin rising from this point. As always, volume is the key. For instance, if the price is dropping toward $55, and the selling volume begins to taper off and buying volume increases, the support is probably still holding. On the other hand, if the selling volume remains the same or increases, then the trend may be holding, and the price may drop below the previous support.

Using support and resistance is not magic or a black-box technique. One main reason for these phenomena is programmed trading. Programmed selling creates a resistance level until all shares are sold. Conversely, programmed buying creates a support level until all shares are bought. In addition, we must factor psychology into the equation. You are not the only one looking at this stock. Thousand of other traders with varying amounts of cash are looking at it, too. And they, like you, see that the stock always seems to bottom out at a certain resistance level.

When you buy the stock based on technical analysis, you are not flipping a coin. You have the odds on your side that many of those thousands of traders will be seeing the same thing that you are seeing and will also be buying. And, what do you know, the stock price begins to rise! Your strategy, of course, must be for you to be among the first to realize that this is the point at which the stock should begin to rise.

If you wait and attempt to trade after the stock price has already begun to move, you will merely be "chasing" the trade, and you may catch it at the wrong time.

Breakouts, of course, are of particular interest to the day trader. A day trader who has been paying attention to both price movement and volume may be able to turn a breakout into an opportunity to buy or sell short. To the dismay of position and options traders, most breakouts never develop into a strong trend of any sort. This is inconsequential to the day trader, however, who is seeking only to get in on about a $1 move in price.

Breakouts may also occur when there is particularly good or bad news about the stock. We'll discuss sources of information and how to use them in Chapter 7, as well as what to do if your stock starts going down right after you've bought it. Right now, though, we want to teach you to recognize the trends. After all, we don't have to make money on 10 trades out of 10 every time. We're shooting for 7 trades out of 10 (that's 70:30).

Remember that the factors we are discussing in this chapter all work in tandem to produce the best trading opportunity for you. As we have discussed, if volume of a stock is trailing off, then interest in it is, too. Thus, even if the price is at a support or resistance level, there may be little further change in price until the volume picks up again. In this instance, go on and look at other stocks, but return to potential ones like this to see if volume is picking up.

Longevity of Support and Resistance   Two indicators of the strength of the support or resistance level are the amount of time that it has held and the number of times that the levels have been tested. A successful test, of course, means that the price has gotten to the trendline and has then pulled away from it, showing that the line is still effective. In the short-term world of the day trader, sufficient support for a stock may be demonstrated by a couple of tests of the trendline over a 10- or 15-minute period.

For example, the day trader is at his computer at the market open watching the movement of XYZ on the minute-by-minute daily chart. The price of XYZ is slowly moving down. When it hits 55¼, it begins to move back up. At this point, the day trader is interested, but does not yet have confirmation that this may be a good trade. He looks at the 200-day chart and finds that 55¼ has served as a support level in the past. He turns his attention back to the daily chart. XYZ lolls up a bit and heads back down. It hits 55¼ and again turns around, this time with a pickup in volume. This shows that the support level of 55¼ is a good one and is holding. The volume increase shows that others have become interested, as well. That's when the day trader enters the trade.

Sometimes, the support level may not be found on a longer-term chart, particularly after a run-up in price, but perhaps simply on yesterday's chart. The day trader may look back to the previous day and notice that 55¼ was a support level then. As long as there is some indication of a support level, accompanied by appropriate volume, there is justification for the trade. This very short term support level, on the order of a couple of days or less, happens because during such a short time frame, most of the players that are causing the stock to perform as it is doing in the short term are still there trading. This lends more confidence to the day trader that the trends are real—another of the many benefits of day trading.

Of course, support and resistance levels on the day trading time frame can be caused by just a few orders being filled. Once these orders have been filled, the support or resistance is gone. But that's okay for the day trader because his time frame is just as short.

In the intermediate term, there may be support or resistance levels that hold over a period of weeks or months. This may be due to selling of large blocks of stock at a predetermined price. In the case of a buyer (e.g., a mutual or pension fund) who doesn't want to pay more than a certain price, the price is probably determined by fundamental analysis regarding what the stock is actually believed to be worth. Thus, each time the price hits or tests, say, the $40 support level, buying takes place. Once all the stock that is wanted has been purchased, the next time that the stock tests this level, it continues on past, creating a good shorting opportunity for the day trader as panic among those who paid $40 and up for the stock bail out.

Because support may be due to preplanned or program buying, each test of the trendline doesn't necessarily prove its strength; rather, it further exhausts it. Thus the day trader must never be lulled into complacency regarding support and resistance levels, but must remain vigilant always and confirm every potential trade with volume.

Over the long term, on the order of months or perhaps years, support and resistance trendlines can indicate their strength, particularly if they have been tested from time to time. In this instance, the trendlines are primarily psychological. Perhaps they began as programmed buying or selling that lasted long enough for other traders to begin to think that the trendlines so formed were significant. Remember, in trading, belief makes it so. Once this happens, the trendlines become a self-fulfilling prophecy. New orders for block trades may even be entered based on these levels, further strengthening them. Position and options traders come in and buy at the resistance line because it always goes up from there, and they sell at the support level because it always goes down from there. Even the day trader may be jumping in if the average daily move is at least $1.

Remember, in trading, belief makes it so.

In the meantime, the company's fundamental value is likely moving on in one direction or the other from the support or resistance. Eventually, someone realizes that the company is worth much more or much less than what it is trading for, and begins to act accordingly. This causes a breakout as the price moves past the trendline on increasing volume. This is the kind of breakout trade that the day trader is looking for. Breakouts are of particular interest because they often generate the kind of multi-dollar-day moves that allow the day trader to take the rest of the month off.

As we discussed, the benefit of day trading on intraday or two-day trends is that just about all of the players will have remained the same; thus the conditions that cause the support and resistance are mostly still in place. For an old trendline that has not been tested in the interim, it is anyone's guess whether it will hold when tested. This uncertainty is even more pronounced when we realize that the players who originally created it may not even be following that stock now. Finally, during a bull market, a lot of stocks that you will be looking at will have done little but rise before they show up on your trading screen. That means there is very little in the way of obvious recent support levels. Thus, the short-term support levels, such as the two-day one, will often be about all you have to work with. But that can be enough.

Support and Resistance Reversals   The Bible tells us that every valley shall be exalted, and every mountain and hill shall be made low. So we learn that once a resistance level has been overcome, it often reverses roles and becomes a support level for the next-higher trading range. Similarly, an old support level, once broken, can become a resistance level for future moves. Again, there is no magic to this, and it is not a black box. As usual, it is psychological. Let's say that LMN has been trading between support and resistance levels of $40 and $60, respectively. Position traders who bought at a support level of $40, only to see the stock price plunge to $25, tell themselves that they will be content to break even if only the price moves back to $40. If it ever does, out they go, the stock price stops at $40 as sellers come into the market, and then goes back down on the selling. Thus, the previous support level of $40 now becomes a resistance level.

Conversely, those who sold short at $60, hoping to make $20 on the ride down to $40, lose if the stock instead breaks out and rallies to $75. They promise to never make that mistake again if only the stock ever goes back down to $60, at which time they will buy and cover their shorts, thus turning the previous resistance level of $60 into a support level.

Support/Resistance Trendlines   Support or resistance levels do not necessarily have to be at the same price each time they are reached. Sometimes, the overall trend of the stock's price can be up or down while moving within the confines of a predictable range. Ideally, you can draw trendlines that encompass these ups and downs. Then you can buy or sell as support and resistance levels are encountered. This is illustrated by the QLT (Figure 5.9) chart we examined earlier.

Convergence of trendlines means the end of momentum in a given direction. When the resistance trendline remains fairly constant while the support-level line begins to converge toward it, fewer sellers are indicated and the stock price may rise sharply. Conversely, when the support trendline remains fairly constant while the resistance level line begins to converge toward it, fewer buyers are indicated and the stock price may fall sharply. We'll elaborate on these principles as we discuss some of the trend patterns in the next few sections.

Consolidation Patterns

Predictive patterns that are found on charts and graphs have a tendency to fall into one of two categories: consolidation patterns and reversal indicators. *Consolidation patterns* are those in which a stock trades for some period between two established upper and lower trendlines. Sometimes, consolidation patterns tend to move laterally, with little indication of a distinct upward or downward movement. Other times they appear to buck a previous trend, but the previous trend typically continues afterward. Consolidation patterns indicate that the market is stepping back and making up its mind. Depending on the type of geometry formed by the bounding trendlines, it is sometimes possible to predict which way a breakout, when it occurs, is likely to go. Because consolidation patterns precede the actual trend of interest, we may also use them as trend precursors. Of course, volume upon reaching a trendline is critical. Let's discuss some consolidation patterns first.

Rectangles or "Trading Range"   When listening to stock reports, you may often hear that a particular stock is in a *trading range*. This means that the price is moving up and down within a certain range and showing no signs of a strong uptrend or a downtrend. On a chart, the price-time graph is such that both support and resistance lines are horizontal; thus the trend forms what is known as a *rectangle*. One reason this happens is that there are people, perhaps institutional investors, who have large buy orders to be filled at a particular set price and others who have sell orders similarly pending.

For instance, one fund may want so many shares at $35, but is not willing to pay more. Thus, when the price begins to fall and hits $35, buy programs kick in and continue until the buying interests other investors who come in and bid the price back up. At the same time, let's say that another fund is divesting itself of the stock and has set $40 as the minimum price at which to sell. Once the price is pushed back up to $40, these sell programs activate and continue until other investors notice that the stock is selling off. Not willing to be left with stock that may continue to decline, investors who bought earlier sell also, exacerbating the downward price move. Note that an increase in volume will occur each time the support or resistance trendlines are tested, signaling whether interest is still present. This continues until one or the other fund is finished trading.

In our example, the trading range is $5. This range is more than adequate, but to be day-tradable, we would like at least a $1 *daily* movement in order to make $1,000 on 1,000 shares. If this is the case, a lot of day traders will be working this stock. In addition, short-term position and options traders will also have joined in. Eventually, however, one or the other fund will have satisfied itself in the number shares it wished to trade. In this instance, once the trendline is hit, volume may increase somewhat, but not as strongly as before. The volume increase will be due to the remaining traders still anticipating that the stock will continue its bouncing between the established trendlines.

Without the institutional trading, however, they may or may not be able to reverse the trend again. If they can, it is unlikely to continue for another bounce. If they can't, the stock will experience a breakout, thus going against the traders in it at that time. Note, therefore, that a rectangle may be either a pause in a previous trend or a reversal of that trend. If the day trader is watching carefully and does not get lulled into the same sense of complacency as the other traders, she may be able to recognize the breakout and go long if it is a breakout of the resistance level or short if it is a breakout of the support level.

Flags   Flags are similar to rectangles in that both trendlines are parallel, but they are tilted up or down, forming a parallelogram instead of a rectangle, and usually occur following a fairly dramatic change in the price trends. The steep line of rapid price changes, of course, forms the "pole" for the flag. The flag is a consolidation pattern when the market slows down to make up its mind regarding the previous rapid price change. If it tilts against the previous trend, it is probably only a pause in the continuance of that trend. If it tilts in the same direction as the previous trend, this signifies a weakening in the continuance of the previous trend and a reversal is likely.

Examine the chart of Triquent Semiconductor in Figure 5.10. The pole of the flag occurred between early October and early November 1998 with a steep 70 percent rise in the stock's price. For the rest of the year, Triquent slowed down, consolidated, and formed a flag pattern dipping in the direction opposite that of the preceding trend, with prices fluctuating in a range of less than $2. Shortly after the first of the year, Triquent tested the resistance level and experienced a breakout on high volume.

Once the day trader finds a stock such as this one, she periodically returns to watch as the price fluctuations within the flag continue. In this example, the dip of the flag against the previous trend is an indicator that the breakout will be to the topside. The trend is such that it is easy to tell when a support or resistance level is about to be tested. In this case, the day trader would pay particular attention to tests of the resistance trendline. The test, accompanied by the very large increase in volume in early January, was the cue to trade.

Triangles   A triangle is an indicator wherein either the upper trendline slopes down and the lower trendline slopes up, or one trendline slopes and the other is horizontal. In all instances, the apex of the triangle points toward the future. Note that, as with the rectangle, any horizontal trendline is usually indicative of institutional or programmed trad-

Figure 5.10 Example of a flag pattern

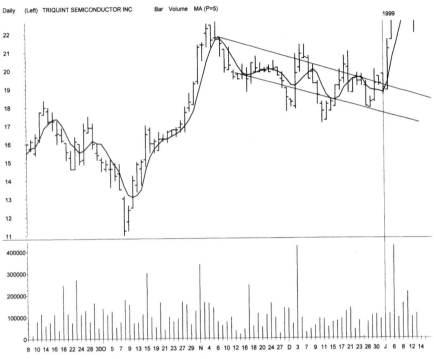

Reprinted with permission of Townsend Analytics, Ltd.

ing at that level. Depending on how the trendlines slant, they fall into three classes: symmetrical triangles, ascending right triangles, and descending right triangles.

A triangle that has a horizontal upper trendline and a lower trendline that slopes up is known as an *ascending right triangle,* which is considered very bullish. An example of this is shown by Pairgain Technologies in Figure 5.11. The ascending (upward-sloping) lower trendline indicates a growing demand for that stock, that is, higher lows. The horizontal upper trendline indicates that institutional selling is occurring at a set price. Note that selling at approximately the $11 level occurred in early October, early and late November, and late January. After the amount available for sale is gone, a breakout occurs on increased volume (early April) and the price pushes up past the upper trendline. The day trader watches for the price to hit the upper, or resistance, level on increasing volume to go long.

Figure 5.11   Example of a triangle pattern

Reprinted with permission of Townsend Analytics, Ltd.

A symmetrical triangle is one wherein the upper trendline slopes down and the lower trendline slopes up. As the stock price bounces between the floor and ceiling, this situation produces a series of lower highs and higher lows. A battle ensues between sellers who are willing to sell for less and buyers who are willing to pay more (i.e., bears and bulls). Of course, we can never discount the fact that thousands of other traders who are watching the stock see the triangle and respond accordingly, as well. Nevertheless, a downward-sloping upward trendline, with its lower highs, is bearish, but an upward-sloping bottom trendline, with its higher lows, is bullish, so the trends tend to cancel out. Thus a symmetrical triangle typically points to diminishing interest in the issue and does not predict whether the stock price will fall or rise at the end of the trend. The market, in effect, is making up its mind. The day trader will want to keep an eye on the symmetrical triangle as the trend makes its way toward the apex. An increase in volume upon the price reaching a trendline is indicative of a breakout if it occurs prior to the apex of the triangle being reached. One that occurs at the apex itself may give a false signal, that is, a breakout to the upside may reverse and vice versa.

The descending right triangle is the opposite of the ascending right triangle. It has a horizontal lower trendline and an upper trendline that slopes down, and is bearish. The descending (downward-sloping) upper trendline indicates a decreasing demand for that stock, that is, lower highs. The horizontal lower trendline indicates that institutional buying is occurring at a set price, creating a support level. Once the desired amount of stock has been bought, a breakout occurs and the price pushes down through the lower trendline. The day trader watches for the price to break the lower, or support, level on increasing volume to sell short.

Pennants Pennants are simply a subset of triangles, where both the upper and lower trendlines slope in the same direction but at different angles. A pattern with both trendlines sloping upward, yielding higher highs and higher lows, is bullish, but a pattern with two downward-sloping trendlines, making for lower highs and lower lows, is bearish.

Broadening Formations Broadening formations are similar to triangles, with the exception that the apex points into the past. As with triangles, broadening formations may be symmetrical, ascending, or descending. A symmetrical broadening formation has an upper trendline that slopes up and a lower trendline that slopes down. This situation makes for higher highs and lower lows. As opposed to a triangle, where price fluctuations eventually settle down, in the broadening formation the price gyrates wildly. Although there is little predictive value per se from a symmetrical broadening formation in that the trends cancel one another, they have historically been a bearish indicator, meaning that the price eventually has a breakout through the bottom trendline and tumbles.

As with the triangle, broadening formations can also have one horizontal trendline. A broadening formation with a horizontal upper trendline and a downward-sloping lower trendline is a descending right (as in right triangle) broadening formation. The horizontal upper trendline is a resistance level indicating a number of shares to be sold at a specific price. Although the lower, downward-sloping trendline indicates lower lows, the descending right broadening formation can be bullish once sellers go away, thus reducing the supply, and the price can continue moving up. Day traders watch for a breakout of the resistance level on increasing volume to buy.

An ascending right broadening formation has a horizontal lower trendline and an upward-sloping upper trendline. The horizontal lower trendline is a support level indicating a number of shares to be purchased at a specific price. Although the upper, upward-sloping trendline indicates higher highs, the ascending right broadening formation can be bearish once buyers go away, thus reducing the demand, and the price can continue moving down. Day traders watch for a breakout through the support level on increasing volume to sell short.

Reversal Indicators

Sometimes, when a trend has been in operation for some time, a pattern begins to develop that portends a reversal in the previous trend direction. Although some of the foregoing consolidation pattern variations can either precede a continuance of the previous trend or be a reversal of it, the three indicators we will discuss here are nearly always indicative of reversals only.

The Double Bottom/Top   A fairly safe way to enter a trade with a predictable trend is to watch for a double bottom or a double top. We will use a double bottom in our discussion here, but the principles apply equally to the double top. A double bottom is based on the same principle as the historic support level, and is most useful to the day trader on the intraday scale. It is effectively two tests of an ultra-short-term support level, perhaps only on the order of a few minutes. Let's say you're in the middle of a trading day. You pull up the intraday chart on a particular stock and see that it has touched a particular bottom earlier in the day and is heading toward it again. Do you buy?

If you do, you want to have some justification to believe that your trade will be better than 50:50. By waiting a bit, you can make a good trade better. Watch the stock for a while. It may continue down to the same level that it hit earlier in the day. Then it stops going down and begins to go up again. You say to yourself, "Gee, I knew I should have made that trade!" But then, the stock stops going up and begins heading down again. In this instance, the stock may be "testing bottom." Once it hits the support level and successfully tests it a second time within a short time period, you should buy. You buy, and the stock begins to go up, but this time it continues going up past where it had stopped just moments earlier.

Waiting for the double bottom, of course, entails the risk that the stock will not test a second time, but will continue going up. On the other hand, however, it greatly minimizes the risk of buying during a breakout and having your stock continue down after purchase.

We cannot overstress that we are now and always talking about investor psychology. *People* make the stock move. They, as you, are watching the stock. They, as you, are waiting to see what will happen. Once they are confident that the intraday bottom just tested is a true support level, they will buy. Hopefully, you will have anticipated the move and bought before they did.

Let's look at a real example. Figure 5.12 shows the two-day, minute-by-minute chart of Ticketmaster. Following the open on December 31, Ticketmaster dropped $3 to $4 per share, to about 55½. This corresponded to the low of the previous trading day. Thus, 55½ provided a support level. In some situations, you might have considered this as a

Figure 5.12   Example of a double bottom

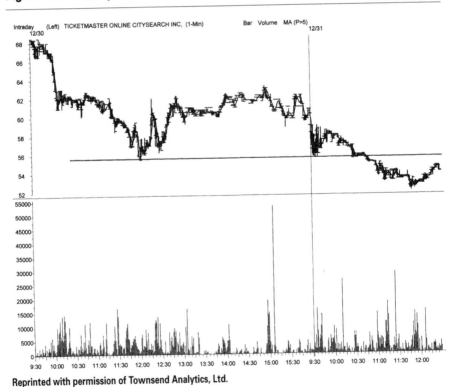

Reprinted with permission of Townsend Analytics, Ltd.

buy signal. But take a look at the volatility. There is no way that any sort of protective stop-loss order you set mentally wouldn't have been hit almost immediately. Nevertheless, the stock price went up a couple of dollars and at about 10:20 proceeded to "test bottom." This bottom test continued for about 20 minutes, but on low volume, after which the support level failed. This is a good example of why two tests are better than one.

Head-and-Shoulders Formations A head-and-shoulders formation indicates a reversal of the previous trend. For example, GHI has been moving steadily upward from $25 to $55 per share. Upon hitting $55, it pulls back to $52½. Then it has a small rally to $57½, and again pulls back to $52½. From there, the price gradually rises to $55. At $55, the price resumes a decline and volume remains low. Thus the $57½ becomes the head and the 52½ on either side form the shoulders of the head-and-shoulders formation.

The situation here is that the stock is attempting to continue to rise in the face of pullbacks, but continued price increases cannot be sustained. The decline on low volume following the right 52½ shoulder indicates that the turnaround is likely complete and interest in the issue has waned. Note that the trading range within a rectangle may also create a head-and-shoulders formation if the trend after the trading range is the reverse of what it was prior to it.

Rounding Formations A rounding formation occurs when a stock price is making a gradual reversal. Reversals can occur at both price peaks and price bottoms. Figure 5.13 shows an example of a classic reversal pattern that included the 1998 bear market and the recovery that followed. A rounding reversal at a price bottom forms a "smile" because of the happiness engendered by a price increase. Conversely, at a price peak, the pattern forms a "frown" because the price is headed down. Your strategy is, of course, to notice that a reversal is occurring when it is beginning and not well into it.

Gaps

Stocks often open at prices different than those at which they closed the previous trading day. Sometimes this difference is so great that the stock opens higher than the previous day's high or lower than the previous day's low. Because there is no overlap of prices in such an instance, a *gap* is said to have formed. If the opening is higher than the

Figure 5.13   Example of a rounding formation

Daily   (Left) SECURITY FIRST TECHNOLOGIES CORP   Bar Volume MA (P=5)
1998

Reprinted with permission of Townsend Analytics, Ltd.

previous high, we have a *gap up,* and if lower than the previous low, we have a *gap down.*

As we have discussed, market makers are responsible for the state of the market. If there has been good or bad news since the last trading day, the market maker will adjust prices accordingly. For example, as we mentioned in Chapter 4, Brazil devalued its currency in early 1999, causing large drops in both the Nasdaq and the Dow. How did the market makers determine at what price a given stock should open? Let's take a look at C-Cube Microsystems. As shown by the two-day, one-minute chart in Figure 5.14, the day before the devaluation, C-Cube sauntered along around 29 to 29½. It opened the next morning at 26¼. There is no magic formula in which a market maker may say, "Let's see. Brazil devalues this much. It owes this amount. It's economy is this big. It trades this volume with the United States. So that means that the stock should open 2⅞ lower than the last close."

To the contrary, market makers have no idea how such an event

Figure 5.14 Example of Brazilian currency devaluation impacting the U.S. stock market

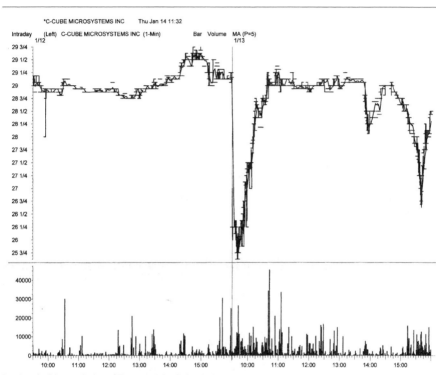

Reprinted with permission of Townsend Analytics, Ltd.

will impact the market. They use their charts and technical analysis just as you do. Take a look at the daily chart of C-Cube in Figure 5.15. The last major lows were during December 1998, when the stock price hovered around 26. Having nothing better to go on, the market maker adjusts the price to near this.

The market maker is, of course, obligated to make a two-sided market, so she is showing her confidence in technical analysis support and resistance levels by using this technique. If it is too low, then she loses when selling shares and, if too high, she loses when buying. Note from our example that although the stock did go down another ½ point after the open, the market quickly realized that the gap down was an overreaction, and the price rapidly recovered to about where C-Cube had closed the day before.

The day trader can use gaps as an opportunity to trade. Gaps are

Figure 5.15   Daily chart prior to Brazilian currency devaluation

Reprinted with permission of Townsend Analytics, Ltd.

usually pretty easy to find simply by watching your greatest percent gainers' and losers' windows right at the open. Significant price changes from the day before early in the trading day are almost always due to gaps at the open rather than to trading following the open, unless some sort of big news just happened to be reported at 9:31 A.M.

For instance, Onsale, Inc., stock opened on a Monday morning with a gap up of over $5 per share (Figure 5.16). In this instance, the stock was already trading near its high of the previous trading day, so there was little to guide the market maker in setting the price. Perhaps he had simply been a purchaser at $97, had noted that the trend had been up most of the previous day, and just wanted to see if he could get $5 out of his trade. The stock stayed around $100 to $105 per share until 9:45 A.M. and then began a precipitous drop that took it to about $50 per share by 10:15. One might say that Onsale went on sale. By 11:30, though, it had rebounded to $75.

Figure 5.16 Opportunities afforded by a gap up

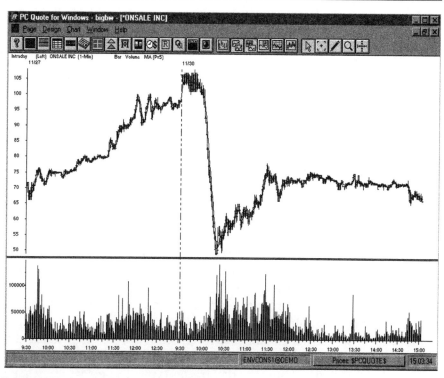

Reprinted with permission of Townsend Analytics, Ltd.

Obviously, there was a lot of money to be made (or lost) here. But only with some difficulty. In the first half hour, the stock was quite volatile, jumping around in a $5 trading range, but not with a particularly high relative volume. The day trader who typically sets a ¼-point loss as a mental stop would have had difficulty trading. To ignore the stop and continue holding 1,000 shares purchased at, say, $102 if the stock dropped to $100 would have meant a $2,000 loss, or a $4,000 loss if the trader were using a 2:1 margin for the purchase. Such a trader would have moved from the realm of technical analysis to that of pure hope, because the rest of the chart is not available and no one knows while selling is taking place whether interest will pick up again to the extent necessary to bail out the purchaser. Thus, a purchase at this time would not have been recommended.

However, the uptick in volume as the price began to slide was an indicator that the stock was a prime candidate to be sold short. Because the stock was moving down rapidly, selling short would also have been difficult. To do this, of course, you would have had to create your own upbid. The day trader who was able to get in at $100 would have ridden this short sale down to a $50 price and grossed $50,000 on a 1,000-share trade in only 15 minutes.

At that time, the huge decline began to bring in bargain hunters almost immediately. The much larger increase in volume would have signaled to the day trader that it was time to exit the trade. Although the price rallied by $25 per share, offering the possibility of another $25,000, the volatile situation with wide price swings would probably have ruled this out.

Being able to identify and to get in on a trade like this is a perfect example of why the day trader must ever work to avoid overtrading and dabbling in the market just for the sake of being there. As we have emphasized before, if there are no good trades, turn off your computer and go out and do something relaxing and enjoyable. Trades like this are worth waiting for, and you don't want to nickel-and-dime your trading account away before one comes along.

This trade resulted from the day trader honing in on a gap, and a short-selling opportunity presented itself. Other opportunities simply come when the market maker is wrong about where she values the stock on the open. If it is too high, it will come down soon, and if too low, it will rise shortly. Thus, the day trader typically seeks to buy gaps down and short gaps up when the technical indicators indicate a trade. Both situations present good opportunities, which is why it pays to keep your eye on gaps.

Gaps on a breakout are also ones to watch. They are even better than regular gaps. Breakouts, of course, indicate that the price has broken through a trendline. Let's assume that a stock has a resistance level of $40. Every time the price reaches that level, selling has usually taken place and the price declines. Once all of the sellers at $40 are gone, anyone wanting the stock will have to bid more than $40, thus producing the breakout. Such a situation can be very bullish. The stock continues to be in demand, and no one is willing to sell at $40, so a breakout occurs. As long as there is an increase in volume to confirm the trend, this would be a good stock to buy. The same thing applies to shorting a breakout of a support level.

Note that there are a lot of thinly traded, low-liquidity stocks that have gaps all of the time. If gaps are a fact of life for the stock you are considering, you should pass. If you are following the rules we are laying out in this book for a good trading stock, however, you will never be pulling up thinly traded stocks in the first place to find that gaps are common for these issues.

Broad Market Indicators

Broad market indicators are the various signposts that the day trader can use to predict the overall tenor of the market. These can be useful in deciding to go long or short and for trend trading, as we will discuss in Chapter 8, "Trade and Grow Rich."

The Long Bond
The long bond describes the daily price and yield of the 30-year Treasury bond. It is the benchmark price and yield that traders watch closely on a daily basis. Although bonds are debt securities, they are interwoven into the equities markets. Changing interest rates impact the securities markets daily. This is because the level of interest rates influences investor perceptions. Such perceptions influence traders' investment psychology and decision making. Let's examine the effect that the debt markets have on the equities markets.

Demand for money increases as the economy expands, because increasing economic growth requires capital and credit. Because capital and credit are limited in supply, economic expansion drives interest rates higher. In such economic conditions, money flows out of the equities markets and into the debt markets where the investor receives a safe rate of return that is considered to be attractive when compared to the risks and returns associated with equities. The rationale for such movement of capital lies in fear and greed.

On the one hand, greed plays a major role because investors are in a position to lock in a level of interest perceived to be high in comparison to the potential return of risk-oriented equities. Furthermore, fear of falling stock market prices, in response to perceived interest rate hikes, wreaks havoc on the equities markets until investors have a greater level of comfort about the eventual level of interest rates. That the uncertain events revolving around perceived interest rate movements stir the much stronger emotion of fear is understandable. Consequently, reduced demand for and heightened supply of equities drives the price down on all but a small portion of the strongest-performing equities.

Conversely, in an economic downturn, declining demand for

money allows rates to fall. In this lower–interest rate environment, stocks again become attractive. Domestic and foreign investors move money from the bond markets into the stock markets under these more favorable circumstances. Either of these situations offers the forward-looking day trader the opportunity to capitalize on the volatility that accompanies this sort of market uncertainty.

The long bond price and yield give the trader the current state of events in the debt market. If yields are falling, it is likely the equities markets will rally. On the other hand, rising yields should have a negative effect on the stock markets. The two aforementioned indicators are just a few of the many important indicators that aid the trader in reacting quickly to changes in the market.

Oversold and Overbought Stocks

When stock prices begin to fall, a bandwagon develops. Let's say a stock that is selling for $50 suddenly begins a decline to $40. Folks who are paying attention to their stocks see it rapidly decline. They panic, and fear causes them to rush and sell, which further drives down the price, say, to $30. At this point, the stock is probably *oversold*. Stocks that are oversold often fall past former support levels. Perhaps $40 was a recent support level for the stock, but panic causes a breakout to $30. In contrast to the herd, the day trader who approaches the market in a calm, rational manner sees opportunity in the overselling bandwagon. When, based on the decreasing volume of sellers, the stock appears to be bottoming out after plunging past a former support level, the time can be ripe for buying.

Of course, the situation works the same way in reverse. When a stock appears to be rising, people get on the bandwagon to buy it, this time out of greed. They reason that since the stock price is rising and everyone seems to want it, then this must be a great time to buy. Often, the price rises precipitously past former resistance levels as the buying frenzy bids the price up higher and higher, at which point the stock may be *overbought*. Again, the day trader waits until the buying volume starts to decrease and sees an opportunity to sell the stock short.

Short-Term Overbought-Oversold Oscillator

The short-term overbought-oversold oscillator represents a moving average of the net differences between advances and declines (issues). This oscillator serves as a helpful reference tool in forecasting the near-term price movements of the market as a whole. Since anticipating broad market moves is the best way to profit in all markets, this indicator should be reviewed weekly. Combining the state of the oscillator with political and economic events that affect and, in many instances, drive the market allows the trader to assess the "true" condition of the market. While reviewing the oscillator, it is important to recognize at all times that good judgment must prevail and that market conditions at any given moment can be unique. Yet, as a guideline, this oscillator is a good tool for gauging the present tone and the future direction of the market.

Over the past five years, this oscillator, utilizing a 10-day moving average, has generally traded between the –400 level and the +400 bar. Figure 5.17, showing the oscillator in conjunction with the Nasdaq composite, presents a compelling argument as to the veracity of the oscillator. Through a comparative analysis of the oscillator with the Nasdaq composite, it is evident that an indicator that portrays the state of the broad market is beneficial to the investor or trader because "a rising tide lifts all boats." Understanding the broad market is essential to understanding the individual segments of it.

Figure 5.17 Overbought-oversold oscillator and the Nasdaq composite

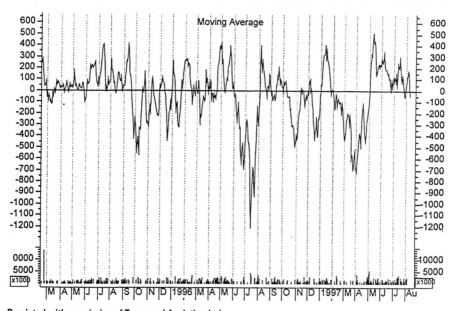

Reprinted with permission of Townsend Analytics, Ltd.

Upside/Downside Volume

Upside/downside volume is the ratio of the daily up volume to the daily down volume. Generally, the construction of the ratio takes into account a 50-day period. It is calculated by dividing the total volume on those days when the stock closed up from the prior day by the total volume on days when the stock closed down. Normally, the indicator tracks the market.

During bull trends, upside/downside volume is decidedly up. Likewise, during bear phases, the upside/downside volume indicator has a downward bias. During market advances, volume of advancing issues is expanding on rallies and contracting during declines. If such a relationship is broken, it serves as a warning of a potential trend reversal. As a broad market analysis tool, the upside/downside volume indicator can be used in conjunction with other technical and fundamental indicators and information to forecast the direction of the general market in the coming months.

New High/New Low Index

Another essential tool for broad market analysis is the new high/new low index. This index, too, emulates the direction of the general market. If the index diverges from the general market trend, it alerts the trader that the move is suspect.

In skittish markets, the various composite averages might move in one direction, say up, but the new high/new low index fails to mirror this rally. Generally, under these circumstances, the market indices reflect a narrow upside move in the high-capitalization blue-chip corporations. Should this bias arise, the trader should be poised for a trend reversal if the rally fails to lift the small- and mid-capitalization issues.

In other circumstances, the index reflects the broad market trend. Given this situation, the trader should trade with the trend, focusing on the strongest stocks in the strongest sectors.

Now it's time to move into the aspects of day trading that make it different from any other type of trading that the investor is likely to have done before. Chapter 6 will discuss the principle tool that makes effective day trading possible: the trading screen and its many windows of valuable information.

chapter 6

timing your trade
for maximum returns

the trading screen and how to use it

In Chapter 5, we walked you through the use of the various graphs and charts used in trading. It is now time to get into the mechanics of the trading screen, where all of the various charts, graphs, and tables that you will use to pick trades are found. For your convenience, Appendix C describes in step-by-step detail how to build your own trading screen so that these tools may be used in the most effective manner.

Our book is not designed as a primer on how to use a home computer, however. We assume that you already have these capabilities and that you are proficient in using a modem and connecting to the Internet. The first thing you will need to do is to sign up with a data-feed service that provides the real-time market access essential to do effective day trading. Most services will provide you with a free-trial-demonstration period. Be sure to specify that you want Nasdaq *Level II* data. Because of the constantly changing and improving nature of data services, please visit our Web sites, brokersaurus.com or LearnTradingOnline.net, for the latest recommendations on data providers.

To run the software and tie into the markets, you will need a computer with Windows 95 or NT, a 17-inch or larger monitor, a modem with at least a 28.8-MHz speed, and an Internet service provider (ISP).

Once you have hooked up to a service you will find several demonstration screens. Each of these provides useful information, but simply moving from one to another really gives you no idea of how to go about using the various windows coherently to be able to make effective trading decisions. Besides, you don't want to be moving from one screen to another anyway. In real trading, by the time you did a lot of screen switching in the middle of a trade, you would probably return to find that you'd just lost all your money.

Of course, it is possible to customize your own screen, or page, into several windows that will give you the appropriately formatted information you need for effective day trading. This is the real Achilles' heel of day trading. Someone who simply gets a direct line to the markets, opens an account with an order-entry firm through which to trade, and starts trading is virtually guaranteed to lose money. The question is, how much time do you want to spend and how much money do you want to lose during the trial-and-error period of designing the optimal trading screen yourself? Starting trading from scratch while trying to figure out how and what to do about a trading screen is definitely an example of "Kids, please don't try this at home!"

Fortunately, we have already done this for you. You may be so advanced that you have laughed at the market background we have provided, chuckled at the rudimentary explanations of technical analysis, and guffawed at our discussion of market psychology. Perhaps you even put our book down a time or two to "drop those two young whippersnappers a line to straighten them out." Even so, this chapter alone will cover the cost of our book many times over. Once you have set up and mastered the use of your trading screen, you will realize just exactly how much time and, more important, money you have saved by being shown how to do it correctly from the start.

In this chapter, we will discuss how to use the optimal trading screen, what windows you want to have open on the screen, and the usefulness of each window to the day trader. Careful attention to detail at this point will help us achieve our goal of having you, as a new day trader, trading profitably from day one. With your money at stake, it is no time for trial and error, only profit.

The Trading Screen

Putting all of the things we have learned and discussed onto a single trading screen that provides you with all of the technical data you will ever need to day trade is, to us, one of the most exciting aspects of our book. The trading screen layout we recommend contains no less than a dozen separate windows of information. Eleven are open and directly in front of you at all times; one is closed, but is in the upper corner of the screen and thus readily available to open with a single click of the mouse.

All of this is designed to allow you to eke out the winning edge, that is, to put the probabilities a little more in your favor and to give you the information you need to make critical decisions in the compressed time frame of the day trader. To be an effective day trader, you need to minimize the things you can't control and maximize those thing you can. The *trading screen* is designed to maximize what you can control by giving you all the information you need when you need it. And it is no less than amazing.

Figure 6.1 shows the overall layout of the trading screen. There are a total of 12 windows on it. We recommend that you set up your screen to look like this one by going through the detailed instructions in Appendix C. This will familiarize you with using the software and eliminate many of the questions you will inevitably have if you simply start using the screen from scratch. (For those who can't get the screen running, you can download the screen from our Web sites at LearnTradingOnline.net or brokersaurus.com.) Here we will discuss why the screen is arranged the way it is, and what all the various windows do for you.

The left portion of the screen, occupying a little over half of it, consists of four Nasdaq Level II market maker windows, one for each of up to four stocks that you may decide to follow during the course of the trading day. There are eight smaller windows on the right-hand portion of the screen. Beginning with the upper left corner of the right-hand portion of the screen is a two-day, minute-by-minute chart showing the real-time price and volume changes over a given time frame for one of the stocks you have selected. Below this are the Nasdaq trends window on the left and the stock time and sales ticker window on the right. Moving to the top right of the screen is a small banner that expands with a click of the mouse to fill the entire screen with a 200-day daily price-volume chart. (Note that any other window can be so clicked to fill the entire screen if desired.) Below that are two short tables. The left one is a price-volume table that sorts the top 10 percentage gainers for any given time during the trading day. The right one is a price-volume table that sorts the top 10 percentage losers at any given time during the trading day. The two longer tables below

Figure 6.1   Trading screen

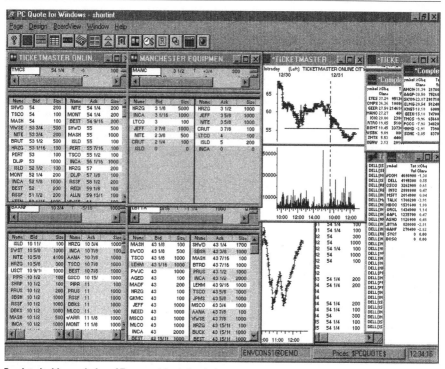

Reprinted with permission of Townsend Analytics, Ltd.

these are the price-change ticker on the left for a short list of stocks that you choose to follow during the day. These are color-coded to show sales of those stocks as either down (red), up (green), or no change (white) from the previous sale. Finally, to its right is a price-volume table that sorts a list of stocks you select (your hot list) from highest to lowest volume.

Skilled use of the information that can be gleaned from this screen setup is what makes highly effective day trading possible. Now we will discuss in detail uses and benefits to the day trader of each of the windows of the trading screen. Although we will attempt to explain and describe what is happening on the windows, to fully understand and follow along, you should be online and have your trading screen up and running as you read. If you are not able to do this, read the chapter anyway, but come back and reread it once you are online.

The Price-Volume Windows

We discuss in other chapters many of the different methods of selecting stocks to trade on a given day. However, if you are, as many do, using your trading screen to select the stocks to trade, you will do this using the three price-volume windows.

The Sort-by-Volume Window

Volume, as you know by now, is one of the prime buy/sell indicators for the day trader. This window is the main one you will use most often in order to determine which stocks to follow. This window will serve as your hot list, that is, a list of the stocks you have personally selected to follow. We have already discussed some of the ways to identify stocks to follow and to place on your hot list, such as the list of short-interest stocks reviewed in Chapter 4. In Chapter 7, "The Trading Day and Its Characteristics," we will provide even more criteria. Suffice it to say here that you can add as many or as few stocks to your hot list as you desire, plus you can save several versions of your trading screen, each with a different list of hot stocks.

Volume is important because it indicates that the stock is *liquid,* that is, a lot of shares are changing hands. Volume is what makes nearly instantaneous trades possible. If you follow a stock with low volume, minutes or longer may go by between sales. You don't want to fool with a stock that no one else is interested in. Worse, you don't want to have bought it and subsequently want to sell it only to find no buyers. Even if you are able to SOES your way out, you will have lost the spread plus commissions.

Volume may also indicate *volatility,* that is, the potential for big moves in the price of the stock. This is the ideal situation for the day trader, because if the stock doesn't move after you've bought it, there is no money to be made. Since market makers haven't been able to keep day traders out of the market, they now attempt to do the next best thing, that is, to try to make the day trader think that the stock isn't moving, and thus get her to sell with no move. Of course, this is the same as buying on the ask and selling on the bid, so the day trader loses both the spread and the commissions. You job is to make sure that the market makers fail at this.

Next to the volume column is the percent-change column. This is helpful in determining volatility. As we have discussed previously, you want to select a stock that has decent volume, but not enough for the price to change so rapidly that you are constantly chasing it. Thus, you will rarely be interested in the stocks at the top of the volume table. You are looking for stocks with moderate volume, say around 50,000 shares in the first half hour of trading, with about a 10 percent price change from yesterday's close. Now you have both volume and volatility. Once you have found such a stock, point your cursor at it and hold down the left mouse button. A half-inch circle will appear. Drag this over to one of your four market maker windows, release the button, and the market maker window for that stock will appear. This also places the stock on the two-day and 200-day charts and on the time and sales window.

The Sort-by-Gainers Window

The sort-by-gainers window offers a somewhat different strategy than that afforded by the sort-by-volume window. These 10 stocks are typically those for which some bit of good news, rumor, or what have you has come out overnight. They will usually fall into one of two categories: stocks whose prices have gapped up on the open and stocks whose prices have jumped following the open. Each of these requires slightly different strategies.

For the gapped-up stocks, the market maker has set a price that she hopes is right for the stock. You want to keep an eye on these to determine whether the market agrees. If the price has been jacked up too much, sellers and profit takers will appear and you will have a shorting opportunity. If too little, bargain hunters will begin to drive up prices, giving you the opportunity to go long.

For stocks that open normally but then begin a rapid price increase, it is apparent that the market has already made its judgment about where the price should be. For these, you want to determine (1) if velocity (momentum) still exists for the move to continue, this time with you on board, or (2) whether the stock has become overbought and is ripe for a turnaround and thus a shorting opportunity. Once you have made your selection, drag the stock over to one of your four market maker windows.

The Sort-by-Losers Window

The sort-by-losers window also offers a different stock-picking strategy than that afforded by the sort-by-volume window. These 10 stocks are usually those for which some bit of negative news has come out overnight. As with the gainers, they will typically fall into one of two categories: stocks whose prices have gapped down on the open and stocks whose prices have dropped following the open. Each requires slightly different strategies.

For the gapped-down stocks, the market maker again sets a price he hopes is right for the stock. As usual, keep an eye on these to see if the market agrees. If the opening price has been placed too low, buyers and bargain hunters will appear and you will have a buying opportunity; if too high, bargain hunters will begin to drive prices down, giving you the opportunity to short the stock.

For stocks that open normally, but then begin a rapid price decline, the market has again obviously made its judgment about where the price should be. For these, you want to determine (1) if momentum still exists for the move to continue, this time with you on board, or (2) whether the stock has become oversold and is ripe for a turnaround and thus a buying opportunity. Once you have made your selection, drag the stock over to one of your four market maker windows.

One thing to take note of is that percent change is relative. If you got a $100 bonus at your office last year and $200 this year, you can brag that your bonus increased by 100 percent. Just don't tell anyone what the actual number was! Similarly, take a look at the Manchester Equipment on the trading screen in Figure 6.1. You'll notice by examining the sort-by-gainers window for the symbol MANC that it was the fourth highest percentage gainer, at 27.27 percent, on the Nasdaq at the time the screen was printed out. However, dragging this stock to a market maker window shows that a gain of only ¾ point on a $2¾ stock was necessary to produce such a large increase. Such low-priced stocks rarely have an average daily movement of $1 that the day trader is seeking. Even if you had gotten in on the entire ¾ move, you would have grossed only $750.

NASDAQ Level II Market Maker Window

Once you have selected one to four stocks to track for possible trading, the Nasdaq *Level II data* window will become invaluable. This window is what makes effective day trading possible, and not having it causes failure for many would-be day traders, or even for those who regularly trade through online brokers. Without it, you might as well call your broker and enter a market order just like everyone else.

Selling Pressure versus Buying Pressure

Access to Nasdaq Level II market maker data allows the day trader to watch market makers lining up on either the bid or ask sides, and thus predict with a 70:30 probability which way a stock is poised to move. In Chapter 5, "High-Probability Trading," we told you that when a stock's price hit a support or resistance level to look for increasing volume to determine whether the stock was a potential trade. Other than a few subtle hints, that's how we left it, and that's how just about every book or article on technical analysis leaves it, too. In this chapter, we finish the job that no one else has. There is a blatantly obvious question that no one raises when discussing technical analysis because it is useless to ask unless access to Level II data is available. Now that access *is* available, we can ask the question: *Just because a stock's price is hitting a trendline, and even if volume is increasing, how do I know from that whether the support or resistance will hold or whether a breakout is imminent?*

The answer is simple: You don't! Period. That is, unless you have access to Level II data. The beauty of Level II data is that you have far more than the basic inside market bid-ask. Figure 6.1 shows the trading screen with the four market maker Level II windows. You may also wish to review the Intel Level II window in Chapter 1, Figure 1.1. Your screen will be in full color; ours here, however, is in black and white, due to printing constraints. The prices in the bid and ask columns are sorted automatically in two ways. First, they are sorted by price, with the highest bid at the top of the bid column followed by successively lower bids and the lowest ask at the top of the ask column followed by successively higher asks. Of course, the highest bid and lowest ask constitute the quote, or inside market. The second sort occurs when several market makers are bidding or asking at the same price level. In this instance, they appear or are *queued up* in the order that their bid at this level was entered (i.e., on a first-come, first-entered basis).

The breaking up of market makers into price levels is the key to using the real power that Level II data provides. On your trading screen, each level will be color-coded so you can get a feel for what is going on just by glancing instead of having to read the actual prices to figure out who is bidding or asking what. In Figure 6.1, we have alternated white and gray for each price level. With this background, we may now answer the question about how to tell whether a turnaround or a breakout is imminent when a stock's price reaches a support or resistance level: Check the Level II market maker window.

This involves examining the depth of each of the different levels at and below the inside market that appear on your Level II window. If there are many market makers at and closely below the inside market bid, and few at each level below the inside market ask, there is depth of support for buying, and the stock price is likely to increase. If the price happens to be at a support level, buying pressure signifies a turn-around. If it is at a resistance level, you probably have a breakout.

Conversely, if there are few market makers at or closely below the inside market bid, but many at and below the inside market ask, there is depth of support for selling, and the stock price is likely to fall. If the price is at a support level, selling pressure signifies a breakout. If it is at a resistance level, the price is likely to turn around.

The third situation occurs when there is roughly equal depth of support on both sides, in which case the stock will probably move little. This is the case more often than not on low volume. Depth of support obviously creates its own volume in a given direction. Of course, there is every gradation between equal depth of support and support for buying or selling, respectively. With experience, you will develop a feel for how much depth of support is necessary to likely cause a significant move in the direction indicated.

To help understand some of these concepts, let's take another look at the trading screen in Figure 6.1. The Ticketmaster market maker window in the upper left-hand corner shows approximately equal interest between buyers and sellers, as evidenced by about the same number and depth of price levels. Baan Company in the lower left appears to show a bit more interest on the buy side than the sell side. Tele-Communications, Inc., the lower right of the four market maker windows, shows a strong tendency on the buy side.

And Manchester Equipment shows roughly the same buy/sell tendencies, but overall, this window best illustrates a low-interest, low-liquidity stock. Only five market makers are present, along with one ECN (INCA or Instinet); ISLD (Island) is listed but, at zero, is not a player. Although not immediately apparent in Figure 6.1, the other three market maker windows can all be scrolled down (note the scroll bar on the right margin of each window) to reveal an even longer list of market makers with lower offers and higher asks than shown in the available space of the window. You won't typically need to do this, however, but the rest of the list is there. Thus whenever you bring a stock to one of your market maker windows and it looks like the one for Manchester Equipment, it's usually better to try another.

Craig McBurney is an engineer. When asked what 3 plus 4 is, he is likely to whip out his calculator and, with a few quick entries, proudly proclaim, "7.0000." Bob Baird is a geologist, so he will ponder for a moment and respond, "Oh, somewhere between six and eight." We make this engineer/geologist distinction to let you know that there is another method to be more precise in gauging the actual strength of the bid and ask sides, and that is to pick the same price differential for each side and add up the number of shares represented. For example, for Ticketmaster, the number of shares being bid between 54 and 51½, a 2½ difference is 4,500; for the ask, between 54¼ and 57, a 2¾ difference (as close as we could get to 2½), is 3,700 shares. This way we detect a little more strength on the buy side.

For Tele Comm, the number of shares being bid between 43⅛ and 43, a ⅛ difference, is 10,100; for the ask, between 43¼ and 43⅜, also a ⅛ difference, it is 2,700 shares. Try this yourself on Baan. First, you'll find that the difficulties are finding price levels that have the same difference from side to side to compare (as with Ticketmaster). Second, it takes time to add up the numbers. Third, what does this exercise tell you that you didn't already know from simply inspecting the number of price levels and thicknesses (i.e., that Tele Comm has stronger buying than Ticketmaster)? Finally, as we learned in Chapter 2, market makers do not have to display orders higher than 1,000 shares anyway, so the 1,000-share bid means *at least* that; in reality, it may be just the tip of a much larger trade iceberg.

So, instead of whipping out your calculator and pushing buttons while the trade is going past you, you'll find that it rarely matters that 3 + 4 = 7.0000 because "somewhere between six and eight" is all you really need. Basically, if you can't tell if there is strength just by looking, it's likely because there isn't much.

As you probably surmised from this exercise, you will, of course, need to quickly learn to compare prices that may be presented in halves, quarters, eighths, sixteenths (*teenies*), and so on. Fortunately, the markets already know they will eventually have to go to a simple decimal system, so that an actual dollar amount will be used: 27.75 instead of 27¾. Why haven't they already done this? Think back to our discussion on SOES (Chapter 2) about market makers doing their best to keep the spreads as high as possible. The difference between the bid and the ask is often about the same as the difference between each price level. What do you suppose would happen to spreads (read *profits!*) if the typical price level difference were a penny!

Market Maker Strategies

Each four-letter symbol in the bid-ask columns of the market maker window represents a market maker. The names of the brokerages represented by many of the market makers you will regularly see on your trading screen are listed in Appendix B. Understanding what the Level II window tells us about the individual market maker's own strategies is another use of the market maker window that can help turn the odds in our favor and make profitable day trading possible.

One such strategy is how market makers refresh their quotes after they have bought or sold at their previous quote. Because market makers do not have to display more than 1,000 shares, regardless of what they really have available to trade, paying close attention to quote updates can provide an outstanding source of information that can reveal the true interest in any given stock. When refreshing quotes, market makers can move the bid or the offer up or down, leave one side at the same level and move the other side, or move one side in one direction and the other side in another direction. Each of these changes furnishes clues regarding the intent of the market maker or the market maker's perception of the near-term movement of the security in question.

In order to interpret these changes rapidly, it is necessary for the day trader to use the color-coded price levels to track the movements of the market maker quote updates. Then the trader can see and interpret these movements as they take place by analyzing and digesting the changes in color. Because each change in price down the list is signified on the window by a different color, it is easy to tell which way the price is moving. In the window, for instance, yellow may be the color of the highest bid and the lowest ask price. If the shares at the highest bid or lowest ask price are all traded, then the next grouping of prices in line moves up and becomes the yellow group.

When there are many marker makers lined up in the bid column at the highest bid price, there is momentum toward buying, and prices may rise. Conversely, when everyone is lining up on the ask side, there is a lot of stock wanting to be sold, and the price may fall. An apparent clockwise rotation of colors (i.e., the bid levels are contracting and the ask levels are expanding) means that the bids at a given price are finding sellers at a lower price and that prices are falling. Counterclockwise rotation indicates that the asks are finding buyers and that the prices are rising. A slowing of rotation may indicate that a reversal of price is imminent and that it may be time to sell or buy. This is also the time to keep an eye on the volume. If volume is keeping up or picking up, it is likely that the price movement will continue. If volume is slowing, then everyone who wants to buy or sell within that particular price range has done so, and a reversal may be coming.

Because market makers are required to make a two-sided market, that is, to be on both the buying and selling sides, the day trader can read an individual market maker's strategy by watching how he refreshes his quotes. If he keeps refreshing his quote at the inside market, this indicates that he is actively in the market, and the day trader should take note of a possible price movement situation. There are only three variations that the market maker can follow. The first is to increase his bid price while increasing his ask price. This indicates he is moving toward the buying action and away from the selling, meaning that the market maker believes the stock is headed higher.

The second is to decrease his bid while increasing his ask price. By doing this, he is in effect moving away from both the buying and the selling action. This means the market maker doesn't wish to actively participate at the moment. If he continuously adjusts his bid so that he does little trading, he may simply be fulfilling his obligation for a two-sided market.

The third situation occurs when the market maker updates both his bid and ask quotes to a lower price, indicating that he is moving away from the buying action and toward the selling. This shows that he believes the price is headed down and he wants to unload what he has.

A market maker could theoretically bid higher and ask less, but this would not make sense and, in practice, would not occur except by accident. Finally, if, in a given security, there is little or no refreshing of market maker quotes, the market is stale and unreceptive to any sort of trading. In this circumstance, the volume is probably low also, and it is advisable to look at other securities. (See Table 6.1.)

Market makers play the market game like others play the game of poker. Sometimes they like to bluff to get a better deal. For instance, let's say that market maker GHIJ is on the next price level down from the inside market bid. This indicates that GHIJ doesn't wish to pay the current quote. However, you may notice that, at the same time, GHIJ is a few levels below the inside market ask, with 50,000 shares for sale. GHIJ may not have 50,000 shares to sell at all, but she wants to create the impression that a lot of stock is coming onto the market so that the price will go down to where she is waiting to buy.

Table 6.1 Market Maker Quote Refreshment Strategies

Bid Change	Ask Change	Interpretation
+	+ or none	Market maker believes prices are going up. Market maker is a buyer.
–	+	Market maker doesn't wish to participate.
– or none	–	Market maker believes prices are going down. Market maker is a seller.
None	None	Stale market.

In this instance, GHIJ will typically be multiple levels below the inside ask if she really isn't a seller. This is because she does not want to run the risk of actually having someone hit her with a buy for all of her shares. If you are in the market for 1,000 shares, you would not be interested in paying any more than the inside ask, and usually less. However, if you are an institutional buyer, and want 50,000 shares for your mutual fund, then you know that an order of this size will drive the price up anyway, and you may well hit GHIJ for the 50,000. Thus, GHIJ will be asking enough so that she is unlikely to be hit, and if she is, she hopes her sale price is high enough so that she may be able to repurchase at a lower price the shares she has just sold.

To prevent even this eventuality, GHIJ may instead tease the market by posting her buy order for 50,000 shares and then remove it quickly upon refreshing. This creates the impression that the 50,000 shares may have sold rather than the order having been removed. Your time and sales ticker, as we will discuss shortly, can assist you in determining which actually happened.

Watching market maker trends even works before the exchanges open in the morning. As 9:30 A.M. nears, you will be able to see the colors changing on your Level II windows as the market makers jockey to get in at what they consider to be the best positions in a given stock before the market opens, as well as which way they are trying to move the price of that stock. These prices change back and forth, and the inside quote in effect at the open determines the opening price of the stock for that day.

Another way to help predict the way a stock may be heading is to observe how quickly a large block of stock for sale moves. A quick sale of a large volume of stock indicates support for price increases. If the block is only nibbled at, or particularly if the seller has to reduce the price to find buyers, then the price is headed lower.

How Market Makers Support a Stock

The market makers, most of whom represent the large stock broker-ages, often come into the market to support the price of the stock of some of their larger clients. For example, if XYZ Corporation is a major client of OPQR Brokerage, and shares of XYZ start to fall, OPQR may come into the market and begin purchasing shares of XYZ in order to support the price and to prevent the sell-off from becoming a panic, which, of course, could wipe out a lot of the share value of XYZ. Keep in mind, however, that even the large market making firms have rela-tively little influence once a bandwagon takes effect and panic or greed begin driving a stock price.

Often, the level at which the brokerage will attempt to support the price of the stock is at a historic support level, as we have discussed previously. This is another of the many reasons that historic support levels may repeat themselves, and thus why technical analysis works. Obviously, reviewing the 200-day chart of the stock being supported is of value.

The Level II window actually allows us to watch and see if broker support is the reason a stock seems to be hitting a support level. If this is so, then we will see shares of XYZ being offered at a certain price, and we will see OPQR Brokerage on the top of the bid column buying up all that is being offered. Once all the stock of XYZ that people want to sell at the support level has been bought by OPQR Brokerage, the selling pressure dissipates and the stock may begin to rise from the support level. This may be a buying opportunity. Conversely, if OPQR finishes buying and drops out, the support may fail, producing a shorting oppor-tunity. All of this is directly on your screen in front of you when you need it.

The Two-Day, Minute-by-Minute Price-Volume Chart

Once you select a stock and add it to your market maker window, the current day's and the previous day's prices and volumes automatically appear in the two-day, minute-by-minute price-volume chart. This win-dow can be customized to show anywhere from one to five days of data. Due to the vast storage space requirements necessary, data older than five days are not retained on a minute-by-minute basis. A one-day, or current day, window is not ideal because it is not immediately obvious that an opening gap has occurred, if yesterday's trend is continuing, or whether a support or resistance level from yesterday is being approached. On the other hand, three to five days of one-minute data tends to be crunched up on the chart. Thus, we selected two days as the best compromise.

This chart is very important because the day trader can draw trendlines on it and then look for support and resistance levels. Volume is always right below the price trend, making it easy to tell if interest is increasing. A glance at the market maker window allows confirmation of the trend direction (i.e., continuance of a trend, breakouts, or reversals). We are using a five-minute moving average for the two-day chart, even though it isn't apparent in the black-and-white diagram. This tends to smooth out the noise in the price fluctuations. However, the minute-by-minute ticks in the graph are usually so close that they virtually form their own trendline, making a moving average less important on this scale.

You will use the tools of technical analysis learned in Chapter 5 on the charts we'll discuss next.

The 200-Day Price-Volume Chart

A moving average can also be utilized on the 200-day, or long-term, chart in the same manner as explained for the two-day chart. This chart is typically 200 days; however, as we discussed previously, if a major change in the market occurred within that time frame, such as the 1998 bear market and recovery, it will not be useful to try to connect current trends with old ones. In such an instance, following the current trend from its beginning will provide the most useful data on support and resistance levels.

The stock trends are similar regardless of the time frame. On the long-term chart, regardless of the exact number of days out, a five-day moving average is helpful in smoothing out the day-to-day fluctuations in the stock price and revealing the underlying trends. Once you have examined the two-day chart and identified some possible support or resistance levels, you will want to review the longer-term chart to determine whether older support and resistance levels are being approached, or tested, again.

The Time and Sales Window

The time and sales ticker window, or *tape,* reports prices and size of transactions, which will be one of the tools you will use as a day trader. It is called the tape because it is the modern-day equivalent of the old ticker tape. Instead of having all the stock prices of an entire exchange whizzing by, however, you will add to the tape the four stocks you have targeted in your Level II windows.

The tape is invaluable for anticipating the near-term movement of a given security. For this, the tape provides a number of clues. In most circumstances, if the tape indicates that all of the most recent trades are coming through at the same price, it is evident that there is an imbalance, perhaps momentary, or perhaps longer in duration, in the supply of and demand for a given security. In this same instance, the tape might also indicate that supply and demand are in equilibrium if all of the trades being reported are consistently trading between the bid and offer.

The size of each trade furnished by the tape also provides valuable clues regarding the nature of the trading taking place. For instance, multiple thousand-lot orders placed on the offer would indicate SOES activity. Likely the stock will run up a level, perhaps two, then come right back to the original level as the SOES traders close out their long positions.

Contrast that to a tape showing blocks of 10,000 to 250,000 shares. Such activity indicates an "institutional" participant. Interpreting the tape under these circumstances is far more complex. If a large block trades at the bid, does it indicate a sell-off and hence lower prices, or does it suggest the seller is completing a large transaction, thus creating a temporary imbalance in supply and demand resulting in an immediate rally? These are the types of questions that can only be answered through experience. Yet without the tape and its subsequent analysis, these questions could not be answered at all.

This window is also useful to track a stock of interest, because each sale is posted with its actual size and actual sale price. As you know, market maker postings, with the exception of those on ECNs, are typically for 1,000 shares regardless of how many shares the market maker wants to trade, if he even wants to trade at all. Regardless of how many shares a market maker is posting, however, the tape tells the tale. For instance, if you see a large sale of stock posted in the Price-Volume Sales window that sells very quickly, it means that there may be a lot of buyers. Conversely, if the block size is being nibbled away and the price is also falling, few buyers at the higher prices are indicated.

The Price-Change Ticker

This window is another one, like the depth of support on the market maker window, that you typically interpret visually. Once you have selected from one to four stocks to monitor on your market maker windows, you can right click on this window in order to add these four stocks. Each time there is a buy or a sell, the selected stock(s) will appear color-coded: green for up, white for no change, and red for down. Glancing at this window from time to time will tell you whether the most recent sales have been up or down. It will be easier for the beginning day trader to simply place a single stock in this window, so as to not have to begin by trying to mentally separate four different stocks at the same time.

The Exchange Ticker

The final window on the trading screen is simply a chart that shows the trend of the Nasdaq stock exchange over the course of the trading day. This helps in determining whether the overall trend of stocks is up or down so that you can go long or short accordingly. Of course, any exchange can be selected, as can any stock, whether Nasdaq or not, for any of the windows on the trading screen. However, watching other markets that cannot be traded except through a broker is of little use to the day trader.

With the foregoing under your belt, let us now proceed to discuss the trading day and how you prepare to meet it.

chapter 7

the trading day and its characteristics

how to pick your stocks and when to trade them

The trading day is made up of several different "trading periods" with distinctive characteristics that must be understood in order to trade successfully. The best times for day trading are from about 9:30 to 11:00 A.M. and around 3:30 in the afternoon. In the morning, you have a lot of folks wanting to get in or out of the market based on overnight news, yesterday's close, or what have you. It is generally better to discipline yourself to not trade as soon as the market opens because prices may be quite volatile at this time and trends can go either way.

Of course, there will be those inevitable trades that you "shoulda" done, which did go up after you wanted to buy. You will remember these. But all those times when the stock did not move in your favor, which you tend to forget, is the reason it is best to wait a while and let the stock you're interested in test for support and resistance. *Woulda, coulda,* and *shoulda* are not in the vocabulary of the disciplined day trader.

Before the Market Opens

You can read any time of the day and check out the latest goings-on of whatever company you may be interested in following more closely.

However, since the *open* is a critical time for trading, it is important that you maximize the information you are getting and minimize the time spent searching for it. When you get up in the morning and are sipping your first cup of coffee, pick up your copy of *Investor's Business Daily* and turn on CNBC so that you will be in top form by the time the market opens.

News and information impact the securities markets on a daily basis. During the trading day, such impact can be moment by moment. Trading and investing decisions are a combination of emotional and rational (sometimes irrational) determinations based, in large part, on both broad-based news (e.g., political, economic, social) and news particular to a given stock. With this in mind, news relating to the markets is necessarily voluminous, complex, and chaotic. The perceptive trader who is able to digest and interpret this constant influx of data properly is in a position to act decisively before the rest of the crowd unravels "the story behind the story." Even though all newspapers arrive at the doorstep at approximately the same time, not all papers are equally informative.

In this chapter, we'll supply you with some information on primary sources of information that will assist you in determining where the market is going, and we'll teach you how to effectively study a given information source. For instance, after reading this chapter you will be able to pick up a paper such as *Investor's Business Daily* and zero in on exactly which sections and what types of articles to read to maximize the quality of information you get while minimizing quantity.

The purpose of your reviewing the news is to determine which stocks may be moving and volatile at any given time. Others may be hesitant to take any sort of action in a volatile market. The day trader, however, is more at home in a volatile market than in any other.

Using *Investor's Business Daily*

Investor's Business Daily (*IBD*) provides *the* best up-to-the-minute news coverage relating to the markets. The newspaper is devoted solely to stocks, bonds, options, mutual funds, currencies and commodities. It is important to scan this paper daily for valuable ideas for the trading day ahead. Pick up a copy of *IBD* before you proceed.

Headline Hopping   Here are some recommendations from William O'Neil, chairman and founder of *Investor's Business Daily,* on his personal strategies for finding winning investments using *IBD:*

- *Front page/page A2:* Quickly glance at the news snippets on the left side of the front page. Scan the headlines of the four major features on the right side of page 1. If interested, read the complete article. Quickly review "Making A Long Story Short" (page A2) for a quick overview of relevant news topics.
- *Economy page/page B1:* Scan the headline for relevant news. Glance at the World Markets section to gain an international perspective.

New America/Computers and Technology Page   Scan the names of the companies profiled. The New America page is a major idea-generating feature. It's important to read up on some of these companies that are growing very rapidly. Mr. O'Neil highly suggests investors cut out this page, save it, track the companies of interest and look for those breaking new high ground.

Check out the fresh ideas on the Computers & Technology page to see if any are relevant to your situation. This page is meant to introduce you to the hardware and software used to solve the problems of corporate America today.

Companies in the News   This is a good in-depth feature for readers interested in the company or the industry highlighted each day. Look at the patterns on the three charts provided. Check the base to examine whether or not the price is extended. Mr. O'Neil suggests brokers and investors tear out this page and keep an alphabetical file. This page has a very long shelf life.

Finding the Stock Market Leaders   Intended to be a very important research device, the Intelligent Tables screen through stocks and reveal those worthy of a second look. Through these tables, Mr. O'Neil keeps abreast of what is really going on in the market, what is moving and what is not. Make this a fast weeding-out process. Winning stocks keep popping up as confirmation of their strength. Mr. O'Neil scans all the exchanges for the subsequently described indicators, but will spend a little more time with the Nasdaq tables and columns as this "exchange" is currently leading the market. Day traders will use Nasdaq almost exclusively.

Greatest Percent Rise in Volume   Note the stocks that are boldfaced (80 EPS and 80 Relative Strength Ranks). Make a hot list of the stocks that stand out and deserve additional researching. Mr. O'Neil makes his list right on the top of the front page of the paper! If you know or recognize a name, jot it down. This list may indicate that something is about to happen.

Most Active/Most Percentage Up in Price   Note the stocks that are going up in price and are trading on high volume. Circle these and add a few to your hot list.

Intelligent Tables A–Z   Quickly scan the remaining stocks traded on the particular exchange. Save time by checking only stocks that are bold-faced (new highs or up a point). Mr. O'Neil looks for unusual moves in price and volume: If price is up significantly, he looks to see confirming action in much greater than usual volume; otherwise, he skips over it. Circle/add to your hot list. Try to scan the entire list in 5 to 10 minutes. The Nasdaq list is long but very important. Quite simply, it generates more ideas. Be certain to cover all ground from A–Z or you could miss something great.

If it is a bad day in the market, also check the underlined stocks (new lows or down a point) and note whether the price is down on high or low volume. If the market leaders are down but with no real volume, the market may be okay. If the leaders are down with two or three times the usual volume, heavy dumping is occurring, and this may provide a sell signal. The Volume % Change column is very important.

Exchange News Columns (Inside the Market, Nasdaq/AMEX Markets)
Scan through highlighted names. Circle/add to hot list those that interest you.

Stocks in the News Charts   Quickly check each chart one by one. Save time by immediately eliminating any with Relative Strength Rank below 80. Circle good bases and research for additional information. Mr. O'Neil usually circles two or three and adds these to his list.

Earnings: Best Ups   Scan very quickly for something that stands out. In a red-hot market you may want to go through these "up" earnings one by one so that nothing gets by your radar.

New High List   Pay particular attention to the top six or seven industry groups for the week. They point to the real leadership in the market.

Beyond that, don't waste your time. Circle names you recognize. Mr. O'Neil usually circles three or four and then checks these companies to see if something is starting to happen. Look for new names in a hot industry sector.

Market Sector Index List   Circle the top four or five indexes. Look at the good versus the bad. Your investigation into the tables should confirm the sector information.

General Market Indicators   Use the information learned by going through the Intelligent Tables to help interpret the market indicators. The indicators give a broad indication, whereas the Intelligent Tables lend insight into which specific industries and sectors are acting better than others.

Quickly glance at all three major indices (Nasdaq, S&P 500, Dow). Look at the change from the prior day's close. Concentrate on the percentage change versus the day before for information about relative action. Glance at the minor-sector charts; circle a few if they are acting right. During tricky periods in the market, Mr. O'Neil spends a bit more time with this page, looking closely at each day's price and volume. He's looking to discern the weakness or strength of the market. Mr. O'Neil also looks at the interest rate charts. These affect the overall market.

What Mr. O'Neil Does *Not* Look At

- Nasdaq Small Cap (having observed after 30 years of model-book research that the greatest stock market winners proved to be stocks greater than $12 in price)
- Futures
- Options
- Bonds
- Overseas markets
- T-bills

This concludes our discussion on how to use *Investor's Business Daily.* All of the information available to the investor today can be narrowed down to specific news items and events upon which day traders should focus their attention.

The day trader should spend 10 minutes a day searching *IBD* for day trading stocks that experienced unusual volume levels the previous day. Usually, there is some sort of news corresponding to the increased activity. These stocks generally will be volatile for a few days until the market has had enough time to assess the news and factor it into the value of the issue. During this time, there are many momentum-related trading opportunities for day traders.

CNBC

CNBC offers up-to-the-minute business news and commentary every weekday with a series of shows beginning at 5:00 in the morning and ending up at 7:30 each evening. When you can't be digesting a newspaper or magazine, such as when you are trading or watching your trading screen, having CNBC on is a must. In just about any trading room you visit, whether it is set up for 30 people or consists of a single day trader in an office, you'll find a television tuned to CNBC. Why, don't you know? Everybody who is anybody listens to CNBC!

CNBC is invaluable to the day trader because breaking news on a company may be reported that could lead the trader to add it to her hot list. Even when nothing particularly newsworthy is going on, CNBC regularly discusses the greatest moving stocks and why they are going in the direction they are. This helps give some depth and a better feel to your understanding of the market and how it works.

Although not a requirement for pure dissemination of information, the various hosts and reporters on the CNBC shows do a lot of kidding around with one another, which helps keep the sometimes dry business of the market interesting and fun. They clearly get along well with each other, and after you've been a regular viewer for a while, you'll probably feel as if you know them personally. Although these folks are referred to as *hosts, anchors,* or *reporters,* such titles don't do them justice. This gives the impression that they are mere facilitators who extract information from whatever "expert" happens to be on the show. Don't be fooled. They are every bit as savvy as their guest hosts and interviewees. Here is the weekday business programming schedule of CNBC, along with some of the highlights of each show.

***Today's Business: Early Edition,* 5–6 A.M.** This hour-long show is designed to give folks who have to get up and run a summary of the news. Hosts are Bob Sellers and Bonnie Behrand. Unless you're a natural "morning person," if you have to be up early enough to see this show, then you're a definite candidate for day trading, if only so you can set your own hours!

Today's Business, 6–7 A.M.   Because we are in a world market, trading is going on somewhere 24 hours a day. This show gives the viewer information on trading floors in Europe, Asia, and emerging markets, as well as domestic and international news featuring live correspondents. Although the day trader may not be trading in these markets, the direction they are moving is often an advance notice of how our own markets might be impacted. Segments include "Stocks to Watch" with Kevin McCullough, CEO interviews, and tips from *Bottom Line Personal Finance Magazine.* Hosts are Tom Costello and Sydnie Kohara.

Squawk Box, 7–10 A.M.   This show covers the hour and a half before the opening bell and continues into the first half hour of the trading day. It features regular visits to the NYSE, where reporter Maria Bartiromo is ready with the latest on which way the trading day and various stocks are lining up. Featured are interviews with Wall Street movers and shakers, CEOs, and mutual fund managers. The host is Mark Haines; however, a guest host from the investment community is often invited. Reporters are David Faber, Kathleen Hays, and Joe Kernen, who keep constant track of which stocks are doing what.

Market Watch, 10 A.M.–Noon   Market Watch begins right after the first half hour of the trading day is over, when most of the initial market volatility is past and the market is gradually settling down toward lunch. The show focuses on business news that is affecting the market as it happens. This type of news can move stock prices and is what the day trader is looking for. Bob Sellers is host for the first hour, followed by Ted David and Consuelo Mack during the second.

Power Lunch, Noon–2 P.M.   Because the market is usually slower at lunchtime due to the plain fact that traders have to eat just like everyone else, *Power Lunch* is able to step back and take a look behind the scenes with interviews of the people making the business news. The focus is often on entertainment, advertising, or the media. Also featured is *Power Lunch*'s "Cool Web Site of the Day," at www.cnbc.wsj.com, which day traders will find of interest. The show is hosted by Bill Griffeth. In accord with the burgeoning interest in day trading, every Monday's *Power Lunch* now has a special feature on day trading.

Street Signs, **2–4 P.M.** Following lunch, the markets typically pick up in a final flurry of trading prior to the close at 4 P.M. Emphasis is on what is affecting the market during the final two hours of trading. *Street Signs* focuses on this activity with reports from the floor of the NYSE by Bob Pisani and with interviews of the professionals on Wall Street, company CEOs, and Washington government officials. Host is Ron Insana.

Market Wrap, **4–6 P.M.** After the 4 P.M. close, *Market Wrap* proceeds to review the events of the day with recaps of what happened and analysis of the causes, with emphasis on what all of this means to investors and market players. David Faber comes in with his "Street Talk" report, discussing developments occurring today that might have an effect on tomorrow's trading, and Joe Kernen discusses the day's winners and losers. On the Friday edition of *Market Wrap,* Bill Griffeth leads a review of the week's happenings and what might be expected in the week ahead. Hosts are Bill Griffeth and Sue Herera.

The Edge, **6–6:30 P.M.** This 30-minute show attempts to keep viewers on the cutting edge of business, industry, and technology trends by discussing where those trends appear to be leading. The emphasis is on forecasting and recommendations from experts regarding how investors should respond to the trends. Tyler Mathisen has a regular segment on mutual funds. *The Edge* is hosted by Sue Herera, with Joe Kernen frequently contributing his analysis of stocks.

Business Center, **6:30–7:30 P.M.** This show is CNBC's equivalent of an evening business news show. It includes segments on what's hot on Wall Street, reading between the headlines, and a review of the entertainment industry. It's hosted by Maria Bartiromo and Tyler Mathisen.

The Open

The initial 30-minute period of the trading day is full of opportunity for quick profits or large losses. During this time of day, the order flow is generally at its peak because everyone has had since the previous trading afternoon to think about what they want to do. Opening prices reflect the sum total of the hype that has accumulated since the previous day's close. For example, Joe Average Investor comes home after a tough day at the office and scans over his newspaper. He may sit back

BROKERSAURUS By Bob Baird and Craig McBurney

Contact us or send us your idea for a cartoon at brokersaurus.com

Artistry by Bill Frauhiger

in his Lazy Boy and catch snippets of the evening news between nods. So armed with valuable trading information, he either logs on to his online brokerage and enters an order or he calls his broker first thing in the morning to place it. Thus, the collective view of "the crowd" dominates the open. And, as we know, the crowd is tossed to and fro by every wind of hype, hot tips, and news. This is one of the reasons that the open, though volatile, can be a good time to trade.

Although greater risk is assumed by the trader at this time of day, opportunities for larger moves also exist, because stocks generally move the most in the early morning when the traders are trying to define the value of the stock for the day. For this reason, even with the reduced control, it is a time when traders can most easily profit if they catch a trend, for a true early morning trend might move anywhere from as few as 3 to as many as 15 Level II price levels or more on a good move. Just one winning trade of that magnitude can propel the trader's earnings well into four figures. Or, on rare occasions, allowing some stocks to trend from the start of the day until their moves lose momentum could allow the day trader's one-day profits to soar to as much as five figures!

Midmorning

Unless the day is unusually active, midmorning is a time to digest the direction of the market and the individual stocks that are being watched and traded. The frenzy of the open is waning and most traders are busy counting their morning winnings or licking their wounds. Although midmorning is frequently marked by a lull in trading activity, the focused trader is still able to uncover numerous momentum and market-making opportunities during this phase of the day.

The key to continued success at this time of day is *focus*. Many traders lose their focus, perhaps only for a trade or two, but this loss of intensity costs the trader both money and, more important, confidence. It is important for the trader's psyche not to give up a portion of the early morning winnings. Moreover, the trader who is able to add to any early morning winnings is riding the crest of the wave as the morning trading winds down. This one point cannot be stressed enough. It is *focus*—a level of concentration exceeding that of others—that separates the successful trader from the mediocre.

Noon

In the middle of the day, the markets are usually fairly slow. This is because it is lunchtime for a lot of people. Even market makers have to eat. If the movers and shakers of the market are in a restaurant, the volume and momentum that a day trader needs just won't be there. Accordingly, the typical noonday strategy can be summed up in two words: *Don't trade!* If the trader does decide to test the waters, the next piece of advice is—don't overtrade. Should the trader disregard both of these recommendations . . . may God be with you.

Midafternoon

Midafternoon is a blend of midmorning and noon. Usually less active than midmorning but more active than the noon hour, it is a time for renewed focus; for here again, the trader can watch those hard-fought gains slip away ⅛ by ⅛. This is not to say there are no opportunities. However, at this time of day, perhaps it is best to buy the bid and sell the offer. Be selective. It is difficult to profit in the early afternoon hours when you are giving up the spread, or even half the spread, on several trades.

The Close

Within the final hour and a half of the trading day, volume and momentum often pick up. This is because everyone is back from lunch, and if anyone really wants to trade, they have a short time left in which to do so. Stocks tend to trend better during this part of the day, offering momentum traders numerous profitable circumstances. With renewed focus, the close provides the day trader a final possibility to pare losses or to increase profits. This final opportunity is very important to the trader psychologically, as it sets the tone for the day to come!

Frequently, the close is a preview of the day to come. If no important numbers or reports are due the next day, the close serves as a guide to the next day's open. This is because closing prices indicate that market players have enough confidence in those positions to carry them overnight. The morning hoopla has died down, Joe Average Investor is back at work and out of the loop for the time being, and the market is dominated by professionals and others who are much more knowledgeable in what they are doing.

Remember, any position you decide to enter late in the trading day must be closed out by the time the market closes, or you are by definition not a day trader. We have thoroughly discussed elsewhere why overnight positions entail a great deal of unnecessary risk.

Chapter 8, "Trade and Grow Rich," provides an in-depth discussion of many of the trading systems and strategies that you may wish to adopt as you develop your own personal trading style.

chapter 8

trade and grow rich
styles and strategies of day trading

The Trading System

The trading system is not a mysterious black box, but simply the sum of the strategies you develop yourself and employ in your trading. There are many hucksters who will sell you their surefire, guaranteed method of making millions in the market. Unfortunately, if such systems ever worked at all, you can be assured that they will not work for you. This is because even a system with merit works only as long as conditions favorable for its operation prevail, usually until so many people find out about it that the impact of whatever the system is supposed to predict is already factored into the stock's price.

The general rule of thumb about surefire trading systems is that they work perfectly up until the time *you* hear about them. As Confederate cavalry general Nathan Bedford Forrest (you know, the guy Forrest Gump was named after) said, "Be thar first with the most." If you can "be thar first" with a new system, it might work. Otherwise, stick to day trading and develop your own system. Of course, there's that gnawing question: If the system works so well and so fast, why isn't the developer down on a Caribbean beach somewhere instead of out hawking it to you?

Make Rules and Trade by Them

In order to make money day trading, it is essential that you discipline yourself to follow your own personal trading system. The most important aspect of the trading system is determining when to sell. You have watched the volume and momentum of the stock. You've looked at the historical charts. You have bought the stock. The question now becomes when to sell. In general, you might want to set a maximum loss of, say, ¼ point. This is a tight stop, and it will not work in volatile markets that are swinging over ¼ point every minute, but it is recommended for all new day traders. By implication, very volatile stocks are not recommended for starting out, either. For position traders, the stop-loss order is typically entered with the trade and is a "hard" stop. Yours will usually be mental, and thus "soft."

Because no one will automatically get you out of the trade, it is just that much more important for you to maintain utmost discipline in consistently following your own rules. Thus, when the stock moves ¼ point against you, you sell it and look for the next trade. At other times, you may wish to set a percentage or dollar amount. You may be tempted to say, "Hey, ¼ point is just 25 cents. So what!" But, remember, for the typical trade of 1,000 shares, ¼ point is $250. Using fractions of points sounds small until the amount they represent is multiplied by 1,000!

For a variation of the ¼-point stop-loss strategy, review Figure 5.14 in Chapter 5. Note that the gap down provided a great buy opportunity for the day trader. The problem is the excessive volatility in the subsequent price rise. Using this strategy, the day trader would have quickly been shaken out of the trade only to see the price continue to increase. In a situation such as this, where the volatility range is about 1 point, the day trader can have the identical risk as with the ¼-point strategy on a lower-volatility stock simply by reducing the number of shares purchased of a higher-volatility stock. For example, 250 shares of a 1-point-volatility stock entails the same risk as 1,000 shares of a ¼-point-volatility stock. In our example, if the day trader had purchased 250 shares, the 3-point gain would have grossed $750.00, not as good as the $3,000.00 that would have been made on a 1,000-share trade, but without the risk.

Having a predetermined contingency plan is like driving down a two-lane highway behind someone who clearly has nowhere to go and nothing to do when he gets there. You wait until just the right time to begin to pass. That's the easy part, just as getting into a trade is easy.

It's being able to safely return to your own lane that counts. When you begin to pass, you fully expect to simply go around and get in front of the other car. And when you trade, you fully expect to make a profit. But, if you are wise, you have a contingency plan, just in case.

What if the other car speeds up? What if someone comes rushing over the next hill or around the next bend sooner than you expected. What if a car pulls out of a driveway directly ahead of you? You ask yourself these questions because you want to preserve life and limb. In like manner, if you value your financial life, you will preserve it with just as much care. The moral to this story is that the successful day trader never enters a trade without a clearly defined exit strategy in place first.

Many times when you are in a losing trade you will be tempted to tell yourself, "This time is different. I can ignore the sell strategy that I originally intended to use because I know that the stock is so good, and my rationale for buying it was so right, that I am going to ride out this drop, so I can ride it back up when it turns around like I know it will." In cases like this, and they will certainly come, just remember this rule: This time *isn't* different. If you stay in a losing trade, in all likelihood you will lose money and, hopefully, learn your lesson.

Another, and worse, thing that could happen is for this to be one of the tiny percentage of times that the stock does in fact turn around and rally. In this event, you will have psychologically convinced yourself that you have the uncanny ability to predict the markets. When you go on to your next trades with your new and false belief, you will lose money on trade after trade, bankrupt your account, have to stop trading, and return to your old job. If you have the tendency to be a "this time is different" day trader instead of one who will discipline yourself and stick to a set of predefined rules, you might just prefer to book the next flight to Vegas or Atlantic City. Your chances are probably better there.

Remember, your number one goal is to not lose money. As the saying goes, watch your nickels and the dollars will take care of themselves. For us, this means that if we watch our losses the profits will take care of themselves. Eventually, you will progress to actually making money without even having to think about it. This will happen naturally as a result of your having learned to not lose money. Even if you have unlimited funds, a small stake is better to start off with because conserving it will teach you well. If you have a large stake as a buffer, you'll tend to get sloppy, a habit that will stay with you and prevent you from ever being truly successful at day trading.

> **Watch your losses and the profits will take
> care of themselves.**

Let the Good Times (Bank)Roll

With the understanding that we are by no means recommending over-trading when we say this, consistent profits will come as a result of the volume of your trades, not by making a few big-dollar ones. Your realistic goal is to day trade for a living, not to day trade for instant wealth. Day trading is your new business. It is not unlike a retail business. Campbell Soup, for instance, may cost $1 a can. Making more money by selling fewer cans at $10,000 apiece is not a very realistic goal. Instead, the goal is to sell four cans a year to every person in America, and make a billion dollars. Bill Gates, look out!

There are very few five-figure trades. Most of the time, your profits will come as a result of making steady gains, together with a few of the inevitable losses. Our goal is for you to consistently turn 50:50 trades into 70:30 ones. Let's say that you did two trades a day, or ten for the week, and you reached your goal of $1,000 on seven and lost the $250 maximum on the other three. That would be $6,250 for the week, or $325,000 on an annualized basis. Even averaging only $500 on the seven trades still comes to $143,000 a year. It's easy to see that you don't have to hit a few big home runs or even do a lot of trading to make money; you just need to do a little trading right.

> **You don't have to hit a few big home runs or even do a
> lot of trading to make money; you just need to do
> a little trading right.**

As a day trader, you will have several specific goals: (1) Bring your trading account balance up to $100,000. This amount is sufficient for you to be able to buy 1,000 shares of any stock up to $100 per share in price that you might want to trade without having to trade on margin. (2) Fill up all your retirement accounts, 401(k)s, IRAs, and so on, to the limit. Once these are maxed out, you want to invest enough in income-earning instruments so you can live off of these investments and have the annual salary that you would like. (3) After that, you can obviously do anything you want. You can continue day trading for fun and profit if you like.

Or, if you believe you have reached the point of knowledge and confidence to be able to trade large-share volumes, you can grow your trading account balance to wherever you'd like and begin to mix it up with the big guns. Another alternative for the seasoned trader is to begin to trade several stocks at once. For instance, you can be actively trading on all four of your market maker windows at once if you have reached the level where you can keep track of them all. This would require $400,000 in a nonmargined account.

Trading Strategies

There are practically as many different trading styles as there are day traders. Trading is a reflection of your unique personality. Because it is such a personal and instinctive activity, all traders eventually develop styles that best suit their own demeanors.

Simply put, day trading follows one of two basic strategies, which may include variations of one or the other or some combination of the two. These two strategies can be likened unto the tortoise and the hare. The fast-paced strategy (that of the hare), used almost universally among the original SOES day traders, is known as *momentum investing*. Because momentum trades, by definition, are made on stocks that are moving, or have *momentum*, it is not as important to make the full spread on a trade. On long trades, the day trader buys the offer, then sells the offer. On short trades, the day trader sells stock on the bid and then closes out the position by buying the stock on the bid.

Using the tortoise approach, certain day traders employ a *market-making* system in attempting to grind out profits in eighths and quarters on a fairly slow-moving stock. Using this method, the day trader rarely gives up the spread, preferring to fade the trend, buy the bid, and sell the offer.

Unlike in the fable, however, day traders using either of these techniques are winners. Both methods if employed properly are profitable. Yet each requires a different trading discipline. Add to the fray the many variations and gradations of each, and the importance of your own personality becomes apparent.

Momentum Trading, or SOES Banditry

Momentum trading came into vogue after SOES was introduced and day traders attempted to work out a strategy that consistently made money. Momentum trading demands swift decision-making skills. Favored among SOES day traders, this style of trading attempts to capitalize on short-term momentum by closing a position outside the inside bid using one of the ECNs. This method, the most widely recognized SOES bandit trading model and used for years by the best SOES day traders, can be done entirely on SOES. Since January 1997, with the advent of proprietary markets, or ECNs, and the prospect of price improvement over the inside market, this type of trading has become even more profitable.

Generally speaking, when momentum is perceived, the day trader will enter into a position using SOES. While the stock still has momentum and is trending in the same direction, the day trader may also use SOES, but will more often attempt to close out the position on one of

BROKERSAURUS   By Bob Baird and Craig McBurney

Contact us or send us your idea for a cartoon at brokersaurus.com

Artistry by Bill Frauhiger

the ECNs by buying the bid or selling the offer, or by buying or selling somewhere between the bid and offer.

To guide their trading decisions, these day traders carefully watch their Level II windows and often rely on observing trading trends in an ECN for timely, valuable feedback regarding momentum in a number of different securities. Noting particularly any locked or crossed market situations, these day traders will jump in immediately and ride the wave of momentum. For example, consider the following inside market:

DEF 25 (bid) × *25¹⁄₈ (ask)*

Using the Level II window, the day trader perceives that the stock is trending up. She enters an order to buy on SOES. Her order is instantaneously executed at the inside market ask of $25⅛. Before ECNs, the day trader would simply let the stock trend up, say, to the following inside market:

DEF 25¹⁄₄ (bid) × *25³⁄₈ (ask)*

At that time, the day trader would simply enter a sell order in SOES for 25¼ and pocket the ⅛ difference between his 25⅛ cost and 25¼. Of course, this required a move of ¼ in the price of the security. Using an ECN, as we will discuss shortly, the day trader may now buy the bid and sell the ask, making a profit of ⅜, or three times as much. Of course, the day trader sticks with the stock as long and as far as the trend goes in her favor before selling.

Now observe the following *crossed market:*

DEF 25¹⁄₄ (bid) × *25 (ask)*

A crossed market, of course, is when one market maker is bidding more for a stock than another is asking, and this occurred more often in the early days of SOES trading. Recall that prior to SEC regulations requiring market makers to honor their quotes, they could enter anything they wanted and not have to actually buy or sell unless they happened to feel like it at the moment. When market makers were still in the habit of being sloppy with their order entries, SOES traders had a heyday. All that was necessary to make money in a crossed situation was for the day trader to SOES the seller at 25, then turn around and immediately SOES the buyer at 25¼, for an instant ¼ profit. This is what made the market makers mad, leading them to give the derisive term *SOES bandit* to those bold day traders who dared to take the market makers at their word.

Market Making

Low-Spread Stocks. With the advent of ECNs, the day trader is now able to not only SOES existing market makers, but to actually *become* a market maker. Market makers make their money on the spread; thus the trader using the market maker approach will likewise attempt to make the spread. Consider the following inside market:

DEF 25 (bid) × 25$\frac{1}{8}$ (ask)

A day trader who recognizes a potential upward trend in DEF will enter his own bid of 25, which will go to the top price level of the Level II window, and buy the shares, just as any other market maker would do any minute of any day. Eventually, the stock begins to trade at a higher price, say,

DEF 25$\frac{1}{8}$ (bid) × 25$\frac{1}{4}$ (ask)

The trader may now place an order at the ask of 25¼ and sell, making a profit of ⅛. Thus the day trader has been able to buy on the bid and sell on the ask. Of course, as long as the stock is trending up, the day trader will continue to ride it up as far as it will go.

In order for the market-making approach to work in this manner, the day trader should look for specific stock characteristics. If a stock meets the criteria, the market-making style of trading can be applied profitably. For a good market-making stock, the standards are as follows:

- The security should be a large-capitalization company.
- The spread should generally be no more than ⅛.
- The stock should have a daily price range of between ¾ and 1 point.

To profit using the market-making style, it is essential to fill both sides of the trade on one of the several ECNs. With an ECN, the playing field is leveled between the day trader and the market maker. Any participant in that market can buy or sell at any level. There are no preferences given or granted to market makers or broker-dealers. In short, it's first come, first served. With this in mind, to buy on the bid or sell on the offer in these ECNs, a company must be highly liquid.

A large-capitalization company provides the necessary liquidity to receive fills outside of the inside market. It is in these securities that institutions and accredited investors take large positions. Inasmuch as they usually won't wish to tip off the general market about their intent to buy or sell large blocks of stock, large investors will often do much of their trading through one of the ECNs. Because the day trader can play market maker in this environment, she has a good opportunity of receiving a fill on an order without surrendering the spread.

Regarding the spread, note that the day trader will be less likely to receive a fill on an order sent to an ECN in a stock with a spread of ¼ or more, which is why we recommend the smallest spread possible. This point of fact is due largely to the willingness of other day traders to trade between the spread. Because, on a liquid stock, there presumably exists a ready supply of day traders willing to trade between the spread, it is unlikely that a day trader will be able to buy the bid or sell the offer in a security with a spread of ¼ or more. That the day trader is forced to give up even ⅛ of a point makes this security unsuitable for the market-making strategy. The goal with market maker trading is to never forfeit even a piece of the spread.

Finally, a stock suitable for market making is one in which there is some price movement, yet not too much volatility. A fine line exists between stocks suitable for market making and those that are not. A stock must have enough volatility that, while trending in one direction, a momentum day trader perceives an inability to close out a position due to compression of market makers at that given level through SOES. Due to this apprehension, the momentum day trader will look to an ECN to close out a position that is running away. It is at this instant that the day trader employing the market-making strategy has the prospect to buy the bid or sell the offer. Should the stock reverse its trend, the day trader is immediately in a profitable position.

High-Spread Stocks You can also become a market maker in certain instances whenever you find a slow stock that could stand being forced into action a bit. First, identify a low-volume stock. Slow-moving stocks often have a wider spread, but they are also less liquid and thus more risky. For instance, let's say that your stock pick is 22 on the bid column and 23 in the ask. Your strategy is to put in an order on an ECN that is

$\frac{1}{16}$ more than the others, or 22$\frac{1}{16}$ in this example. As you'll see on the Level II window, your order, being now the best bid price available, will go to the very top of the bid column.

If you get a seller, immediately switch the stock to the ask column by putting in an order to sell at $\frac{1}{16}$ less than the current ask price, or 22$\frac{15}{16}$. If you get a buyer at your reduced price, then you will have made $\frac{14}{16}$, or 87.5 cents, on your stock. That's $875 on a 1,000-share trade. Not bad for a few minutes work.

Having discussed the two broad trading strategies typically adopted by day traders, a review of the evolution of the individual day trader from "one-stock" trading to "anything-that-moves" trading, as well as other styles, is useful.

Trading Styles

Regardless of which trading strategy the day trader chooses to use, there are many different styles that can be used to accomplish the same goal. These trading styles are basically overlays on the preceding strategies. We'll review some of them now.

One-Stock Trading

As a matter of course, most individuals' trading styles evolve as their knowledge, resolve, and experience grow. In the beginning, most day traders focus their attention on one stock on their hot list in an attempt to understand its characteristics and anticipate its day-to-day moves. This entry into trading is perhaps the best formula to increase the longevity of the day trader's career. One specific reason accounts for this premise.

The beginning day trader is likely being bombarded by an endless stream of data, news, tips, and charts. That this constant flow of data is overwhelming to a day trader recently introduced to this industry is understandable. Should the beginning day trader attempt to bang out trades like an experienced day trader, it is likely that she will "blow out" her account due to one or many rudimentary errors, all of which are part of the learning process. Therefore, the goal is to concentrate and master manageable bites of information from the outset. With this in mind, the day trader will undergo a digestion period during which she focuses her attention on learning one or two things well. Once mastered, the day trader is able to progress to the next level.

Small-Group-of-Stocks Trading

Having attained a level of competence by trading in one stock, the day trader is prepared to begin trading a small group of stocks on his hot list. Such a progression is natural once a certain level of confidence has been achieved with the "one-stock" approach. Again, initially there might be some apprehension as the day trader enters into a new routine with greater parameters and more data to assimilate. However, in due time, the day trader should adjust to the greater flow of information, and when this happens, potential profits should increase. The broader the universe of stocks, the greater the opportunities to catch those stocks that are on the move on any given day.

Anything-That-Moves Trading

The final stage, and the one at which most of the best day traders eventually arrive, is the "anything-that-moves" trading style. This trader's hot list will be large, with additional stocks selected from the sort-by-gainers and sort-by-losers windows. With certain limitations, an expert day trader will employ this trading method. As a momentum day trader, the primary objective is to note any trading imbalances and capitalize on them instantly. The limitations mentioned relate to the day trader's level of experience. Certain stocks may show an imbalance, and yet, in the face of such available figures, the stock fails to move as anticipated. A day trader who has been fooled in this specific security a number of times takes note and refrains from entering into a momentum trade in that given stock even though all the indicators appear to reveal a pending move in the price of the stock.

How Many Stocks to Trade

We have discussed the progression of trading the same stock day after day until its characteristics are learned well, moving on to trading from a small group of stocks over and over, and finally to looking at a large stock-trading pool for any issue that happens to be moving. The question now arises as to how many stocks in which the trader should attempt to have actual open trades at any given time. Most traders will have only one open trade at a time. However, our trading screen setup has four market maker windows open at the same time. This is usually for the purpose of finding one tradable stock out of four good possibilities. Once that stock is chosen and bought or sold short, the day trader then watches that market maker window to the exclusion of all others.

The fact that there are three other windows means that a very experienced day trader has the opportunity to enter into up to three more trades, so that four trades may be open at the same time. This requires total concentration, as well as the skill to immediately recognize shifting trends in any of the open trades while not losing track of what is happening in the others. It will be a while before any new trader will want to attempt having more than one trade going at the same time. Few even very experienced traders will be able to follow four concurrent trades. Obviously, to trade effectively, a day trader wishing to enter into multiple trades in this manner will need multiple amounts of money in her trading account as well.

Among the many approaches available, there are a couple—scalping and intraday trend trading—that more closely pertain specifically to when the trader might end a trade.

Scalping

One of the most important aspects of trading is knowing when to sell, as discussed earlier in the chapter. *Scalping* is a conservative method of trading in which the day trader always closes out a position whenever momentum is perceived, as judged by the Level II window, to be slowing and reversing. For example, volume may be tapering off and the bid and ask now appear to be equalizing, where previously one or the other dominated. The obvious advantage to this trading formula is the limited downside risk; thus it is recommended for beginning day traders. Yet the disadvantages are numerous.

Due to the conservative nature of this style, the day trader frequently is led to close out positions too early. By so doing, the day trader potentially limits the gain. Reentry into the same stock, upon recognition that the trend is indeed continuing after all, frequently comes at a price at least ⅛ worse than the exit price due to price increases after the day trader gets out. Moreover, another in-and-out trade forces the day trader to pay two additional commissions. Therefore, slippage and commissions tend to eat away at profits and exacerbate any losses. Finally, the day trader may be unable to reenter the position if reentry is within five minutes of initial entry. In this case, the day trader may miss out on a major move. To avoid these problems, more-experienced day traders often prefer to trend trade.

Intraday Trend Trading

Many day traders watch the broad market indices, as discussed in Chapter 5, for clues regarding entry and exit points. Following entry, the trend trader will then allow the stock to move freely up and down until it is perceived that the broad market indicators are moving against it. At this time, the trend trader exits the position. As we have emphasized many times throughout our book, it is important to establish trading rules and specific entry and exit points. However, in a high-volatility stock with significant price fluctuations, many day traders would not have entered in the first place, and those who did would likely be shaken out early on. The advantage to this method is that when a stock is truly trending up, the day trader simply rides out the fluctuations and, in the end, achieves greater potential profits by weathering the many headfakes to which scalpers fall prey. Additionally, slippage and commissions incurred in getting back into a trade don't eat away at profit margins.

The disadvantages are found in greater per-trade potential losses. Because trades are allowed to move freely until the broad market indices indicate the need to close out the position, a trade potentially could run ½ point or more against the day trader. If the day trader was wrong in judging the trend, losses can be substantial. This additional risk is a very real consideration when day trading, so trend trading should be used only by experienced day traders.

Doubling Up on Positions

Frequently, a stock will break out from a trading range on higher volume. If the day trader is fortunate enough to catch the initial wave of momentum, there is no need to limit the gain on the security to the initial trade. Should the stock continue to trend, it is likely it will sustain its breakout until the institution or accumulator of shares has finished buying/selling. This may take 10 minutes or a couple of hours. The perceptive day trader will note the market maker doing most of the buying/selling and will accumulate a position paralleling the market maker. This typically involves *doubling up,* or purchasing stock in excess of the average trade volumes the market makers are posting. When the move slows, the day trader closes out the position on an ECN. The risk comes if the price begins to move against the day trader. Such a trader may wish to (1) trade 1,000 shares every five minutes on SOES (this may be a losing proposition if the price is moving quickly against you) or (2) exit more rapidly by using SOES quickly and then entering an ask price on an ECN so as to beat the current inside ask and more likely ensure a sale. Because of the risk involved, this method is recommended for more advanced day traders.

Catching Both Sides of a Move

Some stocks are volatile enough that the better day traders can catch both sides of the move. If a stock is trending up, the day trader takes a long position. When the day trader predicts the stock is due for a trend *reversal* (i.e., its price changes direction), after closing out the position, the day trader takes a short position riding the wave of momentum back in the other direction. Early morning, when stocks are most volatile, is the best time of day to attempt this method of trading. This is a somewhat more advanced trading technique, but, due to the limited risk, may be used by intermediately skilled day traders.

Waiting

As you will find out as you get online and become a day trader, there are simply some days when the market is slow. On a low-momentum day, you may be tempted to buy a stock just to be doing something. Don't. The best rule in this situation: *Wait.* Whereas you may not make any money by waiting, at least you won't lose any of what you already have. The majority of the time, you will get a second chance during the day to get into the stock, and sometimes you may even get a third.

Another mistake is thinking that you *have to* get into a particular trade. After all, you've got a gut feeling that this is going to be the really big one. Or perhaps you believe you have recognized that this particular period of the market has more opportunities than ever before in history and that nothing like it will ever occur again and that if you don't get in and trade, you've missed your once-in-a-lifetime opportunity.

Rest assured that any given trade and any given market period are no different than any time before or any time to come. There is nothing new under the sun. There have always been great opportunities and there always will be. One of our goals in writing this book is to help you recognize them. Anytime you feel as if you *must* trade or that opportunities are passing you by, turn off your computer, go out and enjoy the fruits of your labor, and come back tomorrow fresh and ready to go.

Limit and Stop Orders

Day traders may place *stop orders* or *limit orders* outside the inside market. This feature is important for any day trader using charts or programs that identify good entry and exit points. For instance, UVW may
be trading at $45 per share. Technical analysis may have indicated to
the day trader that $40 is a good support level. In order to not get lost
in the shuffle as this level is approached, the day trader simply uses an
ECN to enter an order to buy at $40. As the stock is at $45, the day
trader's order will go many levels down. As the price moves down, the
day trader's order moves up. The farther down in levels he started, the
less company he has, because few others will be bidding at $40 when
the price is at $45. Thus, when the target price of $40 is reached, the
day trader's order will be at or near the head of the line because subsequent orders at $40 will be cued on a first-come, first-served basis.
The ability to place orders outside the market allows day traders to
reserve their place as far to the front of the line as possible should the
stock ever trade at the desired level.

Mistakes to Avoid

As we have stated repeatedly, your number one goal as a new day
trader is simply to not lose money. Watch your losses, and your profits
will take care of themselves. With this in mind, we offer some additional rules, which, if faithfully adhered to, will further prevent losses.
All of these rules apply to beginning traders. Intermediate and
advanced traders may choose to ignore some of them, but they are well
advised not to forget any.

Entering Too Late (Chasing the Trade)

Chasing the trade means that you recognize the trend only after it has
begun to occur, but you try to get on the bandwagon and buy anyway.
The problem is that, once the trend has started, anyone can recognize
it, and they do. Never get on a bandwagon. If you do, you will be part of
the psychological hoopla jumping on board out of greed. Instead, pull
up a chart on another stock and begin watching its trend, or perhaps
just go for a walk. The day trader must rise above the herd mentality of
the crowd by anticipating the move of the crowd *beforehand.* Getting
on board any bandwagon, either of panic or greed, defeats the entire
purpose of what we are attempting to teach you in this book.

Exiting Too Late

Remember, you bought the stock because your best research led you to believe that the stock was going to move up. What happens if the stock moves down instead? The obvious comment here is that *you were wrong*. If you thought it was going up and it went down instead, then you were wrong, plain and simple. Now is the time that the discipline of a trading system becomes important. We recommend that the beginning day trader determine to limit her downside losses to no more than 25 cents per share. Assuming you have purchased 1,000 shares, 25 cents a share is $250, a not inconsiderable sum to lose in just a few minutes. Add to that, say, a $25 commission going in and out and your loss comes to $300. That's enough. So, rule number one is to not lose money. Sound familiar?

The disciplined day trader sticking with her trading system will *never* just sit and watch the stock go even further down and say to herself, "Well, I have a gut feeling that this stock is going back up, so I'm going to wait out the drop because I know it's going to turn around." Gut feelings are for purchasers of lottery tickets, the vast number of whom are also losers at that game. Remember, the odds of winning yesterday's lottery drawing with yesterday's lotto ticket are only one in 7.1 million less today than they were yesterday. You don't know that the stock is going to turn around any more than the lottery player knows that his number is the winning one. Waiting gets you only deeper into a losing proposition. Don't fall into the trap of feeling that you can't get out of the trade because you will lose too much money by doing so. As we have said, $300 is enough. You were wrong once by buying the stock in the first place. Don't be wrong again by not admitting your mistake and getting out.

The same rule applies on the way up: If your stock is rising but begins to turn around, sell whenever the stock drops ¼ point and take whatever profits you have made on the way up. You don't know whether the turnaround is just a glitch that will shortly reverse itself or if the stock will continue down from there and eat up all your gains. A ¼-point buffer will allow you to not scalp and sell as soon as momentum appears to be reversing, so you'll still be in the stock if the turnaround fails to materialize.

Further, if the stock continues to go up but begins to level off in price as volume begins to go down, it's probably time to sell and go on to a more profitable trade, even if you haven't lost any money . . . yet.

Remember, the day trader looks for stocks with good volatility and volume.

Overtrading

The market offers many opportunities to those who are willing to wait and let it give them its bounties. The key word here is *wait*. With as many stocks as there are to trade, it is likely that one or more trading opportunities exist at any given moment. However, some are better than others. And some are good enough to be worth waiting for, and it is these that the day trader *waits* for. Day traders often make the mistake that simply because they have an account and are online they must be trading as long as the market is open or when others are trading before or after hours. This is a big mistake.

Trading simply for the sake of trading is called *overtrading*. Even assuming you are following your trading rules regarding when to exit a trade, making one trade after another when there are really no good trades to make will result in (1) many small- or no-profit trades, (2) many small-loss trades, and (3) a lot of commissions. All of this, of course, can add up to a pretty significant total loss, meaning that you are nickel-and-diming your account balance away.

Instead, your strategy is to take your own good time and find the best trades. If you work at an office job, when you get there you have to work. If you work outside, when you get to the job site you have to work. If you stay home and take care of the kids, you have to take care of them. Just about every area of labor demands that we participate simply because we are there. Worse, a lot of what we are required to do at work is busywork, or at least it often *seems* like busywork. We have been trained to always be doing something, even if there is really nothing to be done. Fortunately, this is *not* the case in day trading. The day trader is under no constraints whatsoever to trade.

The plain fact of the matter is that sometimes there are no really good trading opportunities. There are two things the day trader can do in response to this situation: For one, she can continue to search her trading screen for the right opportunity and trade only when one presents itself. Or she can shut down her computer, take a jog, go to the golf course, the beach, the movies, or do anything she feels like. This is one of the benefits you will enjoy as a day trader that is nonexistent at other jobs. Take advantage of it. Use this benefit whenever you are tempted to overtrade.

Ways to Lose Money
- No momentum
- Holding overnight
- Too wide of a spread
- Entering too late
- Exiting too late
- Too narrow of a range
- Index in wrong direction
- Trading on the news
- Low volume

Position Trading

Position trading, or short- to long-term trading, is not the same as day trading. Day trading, as we have discussed, is being in and out of the market on the same day, and holding no positions overnight. However, there may be times when you wish to take the risk of staying long term in the market. The principles that you are learning for day trading cannot help but make you a more effective position trader as well. By position traders, we, of course, include not only holders of actual stocks, but those holding options also.

The principles of day trading and position trading are almost identical with regard to when to get into and out of the market. The only real difference is the manner in which the stock's price history will be utilized by each type of trader prior to trading. Thus, the principles in this book will help you become a better investor with your current stockholdings, whether you choose to go on to day trading or not.

Both types of traders will examine the stock's price history, either minute by minute for the past day or two or day by day over the past several months. If the stock is at the bottom of a several-month trading range, and thus may have more upside, both types of traders are interested. The position trader may want to buy the stock to hold for some time and wait for previous highs to again be realized. He will not be concerned so much with missing a recent minute-by-minute bottom by a fraction of a point if he expects the stock to rise by many points over the next few days, weeks, or months.

Of course, if you are not set up with a firm to trade directly from the trading screen, then you had certainly best not care about the exact price at which you buy stock, because during the time you call your broker, wait on hold, tell your broker what you want, have the broker send your order to the trading floor, and finally have the trade actually executed, the price may have changed quite a bit. And don't forget, this process works against you on the way out as well. Thus, even the position trader will be wise to open an account with an order-entry firm, not a regular brokerage, and utilize the same purchasing tools available to the day trader.

The day trader will, of course, prefer that a longer-term low and an intraday low coincide. However, if a stock is bouncing around by a point or so during the day, the day trader will not particularly care if the stock is at or near its high of a few months because she will be out by the end of the day. Her concern is to get in as close to the intraday low as possible. If the stock plummets a few days later, it doesn't matter because she's not in it.

Likewise, both day traders and position traders would like to sell or short at the top of a stock's recent (several-day, week, or month) range. Again, the position trader is not concerned as much with missing the top by a little because he has already realized multipoint gains over the time he has held the stock, but if he is set up as a day trader is, he doesn't even have to lose this. The day trader wants to sell after the stock has risen at least a dollar or so within a single day. Often, a dollar range is a pretty wide range for intraday variations, so she does not want to miss the top by much.

Day trading, then, offers the trader small price gains over an intraday period, which can be repeated day after day at lower risk, whereas position trading offers the investor larger gains over a longer period but at higher risk. If the position trader's stock opens way down one morning due to overnight bad news, there is nothing that can be done. This cannot happen to the day trader. Moreover, the chances are much better on a stock opening lower the next trading day than of it opening higher.

Day trading offers the trader small price gains over an intraday period, which can be repeated day after day at low risk, whereas position trading offers the investor larger gains over a longer period but at higher risk.

If you are position trading, one way to limit your risk is to buy fewer shares. If the stock price goes down, you will lose less. If it goes up, you can make up for the smaller investment by the larger gain over time.

Remember, we are not necessarily advocating position trading per se in this book. We are merely illustrating how the investor who wishes to position trade may do so in a greatly more effective manner by following the principles we lay out here. All investments must be judged in terms of opportunity lost were the funds to be at work elsewhere. For instance, if you have a large proportion of your trading funds tied up in a position trade that may last for several weeks or months to gain $5 or $10 a share, how does that compare with the possibility of day trading to realize several $1 or $2 gains over 5 to 10 trading days?

In Chapter 9, we'll tie up some loose ends and send you off into your new and profitable career.

chapter 9

many happy returns
the end and the beginning

Congratulations! You have made it to the end of our book. This might not be such a big deal for other books of the same length or even longer. But our book is different. It is a book and a course all in one. And it will serve as your constant companion and reference manual for as long as you are day trading—that is, from now on. But before you try out what you've learned with real money, we recommend that you first do paper trading.

Paper Trading: The Psychology of You

No trader, regardless of how much money you may have and are willing to lose, should begin day trading without having done it before or without doing one to two months of paper (i.e., pretend) trading first. As we have discussed, even when beginning actual day trading, it is best to start with a small account, which will make it essential to watch every nickel and conserve the account balance. Paper trading is simply sitting in front of your trading screen, following the strategies and procedures we have taught in this book, choosing a stock, pretending you have bought it, following it after the "purchase," and "selling" it, either at a profit or to cut your losses.

To properly paper trade, you will need to keep a trading log. Your log will list (1) why you entered the trade when you did, (2) the price at which the trade was entered, (3) why you stayed with the trade while you did, (4) the price at which you exited the trade, and (5) why you exited the trade when you did. If you have a printer connected to your computer, you may wish to print the trading screen or some portion of it out both when you buy and when you sell so that you can review your trade and see why it was or was not successful and whether mistakes were made along the way.

Keep in mind that reasons for an unsuccessful trade can usually be easily spotted after the fact. Finding reasons for a successful trade may not be as simple because they may be the same reasons that another trade was unsuccessful. What we mean by this is that sometimes you will make many mistakes when entering or staying in a trade, but the stock will move in your favor anyway—by accident. You may thus have had a profitable trade, but in entering for the wrong reasons or with no real reason, you are likely to repeat the same errors because of one fortuitous success. The next time, the trade is likely to go against you. The best way to avoid this is to pay careful attention to why you are actually entering the trade.

In addition to the whys and wherefores of entering and exiting trades, it is also very important to pay attention to what the stock is doing in the middle of the trade. For instance, your reasons for entering the trade may be as sound as a dollar. You have set a mental ¼-point stop-loss rule. The stock you bought is gyrating back and forth in a ½- to ¾-point range. Eventually, you sell and your reasons for selling are sound. The problem is that you have violated your stop-loss rule in between. Because there is no real risk of losing money, you have adamantly braved the volatility and have refused to be shaken out. And you have prevailed. But you have been lucky. The ½- to ¾-point volatility could easily have turned into a $500, $750, or much greater loss. Thus, day trading is the ultimate game of solitaire, and you cannot afford to cheat.

Paper trading is the best alternative to starting trading with real money, but, unfortunately, it is a poor substitute. When there is no real stake in the trade, the emotions go away. Thus, although the lack of emotions during paper trading is exactly the way all of us should be trading with real money, the fact that we are all human beings and creatures of emotion makes this impossible. As soon as real money,

Illustration by Bill Frauhiger

your real money, comes into the picture, so does emotion. It's just that way.

Thus, at best, paper trading will give you a feel for how some of the mechanical aspects of trading work and perhaps allow you to develop some discipline. To get the most out of day trading, use discipline to treat it exactly the way you would a real trade. In paper trading, if the phone rings or someone comes to the door, it's easy just to answer it and forget about the trade. "After all, it's just make-believe. I'll try it again when I have more time." So, don't do anything during paper trading that you wouldn't do for real with your own money. In a very real sense, paper trading *is* trading with your own money because the principles you learn now will be the same ones you bring to your first day of day trading with real money. If you have messed up on the rules paper trading, well, guess what?

Finally, no matter how good any book is, it cannot address new technologies and rules changes that happen after publication. To address this, we have created a new concept in book publishing, and have set up a Web site, www.LearnTradingOnline.net, that contains a constantly updating "Chapter 13" for ongoing revisions of our book. A link to "Chapter 13" will also be available at brokersaurus.com. Although not even we envision a computer screen taking the place of snuggling up with a cup of coffee and a good book, this will keep you up-to-date until publication of the revised edition of *Electronic Day Trading to Win,* and this is where you can go for the "rest of the story."

Novus Ordo Seclorum

Over two centuries ago, a new country was birthed on the principles of self-government and the idea that the people themselves had the right to select from among their peers those who were to govern and to retain or remove them by free election. Further, this young nation was to be ruled by law and not by men. Of course, we are speaking of the United States. Though these concepts may seem commonplace to us today, they were unknown and radical to a world steeped in the arbitrary rule of kings and emperors. The sense of history that our Founding Fathers felt compelled them to designate their experiment in freedom *novus ordo seclorum*—"a new order of the ages." This is the motto found beneath the pyramid on the back of a dollar bill.

In like manner, the advances that have been made in the ability of the average, everyday person to participate in the market are no less radical a paradigm shift in that arena. You have not just reached the end of a book. You have reached the beginning of something radical and new, perhaps a new career for some, but certainly a vastly improved way of trading for all. Welcome to the ground floor, and, in closing, we are Bob Baird and Craig McBurney wishing you many happy *returns.*

appendix a

the sector indexes

The **S&P Banks Index** (**BIX**) is a capitalization-weighted index of domestic equities traded on the New York Stock Exchange and Nasdaq. The stocks in the index are high-capitalization stocks representing a sector of the S&P 500. The component stocks are weighted according to the total market value of their outstanding shares. The impact of a component's price change is proportional to the issue's total market value, which is the share price times the number of shares outstanding. These are summed for all stocks and divided by a predetermined base value. The base value is adjusted to reflect changes in capitalization resulting from mergers, acquisitions, stock rights, substitutions, and so forth. At last look, the composition of the index included the following companies:

Banc One Corp.
BankAmerica Corp.
Bankboston Corp.
Bankers Trust New York Corp.
Bank of New York Company, Inc.
Barnett Banks, Inc.
Citicorp

CoreStates Financial Corp.
Comerica, Inc.
Chase Manhattan Corp.
Fifth Third Bancorp
First Bank System, Inc.
First Chicago NBD Corp.
First Union Corp.

Fleet Financial Group, Inc.

J.P. Morgan and Co., Inc.

Keycorp

Mellon Bank Corp.

National City Corp.

NationsBank Corp.

Norwest Corp.

PNC Bank Corp.

Republic New York Corp.

SunTrust Banks, Inc.

U.S. Bankcorp. of Oregon

Wachovia Corp.

Wells Fargo and Co.

Fifth Third Bancorp. (FITB) and U.S. Bancorp. of Oregon (USBC) are Nasdaq-listed securities. If the index is trending in one direction, look to trade these securities.

The **CBOE BioTech Index (BGX)** is a price-weighted index of domestic equities. The stocks in the index are representative of small- and medium-capitalization stocks in the biotechnology sector. The index is weighted by the market price of each stock in the index. The percentage movement of higher-priced stocks therefore will impact the index more than lower-priced stocks. At last review, the composition of the index included the following companies:

Amgen, Inc.

Bio-Technology General Corp.

Biogen, Inc.

Calgene, Inc.

Cellpro, Inc.

Centocor, Inc.

Chiron Corp.

Cytogen Corp.

ENZON, Inc.

Epitope, Inc.

Gensia, Inc.

Genzyme Corp.

Immune Response Corp.

Immunex Corp.

Immunomedics, Inc.

IVAX Corp.

Liposome Company

North American Vaccine, Inc.

XOMA Corporation

This index consists almost exclusively of Nasdaq-listed securities. As such, it serves as an accurate bellwether when trading biotech issues.

The **S&P Chemical Index (CEX)** is a capitalization-weighted index of domestic equities traded on the New York Stock Exchange. These are high-capitalization stocks representing a sector of the S&P 500. Recently, the composition of the index included the following companies:

Air Products and Chemicals, Inc.

Dow Chemical Company

E. I. du Pont de Nemours Co.

Eastman Chemical

Ecolab, Inc.

Englehard Corporation

FMC Corporation
B.F. Goodrich Company
W. R. Grace and Company
Great Lakes Chemical Corporation
Hercules, Incorporated
International Flavors & Fragrances
Monsanto Company

Morton International, Inc.
NALCO Chemical Co.
PPG Industries, Inc.
Praxair, Inc.
Rohm and Haas Company
Sigma-Aldrich
Union Carbide Corp.

This index focuses specifically on Big Board issues. Sigma-Aldrich Corp. (SIAL) is the only Nasdaq-listed company. As such, it is of less value to the SOES trader than some of the other indices.

The **CBOE Computer Software Index (CWX)** is a price-weighted index of domestic equities traded on the New York Stock Exchange and Nasdaq. The index is weighted by the market price of each stock in the index. The percentage movement of higher-priced stocks therefore will impact the index more than lower-priced stocks. The index composition contains the following companies:

Adobe Systems, Inc.
Artisoft, Inc.
BMC Software, Inc.
Borland International, Inc.
Broderbund Software, Inc.
Computer Associates International
Electronic Arts, Inc.
Informix Corporation

Microsoft the Corp.
Novell, Inc.
Oracle Systems Corp.
Parametric Technology Corp.
Sybase, Inc.
Symantec Corp.
System Software Associates, Inc.

This index consists almost exclusively of Nasdaq-listed issues. Only Computer Associates is a Big Board stock.

The **CBOE Environmental Index (EVX)** is a price-weighted index of domestic equities traded on the New York Stock Exchange, the American Stock Exchange, and Nasdaq. The index is weighted by the market price of each stock in the index. The percentage movement of higher-priced stocks therefore will impact the index more than lower-priced stocks. The index composition is as follows:

Browning-Ferris Industries, Inc.
Calgon Carbon Corp.
Laidlaw, Inc.
Molten Metal Technology
OHM Corp.

Republic Industries
Safety Kleen Corporation
U.S.A. Waste Services, Inc.
Wheelabrator Technologies, Inc.
WMX Technologies, Inc.

This index contains two Nasdaq-listed securities: Molten Metal Technology (MLTN) and Republic Industries (RWIN).

The **CBOE Gaming Index (GAX)** is a price-weighted index of domestic equities traded on the New York Stock Exchange, American Stock Exchange, and Nasdaq. The index is weighted by the market price of each stock in the index. The percentage movement of high-priced stocks therefore will impact the index more than lower-priced stocks. The following companies are included:

Argosy Gaming Co.	Mirage Resorts, Inc.
Aztar Corp.	Players International, Inc.
Circus Circus Enterprises, Inc.	Primadonna Resorts, Inc.
Grand Casinos, Inc.	Rio Hotel & Casino, Inc.
Harrahs Entertainment	Show Boat, Inc.
International Game Technology	Station Casinos, Inc.
Jackpot Enterprises	Trump Casinos
MGM Grand	

This index contains two Nasdaq-listed securities: Players International, Inc. (PLAY) and Primadonna Resorts, Inc. (PRMA).

The **CBOE Global Telecommunications Index (GTX)** is a price-weighted index of equity securities of firms in the world telecommunications industry. All equity securities in the index trade domestically on the NYSE, AMEX, or Nasdaq. These companies are as follows:

Alcatel Alsthom	GTE Corp.
Atlantic Tele Network, Inc.	Hong Kong Telecommunication
AT&T Corp.	International Caletel, Inc.
BCE, Inc.	Newbridge Networks Corp.
British Telecommunications PLC	Philippine Long Distance Tele.
Cable & Wireless	Telecom Corp. of New Zealand
Compania de Telefonos de Chile	Telefonica de Argentina SA
ECI Telecommunications	Telefónica de Espana SA
Ericsson LM Telephone Co.	Téléfonos de México SA de CV
Geotek Communications, Inc.	Vodafone Group PLC

This index contains ECI Telecommunications (ECILF), Ericsson (ERICY), and some of the foreign telephone companies.

The **S&P Health Care Index (HCX)** is a capitalization-weighted index of domestic equities traded on the New York Stock Exchange and Nasdaq. The stocks in the index are high-capitalization stocks representing a sector of the S&P 500. At last review, the following companies were components of the index:

Abbott Laboratories	HealthSouth Corp.
Allergan, Inc.	Humana, Inc.
ALZA Corporation	Johnson & Johnson
American Home Products Corp.	Mallinckrodt Group, Inc.
Amgen, Inc.	Manor Care, Inc.
C. R. Bard, Inc.	Medtronic, Inc.
Bausch & Lomb Incorporated	Merck & Co., Inc.
Baxter International, Inc.	Pfizer, Inc.
Becton, Dickinson and Company	Pharmacia and Upjohn, Inc.
Beverly Enterprises, Inc.	St. Jude Medical, Inc.
Biomet, Inc.	Schering-Plough Corporation
Boston Scientific	Tenet Healthcare Corporation
Bristol-Myers Squibb Company	United Healthcare Corp.
Columbia HCA Healthcare	U.S. Surgical Corporation
Eli Lilly and Company	Warner-Lambert Company
Guidant Corp.	

This index contains Amgen (AMGN), Biomet (BGEN).

The **S&P Insurance Index (IUX)** is a capitalization-weighted index of domestic equities traded on the New York Stock Exchange and Nasdaq. The stocks in the index are high-capitalization stocks representing a sector of the S&P 500. The index is composed of the following companies:

Aetna, Inc.	Loews Corp.
Allstate Corp.	Providian Corp.
American International Group	Safeco Corp.
Chubb Corp.	St. Paul Companies, Inc.
CIGNA Corp.	Transamerica Corp.
Conseco, Inc.	Torchmark Corp.
General Re Corporation	Travelers Group, Inc.
ITT Hartford Group, Inc.	UNUM Corp.
Jefferson-Pilot Corp	USF&G Corp.
Lincoln National Corp.	USLife Corp.

This index contains Safeco Corporation (SAFC).

The **CBOE REIT Index (RIX)** is a price-weighted index of equity securities of large Real Estate Investment Trusts. The REITs represented in the index have invested a preponderance of their assets in properties. The property portfolios owned by these companies constitute a diverse pool of income-earning real estate investments. All equity securities currently in the index trade on the NYSE or AMEX. The index includes the following:

American Health Properties, Inc.
Avalon Properties, Inc.
CBL and Assoc. Properties, Inc.
Duke Realty Investments, Inc.
Equity Residential Properties Trust
Federal Realty Investment Trust
General Growth Properties, Inc.
Glimcher Realty Trust
Health Care Property Investors, Inc.
HGI Realty, Inc.
Kimco Realty Corp.
Manufactured Home Communities

Merry Land & Investment Co.
Nationwide Health Properties, Inc.
New Plan Realty Trust
Post Properties, Inc.
Public Storage, Inc.
Security Capital Pacific Trust
Simon Property Group, Inc.
Spieker Properties, Inc.
Taubman Centers, Inc.
United Dominion Realty Trust, Inc.
Washington Real Estate Inv. Trust
Weingarten Realty Investors

The **S&P Retail Index (RLX)** is a capitalization-weighted index of domestic equities traded on the New York Stock Exchange, American Stock Exchange, and Nasdaq. The stocks in the index are high-capitalization stocks representing a sector of the S&P 500. The companies are as follows:

Albertson's, Inc.
American Stores Co.
Autozone
Charming Shoppes, Inc.
Circuit City Stores, Inc.
Costco CVS Corp.
Dayton Hudson Corp.
Dillard Department Stores, Inc.
Federated Department Stores, Inc.
Gap, Inc.
Giant Food, Inc.
Great Atlantic & Pacific Co.
Harcourt General, Inc.
Home Depot, Inc.
JC Penney Company, Inc.
Kmart Corporation
Kroger Co.

Limited, Inc.
Longs Drug Stores Corp.
Lowe's Companies, Inc.
May Department Stores Co.
Mercantile Stores Company
Nordstrom, Inc.
Pep Boys—Manny, Moe & Jack
Rite Aid Corp.
Sears, Roebuck and Co.
Sherwin Williams Co.
Tandy Corp.
TJX Companies, Inc.
Toys 'R' Us, Inc.
Walgreen Co.
Wal-Mart Stores, Inc.
Winn-Dixie Stores, Inc.
Woolworth Corp.

This index contains Costco (COST), Charming Shoppes (CHRS), and Nordstrom (NOBE).

The **CBOE U.S. Telecommunications Index (TCX)** is a price-weighted index of domestic equities traded on the New York Stock Exchange, American Stock Exchange, and Nasdaq. The index is weighted by the market price of each stock in the index. The percentage movement of higher-priced stocks will therefore impact the index more than that of lower-priced stocks. The companies are as follows:

ADC Telecommunications	Mobile Telecommunication Technology
Air Touch Communications, Inc.	Nynex Corp.
Ameritech Corp.	QUALCOMM, Inc.
AT&T	Southwestern Bell Corp.
Bell Atlantic Corp.	Sprint Corp.
BellSouth Corp.	Tele-Communications, Inc.
Comcast Corp.	US West, Inc.
Comsat Corp.	Vanguard Cellular Systems, Inc.
DSC Communications	Viacom, Inc.
GTE Corp.	WorldCom
MCI Communications Corp.	

This index contains ADC Telecommunication (ADCT), Comcast (CMCSK), DSC Communications (DIGI), MCI Communications Corp. (MCIC), Mobile Telecommunication Technology (MTEL), QUAL-COMM, Inc. (QCOM), TeleCommunications, Inc. (TCOMA), Vanguard Cellular Systems, Inc. (VCELA) and Worldcom (WCOM).

The **S&P Transportation Index (TRX)** is a capitalization-weighted index of domestic equities traded on the New York Stock Exchange and Nasdaq. The stocks in the index are high-capitalization stocks representing a sector of the S&P 500. The component stocks are weighted according to the total market value of their outstanding shares. The impact of a component's price change is proportional to the issue's total market value. The companies in the index are as follows:

AMR Corp.	Federal Express Corp.
Burlington Northern, Inc.	Norfolk Southern Corp.
Caliber System, Inc.	Ryder System, Inc.
Conrail, Inc.	Southwest Airlines
CSX Corporation	Union Pacific Corp.
Delta Air Lines, Inc.	USAir Group, Inc.

This index doesn't have any Nasdaq-listed securities.

The **Semiconductor Sector Index** (SOX) is a capitalization-weighted index of equities traded on the New York Stock Exchange and Nasdaq. The stocks in the index are high-capitalization stocks representing a sector of the S&P 500. The composition of the index includes the following companies:

Analog Devices, Inc.	Motorola, Inc.
Applied Materials, Inc.	National Semiconductor Corp.
Intel Corporation	Novellus Systems, Inc.
LAM Research Corporation	Teradyne, Inc.
Lattice Semiconductor Corp.	Texas Instruments, Incorporated
Linear Technology Corporation	VLSI Technology, Inc.
LSI Logic Corporation	XILINX, Inc.
Micron Technology, Inc.	

This index is comprised primarily of Nasdaq-listed stocks. Only Analog Devices, Inc., LSI Logic Corporation, Micron Technology, Inc., Motorola, Inc., National Semiconductor Corp., Teradyne, Inc., and Texas Instruments Incorporated are found on the Big Board.

The **Gold and Silver Index** (XAU) is a capitalization-weighted index of precious metals equities traded on the New York Stock Exchange and the American Stock Exchange. The companies listed in this index are as follows:

Barrick Gold Corp.	Newmont Mining Corporation
Battle Mountain Gold Company	Pegasus Gold, Inc.
Coeur D'Alene Mines Ltd.	Placer Dome, Inc.
Hecla Mining Company	TVX Gold, Inc.
Homestake Mining Company	

The **Airline Sector Index** (PLN) is a capitalization-weighted index of long-established and progressive new airline companies. The composition of the index includes the following companies:

Alaska Air Group	Mesa Air Group
AMR Corporation	Northwest Airlines, Inc.
Atlantic Southeast Airlines, Inc.	SkyWest, Inc.
Comair Holdings, Inc.	Southwest Airlines Co.
Continental Airlines, Inc.	UAL Corporation
Delta Air Lines, Inc.	USAir Group, Inc.

This index contains Comair Holdings, Inc. (COMR), Mesa Air Group, Inc. (MESA), Northwest Airlines, Inc. (NWAC), and SkyWest, Inc. (SKYW).

There are numerous foreign indexes that provide a wealth of information relating to and affecting on a daily basis the conditions of our domestic markets. Market Operators, Inc., will provide a list of the foreign indices at your request.

appendix b

market maker list

Symbol	Market Maker
ABLE	Arnhold & Bleichroeder
ABSB	Alex, Brown & Sons
AGED	A. G. Edwards & Sons
ALEX	J. Alexander Securities
ALGR	Fred Alger & Co.
BARD	Robert W. Baird & Co.
BEST	Bear, Stearns
BTSC	BT Securities
CANT	Cantor, Fitzgerald & Co.
CHGO	ABN Amro Chicago
COST	Coastal Securities
COWN	Cowen & Co.
DAIN	Dain, Bosworth
DEAN	Dean Witter Reynolds
DLJP	Donaldson, Lufkin & Jenrette
DRCO	Dillon, Read
ERNS	Ernst & Co.
EVRN	Everen Securities
FACT	First Albany Corp.
FAHN	Fahnestock & Co.
FBCO	Credit Suisse First Boston

GRUN	Gruntal & Co.
GSCO	Goldman Sachs
GVRC	GVR Co.
HMQT	Hambrecht & Quist
HRZG	Herzog, Heine, Geduld
JBOC	J. B. Oxford
JEFF	Jefferies & Co.
JPMS	J. P. Morgan Securities
KINN	John G. Kinnard & Co.
KPCO	Kidder Peabody
LEGG	Legg Mason Wood Walker
LEHM	Lehman Brothers
MADF	Bernard L. Madoff
MASH	Schwab
MHMY	M. H. Meyerson & Co.
MLCO	Merrill Lynch
MONT	Montgomery Securities
MSCO	Morgan Stanley
MSWE	Chicago Stock Exchange
NAWE	Quick & Reilley
NEED	Neddham & Co.
NEUB	Neuberger & Berman
NITE	Knight Securities
NMRA	Nomura Securities
OLDE	Olde Discount Corp.
OPCO	Oppenheimer & Co.
PERT	Pershing Trading Co.
PIPR	Piper Jaffray
PRUS	Prudential Securities
PUNK	Punk Ziegel & Knoell
PWJC	PaineWebber
RAGN	Ragen McKenzie
RAJA	Raymond, James & Associates
RPSC	Rauscher Pierce Refsnes
RSSF	Robertson Stephens
SALB	Salomon Brothers
SBCW	SBC Warburg
SBNY	Sands Brothers & Co.
SBSH	Smith Barney
SELZ	Furman Selz
SHWD	Sherwood Securities
SNDV	Soundview Financial Group
SWCO	Schroeder Wertheim
SWST	Southwest Securities
TORY	Torrey Pines Securities

TSCO	Troster Singer
TUCK	Tucker Anthony
UBSS	UBS Securities
WATH	Waterhouse Securities
WATL	A. B. Watley
WDCO	Wilson-Davis & Co.
WEDB	Wedbush Morgan Securities
WEED	Weeden & Co.
WIEN	Wein Securities
WLSL	Wessels, Arnold & Henderson
WSEI	Wall Street Equities

appendix c

setting up the trading screen

You are no doubt anxious to get started right away and may not initially see the benefit of going through the following procedures to set up the trading screen on your computer. However, doing so is an exercise in itself, and it will keep the simple mechanical techniques of screen setup from becoming a mysterious black box, (i.e., you take it on faith that it can be done, but you have no idea how). The benefit of doing it yourself is that following the process will familiarize you enough with the software that a lot of future questions you may have will be eliminated beforehand, and you will be able to do a little tweaking and customizing of your own screen to suit your tastes—perhaps something as simple as changing the chart colors.

Your final screen should look like the one shown in Figure 6.1 in Chapter 6. The left half of the screen consists of four Nasdaq Level II market maker windows, one for each of four stocks that you decide to follow during the course of the trading day. There are six smaller windows on the right portion of the screen. The upper left, larger graph shows the real-time price and volume changes over a given time frame, usually minute-by-minute data over a two-day period, for one stock you have selected. Moving clockwise, the small chart at the top to the right of the price-volume graph sorts a preselected long list of stocks from highest percentage gainers on down. The next graph sorts your stock list from highest percentage losers on up. The next graph (lower right of screen) sorts the stocks by volume. The window to its left is a short list of stocks you choose to follow during the day, color-coded to show sales of those stocks as either down, up, or no change from the previous sale. The next screen lists sales of a selected stock according to time, price, volume, and so forth. The last small screen shows the ticks of the particular stock exchange you choose to track.

Let's set up the screen from left to right, so we can make sure that everything fits. Note that when we ask you to click something with your mouse, we always mean left click unless right click is specifically stated. For double-click, double-click is specifically stated. You can eyeball the sizes of your windows if you like. Otherwise, we will provide the approximate percentages of the horizontal and vertical areas of the screen that the windows should occupy. To use our method, first measure your effective screen width and height with a ruler (preferably one with tenths instead of eighths). If the effective width is 12.7 inches, say for a 17-inch monitor, 17 percent of the horizontal would be about 2.2 inches, and so on.

Setting Up the Market Maker Windows

First, click on the Market Maker screen setup button along the main button menu along the top of your screen. The Market Maker/Regional Setup window will appear. Under General, enter the symbol for any stock of your choice. Under Columns to Display, click Show Bid/Ask Size and unclick Show Time and Show Status. Then click OK. This gives you a basic market maker window. Move your cursor to the lower right corner of the window and hold down the left mouse arrow to correctly size the window. The window should occupy 50 percent of the vertical area of your monitor screen, and about 28 percent of the horizontal area of the monitor screen. Now right click on the upper portion of the Market Maker window and click on Default Font. Under Font, select Small Font. Under Size, select 6. Click OK. Right click the lower portion of the Market Maker window where the list of market makers is located. Click Font, and select Small Font, Size 6, as before. You now want to make sure that the Name, Bid, and Size columns on the left half of the window and the Name, Ask, and Size on the right half of the window are all visible by dragging the horizontal lines to the right of each of these six column headings to the left until the data in the columns are satisfactorily visible. Repeat this process until you have four Market Maker windows visible. Note that any stock on any exchange may be entered, but market makers will appear only on the Nasdaq. For other stocks, only the individual exchanges are shown.

Setting Up the Intraday Price/Volume Chart

To set up the Price/Volume Chart, click the Chart button on the main button menu. Type in any stock symbol. Under Period, select IntraDay. Under Days Back, select One. Click OK. Right click on the chart. Click Setup Studies. Double-click Volume and Moving Average. Click OK. Scale the chart to about 25 percent of the width of your screen and 53 percent of the height of your screen. Adjust the dividing line between the price graph and the volume ticks so that the price graph occupies the upper two-thirds of the chart. Right click on the chart. Click Change Colors. Under Background Color, select Black. Under Series, select Axis/Labels, and under color, select bright yellow. Select Volume, and under Color, select light blue. Select Moving Average, and under Color, select Purple. Click OK. Right click on the chart. Click Screen Font. Under Font, select Small Fonts, and under Size, select 6. Click OK. Now you can go up and click on the Set Auto Scale and Set Snap Scale buttons on the main menu to adjust the graph proportions to the window. Drag your chart to the top of your screen immediately to the right of the market maker windows.

Setting Up the 200-Day Price/Volume Chart

Now use these same procedures to set up another Price/Volume chart, with the exception that instead of selecting IntraDay under Period and One under Days Back, select Daily as the Period (the chart automatically will default to 200 days). Click the "shrink" button (middle button of three) on the upper right-hand corner of the window. Use your cursor to size what's left of the window to fit in the upper right-hand corner of the trading screen so that only the label shows.

Setting Up the Sort-by-Gainers Board

Click BoardView on the main menu at the top of your screen. Type in *Complete for the title. Make sure the box by Dynamic Reload is checked. Delete everything in the Selected column except for Symbol and Tot Vol by clicking on the items to delete and then clicking the Delete Column button for each item to delete. Under the Avail. Columns column, scroll down the list and highlight % Chg Close. Click the Add Column button to add this item to the Selected column. Under BV Type, select Futures. Under Root, type $PCUQE. Now click the top box under Symbols, and type in any 10 Nasdaq symbols using the Add Symbol button or the enter key. Just to have something to enter, try IMII, CCUR, SSET, ICMT, PMRT, CVAS, NETL, CYBG, DTAM, and PXXI. It doesn't matter what symbols you use because all of them will automatically be replaced with the current top 10 gainers when you are online. Entering 10 symbols simply means you will get a continuous sort of the top 10. Click OK.

Right click the board you have now created. Click Change Colors. Under Background Color, choose the light gray. Right click again. Click Screen Font. Select Small Fonts under Font, select Regular Under Font Style, and select 5 under Font Size. Click OK.

Right click on the board. Click on Column Attributes. Change the Field Width to 4. Click Next. Change Name1 to %Chg, Name2 to Close, and Field Width to 4. Click Next. Change Name1 to Tot, Name2 to Vol, and Field Width to 6. Click OK.

Now size the board to as small as it will go without the scrolling bars appearing, position it in the upper right corner of the screen just under the closed 200-day window bar, and line up the left edge with the left edge of the 200-day bar.

Setting Up the Sort-by-Losers Board

Click BoardView on the main menu at the top of your screen. Type in *Complete for the title. Make sure the box by Dynamic Reload is checked. Delete everything in the Selected column except for Symbol and Tot Vol by clicking on the items to delete and then clicking the Delete Column button for each item to delete. Under the Avail. Columns column, scroll down the list and highlight % Chg Close. Click the Add Column button to add this item to the Selected column. Under BV Type, select Futures. Under Root, type $NCDQE. Now click the top box under Symbols and type in any 10 Nasdaq symbols using the Add Symbol button or the enter key. Just to have something to enter, try IMII, CCUR, SSET, ICMT, PMRT, CVAS, NETL, CYBG, DTAM, and PXXI. Again, it doesn't matter what symbols you use because all of them will automatically be replaced with the current top 10 losers when you are online. Entering 10 symbols simply means you will get a continuous sort of the bottom 10. Click OK.

Right click the board you have now created. Click Change Colors. Under Background Color, choose the light gray. Right click again. Click Screen Font. Select Small Fonts under Font, select Regular Under Font Style, and select 5 under Font Size. Click OK.

Right click on the board. Click on Column Attributes. Change the Field Width to 4. Click Next. Change Name1 to %Chg, Name2 to Close, and Field Width to 4. Click Next. Change Name1 to Tot, Name2 to Vol, and Field Width to 6. Click OK.

Now size the board to as small as it will go without the scrolling bars appearing, position it in the upper right corner of the screen just under the closed 200-day window bar, and line up the right edge with the right edge of the 200-day bar. You want to be able to see both the losers and gainers boards side by side.

Setting Up the Sort-by-Volume Board

Click BoardView on the main menu at the top of your screen. Type in *Complete for the title. Make sure the box by Dynamic Reload is checked. Delete everything in the Selected column except for Symbol and Tot Vol by clicking on the items to delete and then clicking the Delete Column button for each item to delete. Under the Avail. Columns column, scroll down the list and highlight % Chg Close. Click the Add Column button to add this item to the Selected column. Under BV Type, select Futures. Under Root, type $NCDQE. Now click the top box under Symbols and type in any 10 Nasdaq symbols using the Add Symbol button or the enter key. Just to have something to enter, try IMII, CCUR, SSET, ICMT, PMRT, CVAS, NETL, CYBG, DTAM, and PXXI. Again, it doesn't matter what symbols you use, as long as they are real Nasdaq symbols, because all of them will automatically be replaced with the current top 10 losers when you are online. Entering 10 symbols simply means you will get a continuous sort of the bottom 10. Click OK.

Right click the board you have now created. Click Change Colors. Under Background Color, choose the light gray. Right click again. Click Screen Font. Select Small Fonts under Font, select Regular Under Font Style, and select 5 under Font Size. Click OK.

Right click on the board. Click on Column Attributes. Change the Field Width to 4. Click Next. Change Name1 to %Chg, Name2 to Close, and Field Width to 4. Click Next. Change Name1 to Tot, Name2 to Vol, and Field Width to 6. Click OK.

Now size the board to as small as it will go without the scrolling bars appearing, position it in the upper right corner of the screen just under the closed 200-day window bar, and line up the right edge with the right edge of the 200-day bar. You want to be able to see both the losers and gainers boards side by side.

Setting Up the Bid-Ask Ticker

Click on Design in the upper left of your screen. Go down and select Ticker. The Setup Time and Sales window should also open automatically. If not, right click on your new Ticker window and then choose Setup. Under Setup, click Symbol List on the middle left, and then type in any stock symbol, say DELL, in the small white rectangle over the white box. Then click Add. This puts DELL into the symbol list. Under Display on the middle right of the Setup window, select Cascade instead of Jet. In the lower left under data type, click Show Market Makers. Click OK. Your window should be operational if you are online during market hours. Now, let's adjust the font. Right click on the Ticker Window and go down to Font. Under Font, select Small Fonts. Under Font style, select Regular. Under Size, select 5. And under Script, select Western (Western may already be selected). Then click OK. Now all you need do is size your new Ticker Window to occupy approximately 17 percent of the horizontal direction and 58 percent of the vertical direction, and move it to the lower right of your trading screen directly beneath the Sort-by-Gainers and Sort-by-Losers windows. This will cover most of your Sort-by-Volume Window. Then click on your Sort-by-Volume Window to put it over the Ticker Window. That way, you can see the entire Sort-by-Volume window and the pertinent left side of the Ticker Window. The red-for-up and green-for-down colors on the Ticker are what you will be primarily looking for.

Setting Up the Time and Sales Window

Click on Design in the upper left corner of the screen. Go down and click on Time and Sales. This will open a new Time and Sales window. The Setup Time and Sales window should also open automatically. If not, right click on your new Time and Sales window and then choose Setup. Under Begin Time, change 60 minutes back to 6 minutes. Then click the Server button in the lower right. Select Default ($PCQUOTE$) and click OK. Exit the Setup window by clicking OK. Now we want to tailor your colors and font. Right click on the Time and Sales Window again, and go down to Change Colors. In the upper right, click background color and select the light gray. Click OK. Right click again and go down to Screen Font. Under Font, select Small Fonts. Under Font style, select Regular. Under Size, select 6. And under Script, select Western (Western may already be selected). Then click OK. Now all you need do is size your new Time and Sales Window to occupy approximately 17 percent of the horizontal direction and 50 percent of the vertical direction, and move it to the lower right of your trading screen just to the left of your Sort-by-Volume Window.

Setting Up the Exchange Ticker Chart

Click on Design in the upper left corner of the screen. Go down and click on Chart. This will open a new chart window. The Chart Setup window should also open automatically. If not, right click on your new Chart window and then choose Setup. Under Symbols, type in $NDX, meaning Nasdaq exchange. For Period, select Intraday (this may already be the default). For Interval, use 1 Minutes. For Days Back, use 1. For Chart Title, use *$NDX. For Price Server, select Default ($PCQUOTE$). At the bottom of the Setup, only Bar Graph should be checked. Click OK. Now you can go up and click on the Set Auto Scale and Set Snap Scale buttons on the main menu to adjust the graph proportions to the window. To adjust the colors and fonts, right click on the window and select Change Colors. Under Series, select Axis/Labels; then go to Color and choose the bright yellow. Select all the other choices, and go to Color and choose white. Under Background Color, select black. Click OK. Right click again and go down to Screen Font. Under Font, select Small Fonts. Under Font style, select Regular. Under Size, select 6. And under Script, select Western (Western may already be selected). Then click OK. Now all you need do is size your new Time and Sales Window to occupy approximately 19 percent of the horizontal direction and 54 percent of the vertical direction, and move it to the lower right of your trading screen just to the left of your Time and Sales Window.

Trading Screen Download

If you are having trouble getting your trading screen formatted the way we have described, please log on to our Web sites at www.LearnTrading-Online.net or brokersaurus.com. Trade long and prosper!

glossary

AMEX   American Stock Exchange.

analyst   Brokerage employee who utilizes fundamental and technical analysis to predict a stock's price, company earnings, and so on.

ask   Price at which someone is willing to sell stock.

auction market   A physical market, such as NYSE and AMEX, where a specialist acts as auctioneer coordinating buying and selling among many bidders and offerers.

bargain hunter   One who waits for a stock to drop, or go "on sale," prior to purchasing it.

batching   Entering multiple orders at the 1,000-share limit.

bear market   When the market retreats 20 percent from its previous high.

bid   Price at which someone is willing to buy stock.

block   10,000 shares of stock.

breakout   When a stock's price moves past a previous support or resistance level.

broker   Someone who helps you to be that (i.e., *broke*); salesperson who deals in securities.

bull market   Market in which prices are generally increasing.

buy-and-hold   Strategy involving the purchase of stocks for the long term, typically years.

correction   A less than 20 percent pullback in the market from its previous highs.

covering a short   When short sellers repurchase stock to replace or *cover* the stock sold short.

crossed market   When the inside bid is higher than the inside ask.

day trading Technically, any purchase and sale of the same stock within the same day; used here to specifically refer to bypassing brokers, online or otherwise, and trading directly on the Nasdaq exchange by computer.

dealer market Market such as the Nasdaq where no single individual sets a stock's price, but rather the price is determined by competition among many individuals known as *market makers.*

downbid When the bid price is continuing to fall following a previous fall.

downtick When the sale price is continuing to fall from a previous fall.

ECN Electronic Communications Network; a tool used by day traders to directly access the Nasdaq exchange.

equity Stock; ownership of part of a company by holding the stock of that company.

fading the trend When a day trader attempts to buy on the bid and sell at the ask by placing bids and offers in the direction that the market appears to be headed.

fundamental analysis Looks at the fundamentals of a company, that is, such things as price to earnings (P/E) ratio, future earnings potential, dividends, income, debt, management, market share, and a whole host of other aspects; fundamental analysis attempts to determine where a share price *should* be based on the company's current characteristics and future potential.

fundamentalist Someone who looks at a company's fundamentals to determine where the stock price should be.

gap When a stock's opening price is higher than the previous day's high or lower than the previous day's low.

headfake When a market maker attempts to place bids and offers in such a way as to make other traders think a stock is moving in a direction that it really isn't.

inside ask The lowest price at which someone is willing to sell stock to someone else; same as **inside offer.**

inside bid The highest price at which someone is willing to buy stock from someone else.

inside market The highest bid and lowest ask price; same as the **quote.**

inside offer The lowest price at which someone is willing to sell stock to someone else; same as **inside ask.**

institutional client Stock purchasers, such as mutual funds, pension funds, and corporations.

Level I data   The inside market quote; the highest bid and lowest ask price; what typical investors get when they call their brokers.

Level II data   The full table of all buyers and sellers of a stock, showing who is wanting to trade, how many shares they are posting to trade, and at what price they want to trade.

limit order   When the purchaser of a stock sets a maximum price at which he is willing to buy, or the minimum price at which he is willing to sell.

liquid   A stock that is easily tradable.

listed stocks   Stocks bought or sold on an auction exchange, such as the NYSE or AMEX.

locked market   When the inside bid and ask prices are the same.

long   The purchase or sale of stock that you already own.

market limit order   An order entered on SOES to buy at the current inside quote only.

market maker   One of the numerous participants in the virtual Nasdaq market who set stock prices by competition.

market order   An order to trade stock at whatever price happens to be prevailing at the time the order is received.

market timing   A strategy that attempts to buy stocks at the bottom of a bear market and sell them at the top of a bull market; assumes that tops and bottoms can be easily picked.

momentum   A combination of volume and volatility in a stock that keeps its price continuing in the same direction.

Nasdaq   National Association of Securities Dealers Automated Quotations system.

NYSE   New York Stock Exchange.

offer   A price at which someone is willing to buy stock.

order flow   The moment-to-moment incoming buy and sell orders received by specialists and market makers.

OTC   Over the counter; used of Nasdaq stocks.

overbought   After a rapid rally of a stock to prices too high to be sustained, the stock is said to be overbought; a drop may follow.

oversold   After a rapid sell-off of a stock to prices too low to be sustained, the stock is said to be overbought; a rise may follow.

overtrading   Trading simply for the sake of trading.

payment for order flow   If a brokerage does not have its own market maker in a particular stock, it will often pass business (**order flow**) in that stock along to a market maker in that stock in return for a kickback (*payment*).

position   Holding shares in a certain stock.

position trading   Buying and selling stocks with long-term holding times, ranging from months to years.

preferencing   When the day trader selects a particular market maker to which to direct her trade.

profit taking   When a recent run-up in a stock's price brings sellers onto the market to take profits before the stock moves back down.

quote   The highest bid and lowest ask price; same as the **inside market.**

rally   A rapid run-up in a stock's price.

resistance   When a stock's price reaches a high level where the price has difficulty going higher; often the result of programmed institutional selling at that level.

retail client   Small purchaser of stocks, such as the average investor.

reversal   When a stock's price reaches a support or resistance level and turns around from there.

scalping   The conservative practice of buying a stock, holding as long as a trend continues, and then selling as soon as it appears that momentum is slowing.

SEC   Securities and Exchange Commission.

securities   Stocks or equities.

sell-off   A rapid decline in a stock's price.

short   To sell borrowed stock that you do not own in the hope of repurchasing it at a lower price and pocketing the difference.

short squeeze   When a stock that many investors have shorted goes up instead, causing the short sellers to have to buy to "cover their shorts," often causing the stock to rally further.

slippage   Commissions, losing of the spread, and unfavorable price movements in a stock's price between the time the order is placed and when it is filled; all the things that cause the average investor to lose money on nearly every trade.

SOES   Small Order Execution System.

SOES bandit   Derisive name given to day traders using SOES by market makers who were hit, or SOESed, by the day traders, thus causing the market maker to trade at the price he advertised.

SOESed   When the day trader using SOES selects or preferences a specific market with which to trade.

specialist   Acts as auctioneer in a single stock at auction markets such as NYSE and AMEX.

spread   The difference between the inside bid and inside ask.

stock split When a stock's price reaches a price level that appears expensive to the general public, a company will divide the price by a certain amount and multiply the number of outstanding shares by the same amount.

stop order A sell order typically placed just below where a stock's current price to enable the seller to bail out of the stock if a price decline starts.

support When a stock's price reaches a low level at which the price has difficulty moving lower; often the result of programmed institutional buying at that level.

tape The listing for each stock that gives the time, volume, and price for each sale; same as the old "ticker tape."

technical analysis Utilizes charts and graphs to determine where a particular stock's price is likely to be headed in the future.

technician Person who uses technical analysis to predict stock trends.

trading range Used regarding primarily lateral movement in a stock's price with limited up and down movements.

trading room An office already set up with computers and access to the Nasdaq where day traders can come in and trade.

trading screen The computer screen setup that allows the day trader to access current market information and to be able to enter trades.

trend When a stock's price is continuing to move in a given direction, either up or down.

trendline A line drawn across either the price peaks of a stock trend or the price bottoms to emphasize the overall trend.

upbid When the bid price is continuing to rise after a previous rise.

uptick When the sales price is continuing to rise after a previous rise.

virtual market An exchange, completely run on computers, such as the Nasdaq exchange, that allows anyone with the proper setup to participate.

volatility The rate and range at which variations in a stock's price occur.

zero downbid When the bid price is remaining steady after a previous fall.

zero-plus upbid When the bid price is remaining steady after a previous rise.

about LearnTradingOnline.net

Investors have jumped to the next curve—trading on their own using the Internet. LTOnline.net has jumped ahead of them to teach them how to do this successfully, delivering our training directly to their desktop, television, or any CaliberLearning location. For example, there are 130 online brokers. How is it possible that investors will select the correct one for them? Luck? An advertisement?

LTOnline.net's comprehensive training program represents the convergence of two powerful information technologies: distance-learning software and the Internet. At LTOnline.net, cutting-edge applications like videoconferencing and "live market" online training sessions are delivered through a real-time connection. Improving on the "traditional" classroom environment, LTOnline.net drives the development of artificial intelligence software to allow hundreds of students to ask questions synchronously, greatly enhancing the efficiency of the instructor/student exchange.

LTOnline.net's plans include using the leverage and scaling capabilities offered by the Internet medium to create further awareness of the need for investor education. Specifically, as a culture of shareholder awareness develops in Europe in conjunction with increasing Internet usage, LTOnline.net will concentrate marketing activities based on the opportunity presented in each country. Finally, by collaborating with the faculty of international universities in market-friendly economies in Asia, Africa, and South America, and through our Caliber-Learning global partnership, we will teach the principles of investing to the rest of the world. These activities will help create an environment whereby everyone can raise their standard of living through fair and open access to capital markets. Millions of individuals (and therefore societies) worldwide will benefit from investing online through greater awareness of opportunities and increased financial security. These facts obviously have a significant impact in regard to the sustainability of future generations.

about brokersaurus

During the course of writing *Electronic Day Trading to Win,* we realized early on the need to set ourselves apart from the run-of-the-mill dry verbiage and endless black-and-white text that characterizes all too many books of any type on the market today. Originally, we determined to inject a little tongue-in-cheek humor throughout the text to lighten things up and to help drive home some of our points. It quickly became apparent that many of these were amenable to being expressed in cartoon form. And so evolved our new cartoon strip, *Brokersaurus.*

We would like to continue Brokersaurus as a syndicated cartoon in your local newspaper following its introduction here. But Brokersaurus appearing in your paper is not automatic. If you have enjoyed Brokersaurus and would like to keep seeing it on a regular basis, you can help us out by visiting our Web site at www.brokersaurus.com. There you'll find e-mail addresses to editors at the major newspapers, and all you need to do is click on your local paper to send a note telling the editor that someone in their market wants Brokersaurus.

Perhaps you even have some ideas of your own that could be used in Brokersaurus. If so, please visit our Web site at www.brokersaurus.com and tell us. If we use your cartoon idea, we will credit you by name and city on the cartoon and you will receive a personal copy suitable for framing.

The demise of the brokerage industry is but one of many examples of the inevitable *disintermediation* (elimination of the intermediary) process overtaking the marketplace as we know it as a result of the advent of the Internet. We are interested not only in receiving stock market jokes and humor, but also humor regarding the disintermediation process and its effects on other industries—home buying, car buying, and what have you—and you may send these to us in the same manner.

index

Actual-size rule, 52–53, 56
Advisors. *See* Investment advisors
Affirmative determination and SOES, 49–50, 56
After-hours trading, 61
Afternoon trading, 153–154
America Online, Internet connection kits, 70
AMEX:
  as auction market, 24–26
  versus Nasdaq, 14
Analysis, market:
  technical versus fundamental, 91–93
  See also High-probability trading
Analysts, expectations of, 74–77
Analyst upgrades/downgrades, 80–82
Anti-small-investor policies, of brokerages, 41–42, 50–52
Antitrust probe, of money makers, 51–52
Anything-that-moves trading, 165
Archipelago, 67–68
Ask price, defined, 24
Auction market, 24–26. *See also* AMEX; NYSE

Baan Company, as buy/sell example, 130, 135–136
Baby boomers:
  as bull market drivers, 71–72
  as day traders, 8
Back to the Future, Part II, 1
Banks, as market participants, 34–35

Bargain hunters, and market psychology, 70, 73
Barron's, short-interest lists and, 84
Bartiromo, Maria, 150, 151
Batching, defined, 43
Bear market, definition of, 78
Behrand, Bonnie, 149
Benefits of day trading, 15–22
Berkshire Hathaway, 79, 86
Bid-ask price, and the spread, 24
Bid price, defined, 24
Black Monday, 40
Block orders, defined, 52
Bond, long. *See* Long bond
Borrowed securities, 47
Bottom Line Personal Finance Magazine, 150
Brazil currency devaluation:
  as example of investor psychology, 85
  impact on U.S. stock market, 118–120
Breakout:
  defined, 104
  gaps on, 122
  as tool for day trader, 106, 108
Broadcasting, and SelectNet, 62–64
Broadening formation, as consolidation pattern, 114–115
Broker-dealers, institutional clients and, 34–35
Brokers:
  market making and, 27–31
  as salespeople, 19–22

Brokersaurus:
  cartoons, xii, 3, 10, 13, 15, 20, 21, 51, 76,
    152, 160, 178
  evolution of, 209
Buffett, Warren, 79, 86
Bull market:
  defined, 35
  investor psychology and, 71–73
Business Center (CNBC program), 151
Buy-and-hold strategy, dangers of, 16–19
Buying on the rumor, 78–79
Buy/sell decisions, Level II data and,
    134–137

C-Cube Microsystems, as example of
    gapping, 118–120
Charles Schwab, as discount broker,
    70–71
Charts and graphs:
  consolidation patterns, 109–115
  gaps, 117–123
  as market trend indicators, 102–123
  on trading screen windows, 140–141
  reversal indicators, 115–117
  support and resistance, 104–109
  See also High-probability trading
Chasing the trade, 54–55, 169
Ciena Corporation, as example explaining
    volume, 95–96
Clinton, Bill, 37, 79
Closing of market. *See* Trading day
CNBC, as day trader tool, 149–151
Compaq Computer, short-interest list
    and, 84
Computer trading. *See* Online trading
Consolidation patterns, 109–115
  broadening formations, 114–115
  defined, 109
  flags, 111
  pennants, 114
  rectangles ("trading range"), 110–111
  triangles, 111–114
Contraction, economic. *See* Economy
Corrections (market):
  definition of, 18
  as opportunities for day traders, 18–19
Costello, Bob, 150
Covering a short, 84
Crash of 1987, 39–40

Credit policy. *See* Federal Reserve
    System
Crossed market:
  definition of, 60
  SOES banditry and, 161–162
Cycles, economic. *See* Economy

David, Ted, 150
Datek Securities (the Island), 67
Day traders:
  definition of, 15
  goals of, 158–159
  as market makers, 3–4, 32–34
  qualifications of, 6–11
  SOES benefits and, 55–56
  training for (*see* Day trading,
    preparation for)
  See also Day trading
Day trading:
  benefits of 15–22
  versus brokers, 19–22
  versus buy-and-hold strategy, 17–18
  as a career, 2–3, 6–11, 158
  defined, xi–xiii
  mistakes to avoid, 169–172
  preparation for, 175–178, 193–199,
    207–208
  strategies (*see* Strategies for day trading)
  time of day and, 151–154
  See also Day traders
Dealer market. *See* Nasdaq
Debt, versus equity, 23
Deflation, monetary policy and, 36–37
Dell Computer, as example explaining
    volume, 95–97
Direct-access day trading. *See* Day
    traders; Day trading
Disintermediation, defined, 33
Distance learning for day traders, 207–208
Double bottom/top formations, 115–117
Doubling up, 167–168
Downbids, short sales on, 48–49
Downgrades, analyst, 80–82

E. F. Hutton, 82
Earnings reports, market psychology and,
    73–74
ECNs, 58–68
  and after-hours trading, 61

Archipelago, 67–68
explanation of, 58–60
Instinet, 65–67
Island, the, 67
momentum trading and, 160–162
SelectNet, 62–65
selling short and, 60–61
versus SOES, 61–62, 63
Economy, impact on securities markets,
35–38, 123–124
Edge, The (CNBC program), 151
Electronic Communications Networks.
See ECNs
Electronic direct-access day trading. *See*
Day traders; Day trading
Electronic trading. *See* Online trading
Entremed, as example of investor
psychology, 86
Equity, versus debt, 23
Exchange ticker, 143
Exit strategy:
SOES as, 55
stop-loss as, 156–157
waiting too long, 170–171
Expansion, economic. *See* Economy
Expert recommendations, 82–83

Faber, David, 150, 151
Fading the trend:
and ECNs, 58–59
and SOES, 55
Fear and greed as market drivers, 48, 93,
123
Fed. *See* Federal Reserve System
Federal Reserve System, 35–37. *See also*
Monetary policy
Five-minute rule, 45–46
Flag, as consolidation pattern, 111
Flight to quality, 72
Forecasting, market, by analysts,
74–77
Forrest Gump, 1
Freedom, as goal of day trading, 3–4
Full-timers, as day traders, 7
Fundamental analysis, versus technical
analysis, 91–93
Fundamentalist:
defined, 70
price philosophy of, 100–101

Gaps, 117–123
Generation Xers, as bull market drivers,
72
Goldman Sachs, 27
Graphs. *See* Charts and graphs
Greenspan, Alan, 78
Griffeth, Bill, 150, 151

Haines, Mark, 150
Hays, Kathleen, 150
Headfakes:
ECNs and, 60
SOES and, 55, 60
Hedge fund selling, 83
Herera, Sue, 151
High-probability trading, 90–126
broad market indicators, 123–126
charts and graphs, 102–123
overview, 90
price and, 100–101
70:30 trade, 91
technical indicators, 93–102
technical versus fundamental analysis,
91–93
volatility and, 101–102
volume and, 94–100
High-spread stocks, 163–164
Head-and-shoulders formations, 117
Hot list:
sort-by-volume window as, 131
using *Investor's Business Daily* for,
146–147

Indexes, by sector, 179–187
Indicators, market trend:
charts and graphs as, 102–104
consolidation patterns as, 109–115
gaps as, 117–123
Investor's Business Daily and, 148
long bonds, 123–124
new high/new low index, 126
overbought and oversold stocks,
124–125
overview, 93–94
price as, 100–101
of reversals, 115–117
support and resistance levels as,
104–109
upside/downside volume, 126

Indicators *(Continued)*
  volatility as, 101–102
  volume as, 94–100
Individual investors, as market
    participants, 35
Inflation, monetary policy and, 36–37
Insana, Ron, 151
Inside ask, defined, 24
Inside bid, defined, 24
Inside market, defined, 24
Inside offer, defined, 24
Insider trading:
  and buying on the rumor, 78
  versus specialists, 25
Instinet, 65–67
Institutional investors:
  advantages of, 34–35
  online indications of, 142
Insurance companies, as investment
    participants, 34–35
Intel, as example of two-sided market,
    27–28
Interest rates, impact on securities
    markets, 36–37, 78, 123–124
Internet stocks, as example of mass
    hysteria, 88–89
Internet trading. *See* Online trading
Intraday trading advantages, 15–22
Intraday trend trading, 167
Investment advisors, as investment
    participants, 34–35
Investment club members, as day
    traders, 7
Investor perception. *See* Market
    psychology
Investor's Business Daily:
  required reading, 145–149
  short-interest lists and, 84
Island, the, 67

Justice Department, antitrust probe of
    market makers, 51–52

Kennedy, Robert, 6
Kernen, Joe, 150, 151
Kimberly-Clark Corporation, as
    example of market psychology,
    73–74
Kohara, Sydnie, 150

Level I data, defined, 24
Level II data:
  actual-size rule and, 532
  Intel example, 27–28, 31
  as key to effective day trading,
    133–140
  momentum trading and, 161
Limit order:
  as day trading strategy, 169
  definition of, 17
Limit order book, defined, 25
Liquidity, market:
  market making and, 27–28
  and volume, 94–95, 131
Listed stocks. *See* Stocks, listed
Live-auction markets. *See* AMEX; Auction
    market; NYSE
Locked market, definition of, 60
Long bond, as market indicator, 123–124
Long sale:
  defined, 46
  See also Selling long
Low-risk trading:
  SOES and, 53–55, 61–62
  See also High-probability trading
Low-spread stocks, 162–163
LTOnline.net training program, 207–208

Mack, Consuelo, 150
Making a market. *See* Market makers;
    Market making
Making the spread, 29
Manchester Equipment:
  as buy/sell example, 130, 135–136
  as trading screen example, 130, 133
Mandatory order execution, 40–43, 56
Market analysis. *See* High-probability
    trading
Market Knowledge Quiz, 11
Market limit order, explanation of, 54–55
Market makers:
  versus day traders, 32–34
  defined, 27–31
  listing of, 189–191
  and SOES, 40–43
  strategies of, 137–140
Market maker window. *See* Level II
    data
Market making, 162–164

Market order:
  definition of, 17
  explanation of, 54–55
  market makers and, 29
Market participants:
  AMEX/NYSE, 24–26
  individuals, 35
  institutions, 34–35
  Nasdaq, 26–34
Market psychology, 69–89
  analyst expectations and, 74–77
  and analyst upgrades, 80–82
  bull market and, 71–73
  buying on the rumor and, 78–79
  earnings reports and, 73–74
  and expert recommendations, 82–83
  and index fund changes, 89
  mass hysteria and, 87–89
  overview, 69–71
  short-interest lists and, 83–85
  stock splits and, 79–80
  world news and, 85–87
Market timing. *See* Online trading;
  Trading day
Market Watch (CNBC program), 150
Market Wrap (CNBC program), 151
Mass hysteria, investor psychology and,
  87–89
Mathisen, Tyler, 151
Men in Black, as example of investor
  psychology, 86
Military action, impact on stock market,
  79
Momentum, defined, 94
Momentum trading, as strategy, 159–162
Monetary policy:
  buying on the rumor and, 78
  impact on stock market, 35–37
Money magazine, 22
Morning trading, 151–153
Mutual funds, day trading and, 19–22

Nasdaq:
  after-hours trading and, 61
  as dealer market, 26–34
  Level II market maker window, 133–140
  versus NYSE, 14
  and overbought-oversold oscillator, 125
  and SOES, 39–43

National Association of Securities Dealers
  (NASD), 39–43
National Association of Securities Dealers
  Automated Quotations system. *See*
  Nasdaq
National Market Stocks (NMS), and SOES,
  40
New high/new low index, 126
News, daily:
  on CNBC, 149–151
  impact on securities markets, 85–87,
  145
  from *Investor's Business Daily,* 145–149
New York Stock Exchange. *See* NYSE
NMS. *See* National Market Stocks
Notice-To-Members (NTM) 88-61, 43
NTM 88-61, 43
NYSE:
  as auction market, 24–26
  history of, 12–14
  versus Nasdaq, 14

Offer price, defined, 24
Oil sector, as example of investor
  psychology, 85
O'Neil, William, on winning investment
  strategies, 145–149
One-stock trading, 164
1,000-share rule, 43–44, 56
Online traders, as day traders, 7
Online trading, 127–143
  exchange ticker, 143
  Nasdaq Level II market maker window,
  133–140
  price-change ticker, 143
  price-volume windows, 131–133
  setting up, 127–128, 193–199
  time and sales window, 142–143
  trading screen, 128–130
  two-day, minute-by-minute price-
  volume chart, 140–141
  200-day price-volume chart, 141
Onsale, Inc., as example of gapping,
  120–122
Opening of market. *See* Trading day
Order flow, defined, 34
Order-handling rules, 50–52
OTC. *See* Over-the-counter (OTC) market
Overbought-oversold oscillator, 124–125

Oversold and overbought stocks, as buy/sell indicators, 124
Over-the-counter (OTC) market, defined, 27
Overtrading, 171–172

Pairgain Technologies, as example of triangle pattern, 112, 113
Panic of 1907, 36
Paper trading, 175–178
Part-timers, as day traders, 7
Payment for order flow, defined, 30
Peaks and valleys. *See* Charts and graphs
Pennant, as consolidation pattern, 114
Pennzoil, as example of investor psychology, 89
P/E ratio, bull market and, 72
Perception, investor. *See* Market psychology
Pfizer, as example of investor psychology, 85
Pisani, Bob, 151
Politics, impact on stock market, 35–38
Position, defined, 30
Position traders:
    definition of, 17
    investor psychology and, 87
    See also Position trading
Position trading, 172–174. *See also* Position traders
Power Lunch (CNBC program), 150
Predictions, market, by analysts, 74–77
Preferencing:
    and Archipelago, 68
    market makers and, 41
    and SelectNet, 62–64
Price, as market trend indicator, 100–101
Price-change ticker, 143
Price-to-earnings ratio. *See* P/E ratio
Price-volume windows, 131–133, 140–142
Professionals, as day traders, 7
Professional trader, as defined by NASD, 44–45
Professional trader rules, SOES and, 44–45, 56
Profit taking, investor psychology and, 87
Psychology, market. *See* Market psychology

QLT Phototherapeutics, as example of trendlines, 102–104
Queuing up, advantages of, 65
Quote, defined, 24
Quote refreshment strategies, 139–140

Rally, defined, 34
Ray-Ban, as example of investor psychology, 86
Recession, monetary policy and, 36–37
Rectangle, as consolidation pattern, 110–111
Resistance level:
    defined, 104
    See also Support level
Retail clients, as market participants, 35
Retirees, as day traders, 8
Reuters (Instinet), 65–67
Reversals, trend:
    catching both sides of a move, 168
    indicators of, 115–117
    of support and resistance levels, 108–109
Risks of trading:
    and ECNs, 61–62
    minimizing, 169–172
    and SOES, 53–55
Rounding formations, 117
Rules for day trading. *See* Strategies for day trading

S&P 500:
    effect on market psychology, 89
    major indexes, by sector, 179–187
    as measure of stock performance, 86–87
Savings and loans, as market participants, 34–35
Scalping, 166
Screen, trading. *See* Online trading
SEC:
    probe of market makers, 51–52
    and SOES, 44–45
Sector indexes, 179–187
Securities and Exchange Commission. *See* SEC
Securities markets. *See* Stock market
SelectNet, 62–65
Selectron, as example of investor psychology, 89

Sell/buy decisions, Level II data and, 134–137
Sellers, Bob, 149, 150
Selling long:
   bull markets and, 73
   SOES and, 46–50
   See also Long sale
Selling short:
   ECNs and, 60–61
   market psychology and, 83–85
   SOES and, 46–50
Sell-off, defined, 34–35
Sell strategy. *See* Exit strategy
70:30 trade:
   as goal of day traders, 91, 158
   Level II window and, 134
Short-interest lists:
   psychology of, 83–85
   sort-by-volume window and, 131
Short sale:
   defined, 47
   See also Selling short
Short-sale rule, 46–49, 56
Short squeeze, 84
Slippage costs, 24
Small-group-of-stocks trading, 165
Small Order Execution System. *See* SOES
Smart trading, explanation of, 65
SOES, 39–57
   versus ECNs, 61–62, 63
   history of, 39–40
   rules for, 40–53, 56
   trading possibilities and, 53–57
SOES banditry, as trading strategy, 160–162
Sort-by-gainers window, 132
Sort-by-losers window, 132–133
Sort-by-volume window, 131–132
Specialists, auction markets and, 25–26
Spread:
   defined, 24
   market making and, 28–29, 162–164
Squawk Box (CNBC program), 150
Standard & Poor's 500 Index. *See* S&P 500
Stock market:
   economic factors influencing, 35–38
   overview, 22–24
   participants, 24–35
Stocks, listed, definition of, 25
Stock splits, psychology of, 79–80

Stop-loss order, as an exit strategy, 156–157
Stop order, as day trading strategy, 169
Strategies for day trading, 155–174
   anything-that-moves trading, 165
   catching both sides of a move, 168
   doubling up, 167–168
   intraday trend trading, 167
   limit orders, 169
   market making, 162–164
   mistakes to avoid, 169–172
   momentum trading, 160–162
   number of simultaneous trades, 165–166
   one-stock trading, 164
   position trading, 172–174
   scalping, 166
   small-group-of-stocks trading, 165
   SOES banditry, 160–162
   stop orders, 169
   systems and rules, 155–159
   waiting, 168
Street Signs (CNBC program), 151
Support level:
   defined, 104
   longevity of, 106–108
   and resistance level, 104–109
   reversals, 108–109
   trendlines, 109
Symbols, for major market makers, 189–191
System of day trading. *See* Strategies for day trading

Tape:
   defined, 30
   as online time and sales window, 142–143
Technical analysis:
   versus fundamental analysis, 91–93
   See also High-probability trading
Technical indicators. *See* High-probability trading
Technician, defined, 93
Teenies:
   defined, 48
   ECNs and, 61
   on Level II windows, 136
TeleCommunications, Inc., as buy/sell example, 130, 135–136

Ticker tape. *See* Tape
Ticketmaster:
  as buy/sell example, 130, 135–136
  as example of double bottom
    formation, 116–117
Time and sales window, 142
Time value of money, buy-and-hold
    strategy and, 16–18
Timing. *See* Online trading; Trading
    day
Today's Business (CNBC program),
    149–150
Trading, high-probability. *See* High-
    probability trading
Trading day:
  before market opens, 144–151
  closing of market, 154
  midafternoon, 154
  midmorning, 153
  noon, 153
  opening of market, 151–153
Trading online. *See* Online trading
Trading Places, 24
Trading range, defined, 110
Trading room, at-home trading versus, 5–6
Trading screen. *See* Online trading
Trading strategies. *See* Strategies for day
    trading
Treasury bond, as market indicator,
    123–124
Trend channel, defined, 104
Trend reversals. *See* Reversals, trend
Trendlines:
  explained, 102–104
  market psychology and, 107–108
  support/resistance, 109
  See also High-probability trading
Trends:
  as tool of market analysis, 102
  See also High-probability trading
Triangle, as consolidation pattern,
    111–114
Triquent Semiconductor, as example of
    flag pattern, 111, 112
Two-day, minute-by-minute price-volume
    chart, 140–141

200-day price-volume chart, 141
Two-sided market, defined, 27

U.S. Treasury bond. *See* Treasury bond
Upbids:
  ECNs and, 60–61
  SOES and, 48–49
Upgrades, analyst, 80–82
Upside/downside volume indicator, 126
Upticks, upbids versus, 49

Velocity, defined, 94
Viagra, impact on stock market, 86
Virtual market:
  versus auction exchange, 26
  Nasdaq as, 26–27
Volatility:
  defined, 94
  as friend of day traders, 18
  impact on day trading, 156
  as market trend indicator, 101–102,
    131–132
Volume:
  defined, 94
  as market trend indicator, 94–100

Wage pressures and monetary policy,
    37–38
Wall Street Journal, The, short-interest
    lists and, 84
Washington Post, The, on day trading, 2
Web sites:
  day trader distance learning, 207
  McBurney and Baird online trading,
    129
  Power Lunch, 150
Wiggles and jiggles, 55
Windows 95, Windows NT, 127
Winning ideas from *Investor's Business
    Daily,* 145–149
Women, as day traders, 8
World news, impact on securities
    markets. *See* News, daily

Zero downbid, 48
Zero-plus upbid, 48

about the authors

Craig McBurney is the founder and chief thinking officer of a Web-based, investor education company, LearnTradingOnline.net. He grew up in Fairfax, Virginia, and attended Virginia Tech, where he studied civil engineering until becoming overwhelmed with boredom. In 1996, after training with a major securities firm, he began trading on his own. McBurney spent the beginning of his day trading career like most people . . . losing money. He quickly recognized the need in the marketplace for quality training but was unable to find a true mentoring-style program. This was the catalyst for launching Trade-Mentor, the predecessor to the distance-learning training available at www.LearnTradingOnline.net.

McBurney has an avid interest in sailing, having attended the Landing School of Yacht Design in Kennebunkport, Maine. He then relocated to the British Virgin Islands, where he was employed as the director of Offshore Sailing School in Tortola. He is currently combining his death-defying entrepreneurial pursuits with his sailing addiction to launch the Caribbean TriFoil Racing League. Go to TriFoilRacing.net to experience "speed sailing"—the ultimate extreme sport.

McBurney resides in Potomac, Maryland, and is the mostly sane, single parent of three incredible daughters, Casey, Tressie, and Kennya. He is looking forward to the day when his offspring can feed and shelter themselves so he can cancel his life insurance and fly a hang glider again.

Bob Baird, Ph.D., is an independent investor who operates his own firm, Environmental Consulting, Inc., in Glen Allen, Virginia. He was born in Waco, Texas, and grew up in Paducah, Kentucky. He attended the University of Kentucky at Lexington, where he received both bachelor's and master's degrees in geology. His work there on the Central Kentucky Mineral District was published in *Economic Geology.*

Afterward, he was employed by Mobil Oil Corporation as a research, exploration, and production geologist in the Dallas, Denver, and Stavanger, Norway, offices. Papers on his work there on petroleum generation in the Norwegian North Sea and Australian Northwest Shelf were published in the *Bulletin of the American Association of Petroleum Geologists* and the *Journal of Petroleum Geology.*

Baird then went on to continue his studies at Virginia Tech, where he earned a Ph.D. in geology and taught geology to undergraduate students. For the latter, he received the C. G. Tillman Award for Excellence in Undergraduate Teaching. Papers on his research in the Charlotte Geologic Belt of south-central Virginia have been published in *Southeastern Geology* and in a *Geological Society of America Special Publication.* Utilizing his education background, Baird works closely with McBurney in the Education Division of LearnTradingOnline.net, and he is coordinator of the Brokersaurus cartoon series.

Subsequently, he worked both in the private sector and for the Virginia Department of Environmental Quality before founding Environmental Consulting, Inc., which specializes in soil and groundwater contamination assessment and cleanup of petroleum leaks and spills, and provides environmental site assessments for real estate transactions.

He is an elected director on the Henricopolis Soil & Water Conservation District Board, which oversees soil and surface water conservation practices in Henrico County, provides conservation materials and education programs for the school system and the general public, and encourages voluntary best-management practices for the county's farms.

Baird was also appointed by former Virginia governor George Allen to serve as a member of the Virginia Board for Geology. The Geology Board regulates the practice of geology in Virginia and provides testing and certification of professional geologists. Baird himself is certified as a Professional Geologist in both Virginia and North Carolina.

When not hot on the trail of the extinct Brokersaurus, Baird turns his attention to American history as a Civil War reenactor with F Company, 21st Virginia Regiment, and as a member of the Central Virginia Relic Hunters Association and the Richmond Civil War Round Table, and he is active in battlefield preservation. He is also a member of the Innsbrook Rotary Club.

Baird and his wife, Martha, reside in Glen Allen, Virginia, and are the parents of married daughter, Kym, and teenage son, Robby, an aspiring classical pianist and composer.